CW00553655

Underworlds

UNDERWORLDS

ORGANIZED CRIME IN THE NETHERLANDS 1650–1800

Florike Egmond

Polity Press

First published in 1993 by Polity Press in association with Blackwell Publishers

Editorial office:
Polity Press
65 Bridge Street
Cambridge CB2 1UR, UK

Marketing and production:
Blackwell Publishers
108 Cowley Road
Oxford OX4 1JF, UK

238 Main Street
Cambridge MA 02142 USA

ISBN 0 7456 0644 X

British Library Cataloguing-in-Publication Data
A CIP catalogue record for this book is available from the British Library.

Library of Congress Cataloging-in-Publication Data
Egmond, Florike.
Underworlds : organized crime in the Netherlands 1650–1800 / Florike Egmond.
p. cm.
Includes bibliographical references.
ISBN 0–7456–0644–X (alk. paper)
1. Organized crime—Netherlands—History. I. Title.
HV6453.N4E354 1993
364.1′06′09492—dc20 93—26455
CIP

Typeset in 10 on 12 pt Sabon by Photo·graphics, Honiton, Devon
Printed in Great Britain by TJ Press Ltd, Padstow, Cornwall

This book is printed on acid-free paper.

Contents

III Ethnicity

IV The Changing Structure of the Rural Underworld

V Conclusion

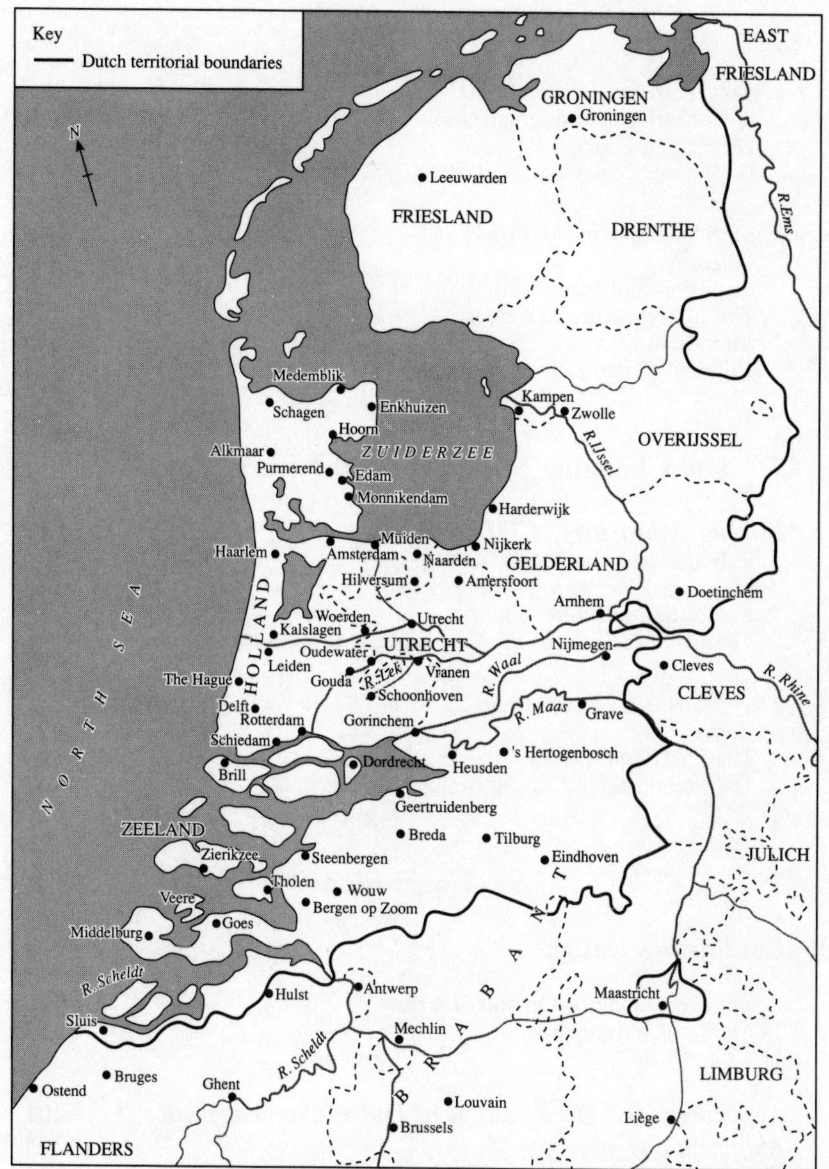
Key
Dutch territorial boundaries
N
NORTH SEA
EAST FRIESLAND
GRONINGEN
Groningen
Leeuwarden
FRIESLAND
DRENTHE
R.Ems
Medemblik
Schagen
Enkhuizen
Hoorn
Alkmaar
ZUIDERZEE
Purmerend
Edam
Monnikendam
Kampen
Zwolle
R.IJssel
OVERIJSSEL
Harderwijk
Haarlem
Muiden
Amsterdam
Naarden
Nijkerk
GELDERLAND
Hilversum
Amersfoort
Doetinchem
Arnhem
HOLLAND
Woerden
Utrecht
Kalslagen
UTRECHT
Oudewater
Leiden
Nijmegen
Cleves
The Hague
Gouda
R. Lek
Vianen
R. Waal
R. Rhine
Schoonhoven
CLEVES
Delft
Rotterdam
Gorinchem
R. Maas
Grave
Schiedam
's Hertogenbosch
Brill
Dordrecht
Heusden
Geertruidenberg
ZEELAND
Breda
Tilburg
Zierikzee
Steenbergen
Eindhoven
JULICH
Tholen
Wouw
Veere
Bergen op Zoom
Middelburg
Goes
BRABANT
R. Scheldt
Antwerp
Maastricht
Hulst
Sluis
Mechlin
R. Scheldt
Bruges
LIMBURG
Ostend
Ghent
Louvain
Liège
Brussels
FLANDERS

Map of the Dutch Republic

Preface

Anthropologists used to thank the subjects of their books, their 'informants', the people with whom they spent a lot of time, who have occasionally become friends, and who formed one of their principal interests during their period of research. It seems unfair that I cannot do the same. Although 'bad company' in some respects, the protagonists of this study have become, if not exactly friends, familiar and fascinating figures during the years I spent reading their interrogations and sentences in the Dutch archives. In fact, it was the wealth of personal details offered by the eighteenth-century dossiers of the twin brothers Frans and Jan Bosbeeck (captains of the Great Dutch Band) that convinced me of the value of the Dutch criminal records in the first place, and inspired my attempt to gain access to as yet unexplored 'underworlds'.

I would never even have come across these dossiers, however, if the work of Anton Blok, Richard Cobb, and Olwen Hufton had not put me on the twin tracks of organized crime and the history of ordinary, poor, and quite often marginalized people. Anton Blok has been closely associated with my research in the criminal records. Our discussions about many kinds of organized crime, about history and anthropology; and about themes such as ritual, language, names, and mentalities have always been animated, enjoyable, and stimulating both when we agreed and – perhaps even more so – when we did not. If I have disregarded some of his pertinent suggestions, I hope at least to have borne in mind his repeated advice: try not to bore your readers.

Besides introducing me to the world of crime and the ways of life of marginal and mobile groups in the past, research in the field of historical crime and criminal justice has brought me into contact with a wide circle of colleagues. The meetings of the International Association for the History of Crime and Criminal Justice and of its Dutch branch, the Werkgroep Strafrechtsgeschiedenis, have been especially stimulating –

not least thanks to the continued efforts and organizing abilities of Herman Diederiks, Sjoerd Faber, and Pieter Spierenburg. I would like to thank both Faber and Spierenburg for generously letting me peruse their extracts of several series of criminal sentences. It has always been a pleasure to talk about crime and the law with Cyrille Fijnaut and Frank Bovenkerk. Their expert knowledge of modern crime and police organization invited fruitful comparison. Meetings and discussions with Peter Burke, Robert and Esther Cohen, Carlo Ginzburg, Peter Mason, and Jim Sharpe have been especially important to me. Their company, like their work, has invariably been inspiring and I am grateful for their valuable and encouraging suggestions. I would not have exchanged Peter Mason's 'bad company' for any other.

Without the financial support of the Nederlandse Organisatie voor Wetenschappelijk Onderzoek and the cooperation of numerous archivists in many different parts of the Netherlands and Belgium it would have been impossible to undertake this project. I wish to acknowledge in particular the support of the staff of the Algemeen Rijksarchief at The Hague, the state archives of North Holland, North Brabant, and Zeeland, and the municipal archives at Amsterdam and 's Hertogenbosch.

This study is a revised version of my 1991 dissertation 'In Bad Company'. I am grateful to Arend Huussen, my supervisor, whose comments and advice have been extremely helpful. I have taken my time in producing several versions of chapters and may well have tried his patience, and also that of my students at the University of Amsterdam, who had to listen when I tried out ideas during seminars on historical crime, popular culture, marginality, and criminal justice. The informal meetings of a group of historians and anthropologists at Amsterdam have been equally stimulating.

Finally, I would like to thank Peter Mason, Anne Gevers, Mayke de Jong, Els van der Borg, Herman Roodenburg, Jim Sharpe, Arnold Labrie, Mattijs van de Port, Gerard Rooijakkers, Elisabeth Honig, Henk van Nierop, and Jeremy and Inga Boissevain. All of them have been patiently listening to my tales about crime and criminals for years. I am grateful to them for being great companions.

Part I

Introduction

1

In Bad Company

In August 1731 a local court in South Holland condemned the nineteen-year-old Andries Jansz to death by hanging for burglary, numerous thefts, violence, and association with church robbers and murderers. Like several other eighteenth-century thieves and vagrants, he was nicknamed The Glory of Holland (Roem van Holland).

This book is about people like him, who were regarded as a far from glorious element in Dutch society. It concerns men and women involved in rural organized crime in the course of the seventeenth and eighteenth centuries, and explores their criminal activities as well as their customs, forms of association, family relations, languages – in short, their way of life. Nearly all of these people were living on the fringe of established Dutch society, which regarded them as a marginal menace. Until recently they have also been excluded by most historians: respectable historiography had very little interest in criminals, vagrants, and similar outsiders. If it dealt with the history of crime and criminal justice at all, its concern was with the courts, with criminal prosecution rather than with the defendants and their considerations. For a long time, as a consequence, they have led a marginal existence in the anecdotes of local historical journals and in cases of legal history.

Compared with France, Germany, and England,[1] the position of vagrants and professional criminals in Dutch historiography has been especially weak, perhaps because they were so hard to fit into the placid, prosperous, well-ordered, egalitarian, and often rather dull image of the Dutch Republic. Rural bands constituted an unsuitable element in the Holland-centred presentation of Dutch history, with its emphasis on towns and on a pacified, town-influenced countryside. This compelling representation of life in the early modern (seventeenth- and eighteenth-century) Netherlands left very little room for organized crime, brutal violence, or social marginality, except when such topics were needed for an examination of the issue of Dutch tolerance. Schama's much discussed study of Dutch culture during the golden age (1987) has helped to reveal some of the more fascinating sides of Dutch history, but by strengthening the impression of cultural homogeneity he too appears to have fallen into the trap of believing what the Dutch themselves wanted (and still want) to believe about their own society: that it lacked significant class and cultural differences. (The main point of this representation is, of course, that it denies the basis for social conflict). The position of vagrants, thieves, robbers, and burglars is not much better in the by now considerable number of studies on Dutch criminal history (among them the excellent Faber 1983, Huussen 1976, 1978, and Spierenburg 1984), many of which, moreover, tend to concentrate on urban crime and justice. Again, their cases usually serve either as anecdotal illustrations or as material for discussions of criminal procedure, types of crimes, and forms of control and punishment – discussions which reflect a considerable preoccupation with order. The people on the wrong side of the judicial bench have thus been losers twice over.

Working Definitions

It is no coincidence that even a simple and convenient descriptive term for these people seems to be lacking. Apart from its negative connotations, 'criminals' is much too wide; 'organized criminals' sounds ridiculous; 'vagrants' or 'thieves' covers by no means all of them, while many vagrants in the strict sense of the term were not involved in organized crime at all; 'defendants' is far too legal, and so on. There is good reason, then, to begin by taking a closer look at terminology and concepts, both modern and early modern.

The term 'organized crime' immediately evokes drug-dealing, mafia-like organization and international connections. Yet, as Mary McIntosh has shown, in spite of these modern connotations it can be used to cover historical types of crime as well.[2] After all, criminal organization existed before the twentieth century and it would be confusing not to call it thus. Besides, the invention of a new concept for historical organized crime would immediately raise none too interesting questions about the exact point of transition from the one to the other. To subsume modern mafia and ancient robber bands under the same concept – regarding them as members of one family – may eventually help to elucidate both the differences between and the similarities in modern and not so modern forms of organized crime.

It should be made clear, however, in what sense 'organized crime' is used here, and how it relates to early modern concepts and notions of crime: an uneasy relation in some respects, which precisely for that reason assists us in formulating the main questions of this study. The modern notion of 'organized crime' has the advantage of referring both to a set of criminal offences (rather than to a single one) and to the way in which people cooperate and organize themselves (rather than to their actual number or to particulars of their organization). My selection of relevant cases from the huge stock of Dutch criminal sentences of the period 1650–1800 is based on this approach.[3]

Instead of looking for specific crimes, such as theft, robbery, burglary, murder and robbery, arson and robbery, or for particular forms of organization, I have collected all groups numbering more than four people which committed serious property crimes in the Dutch countryside (ranging from picking pockets to murder and robbery) and went about their criminal business in an organized, professional way (assuming specialization, planning, and some measure of continuity). This meant going through all the criminal sentences and many of the accompanying dossiers of over three hundred courts with full competence in criminal cases in the Dutch provinces of Holland, Zeeland, and Brabant. Covering a long period, ending with the last years of the eighteenth century when the criminal law as well as the judicial and administrative organization of the northern Netherlands were transformed, necessitated limiting the area to these three adjacent but very different regions: urbanized and densely populated Holland (that is, the modern provinces of North and South Holland) with its shipping and fishing industries, harbours, artisans' workshops, trade, and commercial agriculture; rural and predominantly agricultural Brabant (modern North Brabant); and, lastly, Zeeland, which in many respects proved to be intermediate.

The resulting collection comprised a large number of extremely diverse bands, networks, and groups. This wide range of groups operating in rural parts of the northern Netherlands is in itself worthy of note, for it plainly contradicts McIntosh's model, which links specific forms of criminal organization to particular types of societies and thus implicitly to phases of modernization. Following her argument, only two varieties of organized crime could have existed in the Dutch Republic: craft crime in the urbanized zones – possibly as part of a larger criminal underworld – and picaresque bandits or outlaws in rural areas (see McIntosh 1975). Such a strict division of urban and rural spheres makes no sense in the Netherlands and especially in the urbanized western provinces. The diversity of organized crime in the early modern Netherlands, moreover, clearly precludes any further attempts at rigid classification.

The use of the non-indigenous and non-legal concept 'organized crime' also had other advantages. It prevented a too early exclusion of cases relevant for the purpose of taking stock of the many different types of criminal organization and reduced the risk of following too closely in the footsteps of the Dutch courts of this period. Why this should be a dangerous procedure will be discussed shortly. In order to appreciate some of the dangers, we should first take a closer look at the terminology used by early modern Dutch courts. The questions raised by these contemporary concepts help to structure the present inquiry into the activities, organization, and culture of groups involved in rural organized crime in the Netherlands in the seventeenth and eighteenth centuries.

Contemporary Concepts

General, abstract terms covering, for instance, a whole category of offences (such as 'property crime') were nearly absent from the language used in early modern criminal trials and sentences. (This applies not only to the Netherlands but also to most of its neighbouring countries.) Neither the court members nor the defendants talked of 'aggravating circumstances' or 'crimes of violence'. Instead, the criminal records present an abundance of concrete and often immensely detailed descriptions of the offences committed, the exact circumstances, and the specific perpetrators. An Amsterdam sentence from 1714, for example, characteristically does not summarize Cornelis Coster's offences as burglary under aggravating circumstances but as 'notorious housebreaking in the countryside, and this at unseasonable times, using force and violence, and robbing the country folk of their possessions'.[4]

The terms most commonly used for offences committed by the groups discussed here include: housebreaking or burglary (*huijsbraak*), theft (*diefte, dieverij*), qualified burglary (*gequalificeerde huijsbraak*), notorious or notable housebreaking (*notoire* or *notabele huijsbraak*), breaking, entering, and stealing (*diefstallen met inbrekinge*), acts of violence (*geweldenarij*), ruffianism (*straatschenderij*), wantonness (*moedwilligheid*), insolence (*insolentie*), begging in a group (*troepsgewijs bedelen*), subsisting on robbery and begging (*leven op roof en bedelen*), robbery (*roof*), church robbery (*kerkroof*), raids (*rooftochten*), vagrancy and begging under false pretences (*vals bedelen en vagebonderen*), tramping and begging (*schooien*), villainy or roguery (*schelmstukken*), disturbing peace and order on the public roads (*de publieke wegen te ontrusten*), extortion and exactions (*afdreijgen en exactien*), freebooting and theft (*vrijbuit en dieverij*), and finally a 'godless', sinful way of life (*goddeloos leven*). Convicted women were often reproached for their 'dissolute and abominable way of life' (*leijdende een desoluijt ende abominabel leven*) and their licentious behaviour because they were 'living with famous thieves' (*bouleren met fameuse dieven*).

Such a proliferation of descriptive terms may be found in criminal sentences pronounced by courts all over the Dutch Republic, but regional differences did exist. Compared with the southern provinces, sentences from the urbanized, western part of the Dutch Republic are more restrained in form and phrasing. The Brabant courts appear to have made a consistent effort to express in baroque phrases the nature of the offences as well as their extremely objectionable character. In elaborate and lengthy expositions they describe and define what is perhaps best rendered as 'enormities' or 'disproportionate acts of violence' (*enorme feitelijkheden*), 'violent begging and intolerable quartering' (*geweldige schooierije en ondragelijcke inlogeringe*), and 'enormous and horrible evil doings' (*enorme en afgrijselijcke forfaiten*).

Descriptions of offences present regional and even local differences in style and idiom, but almost no important changes over time. The same applies to the less colourful terms for the groups involved. All records, whether from the 1680s or the 1790s, frequently refer to 'company' (*compagnie*), 'troop' (*troep*), 'band' (*bende*), and 'plot' or 'confederacy' (*complot*). 'Society' or 'association' (*societeit*), 'bunch' (*rot*), and 'party' (*parthije*) were used more rarely. Until the appearance of 'robber band' (*roverbende*) in the 1780s, no new terms were introduced. The word 'band' occurs more often in the southern than in the western provinces.

What exactly did the judges mean when they used these terms? Dictionaries are not much help in this respect, since, unlike the criminal sentences, they do not distinguish a band from a company or an association from a troop in terms of coherence and hierarchy. The courts used 'troop', 'society', 'confederacy', 'company', and 'band' as a series of related terms, a continuum ranging from a relatively loose-knit, dispersed, amorphous association to a coherent group with a hierarchical structure. The attributes most often mentioned in connection with the word 'band' are leadership and hierarchy. A band is nearly always someone's band, and is usually designated by the name of its leader: 'the Rabonus Band', or 'the band and association of famous thieves of Heintje van Goch'. As a corollary, the notion of 'band' is used to define a captain's role: 'who is captain of a band'. A band may also be referred to as a separate society with its own customs and even its own language. 'Troop' and 'bunch', on the other hand – and to a lesser extent 'association' – are hardly ever connected with hierarchy or leadership; 'company' is somewhere in the middle. (The secondary meaning of the Dutch terms *bende* and *troep* – rubbish, mess, dirt – suggests a lack of order that seems to be in plain contradiction with the close-knit and hierarchical structure associated with bands. Could it refer to the social position of these groups – outside the social order, as persons out of place – rather than to any lack of internal order?)

As far as forms of wider organization are concerned, a general term, such as 'underworld', is again conspicuously absent from Dutch judicial language. Descriptions of particularly extensive bands occasionally reveal fears of a conspiracy as well as abhorrence at their activities, but they never hint at collusion between different groups. Typically, it is by adjectives and not by a single substantive denoting a fixed structure that the sentences refer to these extensive bands and their activities. Whether this signifies that the idea of a dangerous, subversive counter-society was not taken seriously by the courts at the time and, if so, whether they were right in doing so, will be discussed later (see especially Chapters 2 and 9). In several other European countries the notion of an underworld certainly seems to have been more conspicuous. French and Italian criminal sentences sometimes speak of hierarchically structured criminal organizations; the activities of 'thief-taker general' Jonathan Wild in eighteenth-century London were famous; and picaresque stories as well as tales of secret and criminal counter-societies were produced in large numbers all over Europe.[5] The ones sold in the Dutch Republic during the eighteenth century, however, were almost without exception translations of Spanish, Italian, or French tales.[6] Were indigenous bands not spectacular enough to be used in tales, or did they perhaps lack a subversive quality?

Dutch terminology for the offenders themselves again shows mainly continuity. Special phrases were occasionally employed for Jews or gypsies, but the standard expressions may be found all over the Dutch Republic and were used throughout the seventeenth and eighteenth centuries: thieves (*gauwdieven*), burglars (*huisbrekers*), famous thieves (*fameuse dieven*), pickpockets (*zakkenrollers*), cutpurses (*beurzensnijders*), vagrants (*landlopers*), beggars (*bedelaars*). Less common were 'robber' (*rover*), 'highway robber' (*struikrover*), 'villains' (*boeven* or *booswichten*), 'violent person' (*geweldenaar*), 'rascals' (*deugnieten*), 'famous rogues' (*fameuse schelmen*), 'infamous persons' (*infame personen*), and 'evil doers' (*kwaaddoeners*). More colourful expressions – such as 'inveterate rogues' (*aartsschelmen*), 'excessive extortioners' (*verregaande knevelaars*), and 'confounded rascals' (*spitsboeven*) – appear more frequently in the south. During the whole of the period 'bandit' occurs only once in the records: in the first quarter of the seventeenth century, when it was used in its original meaning of banished person. (In Dutch language and literature since the nineteenth century both 'band' and 'bandit' – *bende* and *bandiet* – have been associated with a Mediterranean setting. The entry for *bandiet* in a current Dutch dictionary refers to its Latin-Italian origin and mentions only Italian, Turkish, and Greek literary examples.)

Dutch judicial terminology describing offences, offenders, and their forms of cooperation thus remained largely unchanged during the period 1650–1800. A late eighteenth-century judge might have skipped some of the elaborate terminology of the 1670s. His predecessors of the mid seventeenth century would have been surprised at the length and detailed character of a 1798 sentence. Neither would have had any problems in understanding each other's sentences, though a few minor changes should be mentioned. Some of the baroque terms – such as 'ruffians' (*calissen*), 'wicked scoundrels' (*snoode guijten*), and 'rogues' (*boeffgesellen*) – had already become old-fashioned by the beginning of the eighteenth century. Others, which continued and still continue to be used, began to lose their extremely negative and pejorative meaning in the course of the eighteenth century. By the middle of the nineteenth century *schelm*, *schavuit*, and *guit* – like their English equivalents 'rascal', 'rogue', and 'scoundrel' – usually referred to naughty children; in 1700 there had been nothing playful about their meaning.

These shifts may be regarded as different aspects of a process of semantic change. Expressions and terms which lost most of their negative meaning or even disappeared completely shared a strongly moralizing and censuring message. They were replaced not by newly invented pejorative terminology but by more neutral terms like 'thief' and 'burglar'. Such changes formed part of a general standardization and formalization of the Dutch language, which entailed a reduction of both flamboyant idiom and regional variation in written language. (The somewhat less ornate style of criminal sentences pronounced in the big towns of Holland compared with the elaborate and often verbose style of the south may point to regional differences in the progress of this development.) The narrowing down of juridical definitions and the standardization of terms used to describe offences may also be interpreted as an aspect of increasing juridical professionalism, but this remains an inadequate 'explanation' of a notable development. Whereas seventeenth-century sentences often resound with a sense of very personal outrage felt by the local judicial authorities, by the late eighteenth century these same courts censured and condemned from a far superior, morally elevated, and apparently unassailable position. The sense of personal outrage had largely gone.

Perhaps we are dealing here with a set of interrelated developments: a growing gap between the authorities and the groups involved in illegal activities; formalization of the means (including language) to repress and contain them; and, possibly, the concomitant growth of a sense of increasing personal safety among those 'in control'. But even if this was the case, it should be remembered that these were only slight changes over a long period. Continuities prevailed in the vocabulary used to portray organized crime in the Dutch Republic during the seventeenth and eighteenth centuries.

Regional differences, on the other hand, were pronounced. The more frequent occurrence of the term 'band' in the southern sentences may, of course, simply betray regional differences in the perception of organized crime: perhaps southern courts were more prone to regard people cooperating in illegal activities as a coherent, threatening group. It may also relate to actual differences between groups: in Brabant close-knit bands with a hierarchical structure and a captain, in Holland and Zeeland more random coalitions. Another, even slighter regional divergence in terminology points in this direction. The courts in Holland often refer to travelling or stealing 'in company'. In Brabant the same term is used as a substantive: a company.

This brief survey of the vocabulary of the Dutch criminal courts suggests three problems which direct the following explorations of the world of rural organized crime in the Netherlands in the seventeenth and eighteenth centuries.

Patterns in Crime

First we may ask whether the virtual absence of long-term change in the courts' vocabulary indicates continuity in forms of criminal organization. Of course, it might only reflect continuities in the courts' perception of crime, but the large number of independent courts seems to make this a very unlikely possibility. Correspondingly, regional variation in terminology might be interpreted as a sign of actual variation in the structure and organization of bands operating in different parts of the Dutch countryside. These questions open up the wide field of 'patterns in crime'.

This book is not a study of fluctuations in the number of robberies, or of relations between property crimes and crimes of violence, of total numbers of people involved in organized crime, or even of decreasing and increasing numbers of convictions. Here 'patterns' means qualitative patterns in crime, though some apparent fluctuations in rural band activity will be discussed as the occasion arises. There is a dual reason for this restriction to qualitative aspects. During the past twenty to thirty years much sophisticated quantitative research on historical crime has been carried out in the Netherlands and in Britain, Germany, Belgium, France, and Italy. In so far as it has resulted in statements about increases and decreases of particular crimes, or about changes in the predominance of certain types of crimes – such as the famous 'violence au vol' thesis – the conclusions are disputable even after decades, while the results tell us more about the viewpoints, preoccupations, and priorities of the courts than about the crimes or their perpetrators.[7] A quantitative approach thus seems hardly conducive to a closer acquaintance with the defendants, the main focus of this study.

More specifically, the Dutch criminal records of the sixteenth, seventeenth, and eighteenth centuries – like many other early modern records – by their very nature undermine attempts at quantification. It is not only that series of sentences are marred by small gaps and influenced by differences in registration; such minor defects characterize even the best kept archives. Often the gaps are much more substantial, whole files have gone, and the criminal records of several small jurisdictions have disappeared completely. These major lacunae preclude any reliable statements about the numbers of people involved in organized or any other type of crime. Nor is there any way to decide whether more or fewer sentences were pronounced per thousand inhabitants in 1620 than in 1795. Even supposing that all criminal records had been preserved – and disregarding the famous 'dark figure' problem of undetected, unregistered, and unprosecuted crime – we still would not be able to calculate the actual amount of serious crime (in the sense of criminal activities) during this period because of a particular characteristic of early modern Dutch justice: frequently sentences against professional thieves and burglars present only as much evidence as was deemed necessary to obtain a conviction. Except in some cases of unusual importance, neither the prosecuting bailiffs nor the judges were interested in establishing the number of robberies committed by a particular defendant, never mind in tracing criminal curricula. The courts valued reliable evidence, especially if it concerned offences committed within their own jurisdiction, but a theft in a neighbouring territory – even if it was only 10 kilometres away – was of secondary importance unless needed to prove a long-standing criminal involvement. There is not much point, then, in trying to calculate the chances of getting robbed in an early modern town as compared with the countryside, let alone in trying to compare such computations with modern statistics. Any such attempt is doomed to failure by the difference in aims of early modern criminal justice.

Yet, precisely because of the extreme fragmentation of Dutch criminal justice, we can indeed say something about qualitative patterns in crime, which comprise regional differences and changes in criminal styles as well as the varying involvement of particular groups. I am using the term 'criminal style' here to cover not only types of criminal activity and ways of committing these crimes (such as burglary, robbery, particular uses of violence, the manner of transporting booty, etc.) but also social and organizational aspects of the groups involved (such as size, coherence, mixed or homogeneous sociocultural background, and egalitarian or hierarchical structure).

Unlike the English system, where judges and their assistants based in London toured the countryside, Dutch criminal justice was characterized both by territoriality and by extreme decentralization. ('Decentralization' and 'fragmentation' are the wrong terms to use: during no previous period had Dutch justice and administration ever been centralized or united.) At any moment during the whole of the early modern period more than three hundred largely independent, urban or rural first-instance courts dealt with criminal cases in the provinces of Holland, Zeeland, and Brabant. Some courts handled many cases each year, others pronounced a criminal sentence only once every ten to twenty years, depending on the size of their territory and the number of inhabitants. While the competence of each of these individual courts ended at the borders of its territory, it was unlimited in terms of validity: practically speaking, there was no appeal in criminal cases. The role of the provincial high courts of Holland and Zeeland (Hof van Holland en Zeeland) and of Brabant (Raad van Brabant) as appeal courts was generally restricted to civil cases. With respect to particular crimes, categories of people, and territories they might act as first-instance criminal courts, but the bulk of all criminal cases was dealt with by local first-instance courts. (For a survey of the organization of Dutch criminal justice and the relevant literature see Appendix.)

Because of the virtual independence of these courts, it is extremely unlikely that specific local prejudices and circumstances, personal involvements, idiosyncrasies and preconceived notions of court members – that is, judges and bailiffs – completely 'shaped' the information presented by these records as a whole. ('Independence' does not imply a total lack of outside influence. Since most court members had had no legal training whatsoever, they were supposed to ask for the advice of professional legal experts in major criminal cases. The decision remained theirs, however.) If, for instance, only one Dutch court had suddenly started to convict Irish and English vagrants in the course of the 1620s, the reason might have been a change in its prosecution policy. In fact, at least a dozen different courts began to condemn Irish and English vagrants in the 1620s, but stopped doing so in the course of the 1630s and early 1640s. While providing no reliable evidence on numbers and amounts, the records of the 'three hundred' courts can thus be compared and used as a check upon each other.

While tracing 'patterns in organized crime' in the Netherlands, we may try to determine if, how, and to what extent they fit in with the ones suggested by Hobsbawm, Blok, Weisser, Beattie, Hay, and several other scholars with respect to banditry and organized crime in different periods and regions. Nearly all of them based their ideas on fragmentary evidence, single cases, literary sources, or a mixture of these, and not on systematic research covering a long period and including all the extant criminal records. This is not a comparative study, however, and nor am I interested in testing theories or vindicating models, let alone in generalizing from 'the Dutch case'. The case-studies, which together make up Parts II, III, and IV, consist of unique and specifically Dutch examples and serve no ulterior purpose. They cannot be turned into generalizing statements without either reducing them to so-called essentials or putting them on the rack and stretching them – both of which seem particularly obscene in this context. Yet these same case-studies are more than anecdotes. The evidence offers glimpses, suggestions, and hints, which often implicitly pertain to broader themes raised by the above-mentioned authors, such as links between banditry and popular protest, connections between stigmatization of particular occupational or ethnic groups and their involvement in crime, the ever present theme of poverty as an incentive to property crime, relations between warfare and crime, the issue of state formation and banditry, the geography of crime, and the regional distribution of banditry in early modern Europe.

Chapters 3 and 4 examine the geography of organized crime and relations between warfare and organized crime, starting from the regional and occupational background of band members active during the second half of the seventeenth century. Several 'southern' regions, such as Brabant, had only become part of the Dutch Republic in 1648; active warfare was still going on there during the 1630s and 1640s. Holland and Zeeland, on the other hand, had always formed the core area of the Netherlands; no actual fighting had taken place there since the late sixteenth century or the first years of the seventeenth century. Were military bands active both in Holland and in Brabant, and can we find any connection between the formation of new bands and the end of phases of warfare? Is there any proof to substantiate the stereotypical image of bands consisting of deserters and dismissed soldiers? Did former soldiers get involved in organized crime because they were poor and out of work, or did they have other reasons too? Finally, does the evidence in any way support Hobsbawm's suggestion that certain types of rural banditry should be regarded as *social* banditry, as inarticulate forms of social protest (1981)?

Chapters 5 and 6 likewise address the themes of geography and poverty, but here the focus is on ethnicity, stigmatization, mobility, and social exclusion. Gypsies as well as Jews played a prominent role in the bands of the period 1690–1800. Why did they, and how were they able to reach this position? Did the social exclusion of gypsies and Jews contribute to their involvement in crime? Should we interpret their illegal activities simply as one of the few means open to them to provide for themselves, or also as covert signs of protest, resentment, and even rebellion? While both gypsies and Jews were stigmatized by the Dutch authorities and by the established Dutch population, they differed in nearly every other respect, including criminal style, social and legal position, and form of exclusion. Did these ethnic minorities cooperate at all when involved in criminal activities?

This raises the problem which forms the main theme of Chapters 7 and 8: the question of internal solidarity and coherence in the world of crime – as indicated by cooperation among bands from different regional and cultural backgrounds – which, indirectly, reflects again on the issue of rural theft and robbery as the inarticulate revolt of the powerless. The geography of crime, poverty, and non-ethnic social exclusion are discussed as subsidiary topics in this part. The second half of the eighteenth century is known as a period of population growth and of a widening gap between rich and poor – in the Netherlands no less than in other parts of western Europe. Terminology used by the late eighteenth-century Dutch courts expressed their moral censure of the vagrant poor and did indeed point to a sharp social division. We may well ask whether the growing numbers of vagrant poor ever joined forces and formed an integrated underworld during this period. How far did cooperation between bands from different backgrounds go? Did it ever reach the stage when we may speak of a counter-society?

The layout of this book thus reveals a shifting emphasis within a set of overlapping and recurring topics in the analysis of rural organized crime. The thematic organization roughly coincides with a chronological sequence: Part II deals with the second half of the seventeenth century, continuing up to about 1720; Part III focuses on the period between 1690 and the 1760s; Part IV briefly returns to some early eighteenth-century configurations before concentrating on the second half of the eighteenth century. This shifting emphasis in itself implies that no single approach suggested by the authors mentioned above (and by several others as well) is in itself enough to come to grips with organized crime in the early modern Netherlands, but that several of their ideas put together – each time in a different combination – are helpful. The case-studies also suggest some other patterns.

Primarily, though, the combination of systematic research (using serially organized records) and a micro-historical approach[8] (concentrating on especially well-documented examples) here serves to particularize without falling into the trap of anecdotal history. The purpose is to show how familiar, recurring, and new elements join to form unique combinations linked by family resemblances (see Wittgenstein 1958; cf. Ginzburg 1990a, 1990b, and Blok 1975). This applies not only to the bands themselves but also to the varying combinations of, for instance, geographic, ethnic, and economic aspects affecting forms of criminal organization.

Marginal Cultures

The second theme directing this study consists of a range of topics which may perhaps best be characterized as aspects of the historical anthropology of marginal groups. (It will be obvious that I am using the word 'marginal' in the sense not of historically unimportant but of less powerful, and socially irrelevant according to the views of contemporary established society.) Seen from this perspective, the fact that certain people were convicted for illegal activities which were part of their way of life as a group primarily offers a means of gaining access to the people involved: to the defendants and their world. The emphasis here is on everyday existence, on illegal as well as legal professional activities, patterns of mobility, customs and beliefs, contacts with colleagues, friends, associates, and kin, family life, gender relations, rituals, language and names. Very little information can be found about certain important aspects of their lives: I would have liked to know more about relations between men and women, fights and insults, honour, attitudes towards children, love and anger, friendship and humour, their ideas about themselves and about different groups, about religious beliefs and the stories they told each other. By piecing together biographical details and other fragments of information it is none the less possible to portray bands, networks, and families involved in crime, and to get some idea of life at the fringe of society.

This exploration of marginal cultures again links up with problems raised by contemporary terminology. Earlier, the notion of an integrated criminal underworld was brought up. Now we may ask some related questions which focus on the social and cultural implications of marginality rather than on organization and cooperation. These points are closely connected both with the wider issue of social hierarchy and its cultural implications and with the related problem of the links between infamy and defilement, between impurity and crime (on these links see especially Blok 1989, 1991). The censuring and often pejorative terminology used by the courts pointed to a clear division between the established Dutch and the more mobile and (if only for that reason) disreputable inhabitants of the Netherlands who were convicted for theft, burglary, or robbery. We need to know much more about the latter's way of life, however, before we can decide whether we are dealing with a separate, dishonourable, infamous section of Dutch society – a *Gaunerschicht*, a *classe dangereuse* (to use an anachronistic term once again) – as the courts seem to suggest. Did these groups in fact constitute one or more separate underworlds?

The recurring theme is thus the question of whether crime – in the sense of a regular involvement in illegal activities – decisively structured the way of life, the culture of these groups. As the case-studies will show in more detail, the link between crime and group culture in the early modern Netherlands was a complex one. Instead of groups developing secret languages for criminal purposes, for instance, we find that many of them turned dialects and professional idioms they were already using outside the context of illegality into an asset in the business of crime. The same is true of many types of organization and mobility. Most bands of thieves and robbers active in the Dutch Republic did not devise totally new forms of cohesion, hierarchy, or communication; nor did they suddenly develop new patterns of travel or occupational expertise. The criminal styles of nearly all of them directly or indirectly derived from qualities, attributes, and forms of organization that were part of their way of life irrespective of organized crime. Such 'tactical qualities' were among the resources enabling these groups to operate more or less successfully as thieves, burglars, and robbers (on 'tactical power' see Blok 1988, pp. 113–14). They help us understand how particular groups became prominent in the criminal business while others did not. This is not the same thing as stating that tactical qualities explain why these groups were involved in criminal activities. After all, not every mobile person who knows how to handle a gun becomes a robber.

In so far as they concern the connection between organized crime and group culture, the case-studies might raise questions about relations between social marginality, infamy, and crime in the Netherlands compared with other European countries, or even with non-European societies. Such comparative matters are not discussed here, mainly because I doubt whether there is any 'Dutch' pattern that could be compared with a 'French', 'German', or 'English' one – to say nothing of an 'early modern European' pattern that might be contrasted with, for instance, connections in India between low caste, impurity, and criminal involvement. By going into particulars instead of generalizing I hope to demonstrate the complexity of this relationship, even within the small area of the northern Netherlands and the limited period of about 150 years. This precludes simple answers to questions such as whether marginality or stigmatization caused certain groups to become involved in crime, or were they stigmatized because of their criminal activities?

Much more interesting than this either or problem are the implications of the fact that most of the groups involved in crime did not develop totally new languages, customs, rituals, and forms of organization but adapted former customs or simply continued their usual way of life. It follows that the criminal records, besides allowing us to study crime and its organization in the past, also form a veritable treasure trove of information about a much wider, not necessarily criminal segment of society, which consists largely of people who are almost impossible to trace in any other type of historical record. To mention only one example: apart from the criminal records, the only available sources in the Netherlands concerning gypsies during the early modern period are a handful of pictures, some moralizing and exoticizing poems, a few folk-tales, the placards issued against gypsies by the Dutch provincial and local authorities, some dubious remarks by contemporary historians, and fragmented (mostly unexplored) references in local archives to minor conflicts between rural inhabitants and gypsies. As far as we know, there is no form of registration (marriage, burial or baptism – some gypsy children were baptized in either Roman Catholic or Protestant churches, but the use of different names makes it hard to identify them in church registers) and gypsies did not leave their own stock of documents. Compared with these fragments, the value of the huge mass of criminal records concerning gypsies – even though they offer a distinctly coloured view – is obvious.

Of course we should not be naïve about the importance of illegal activities in the lives of these people. Crime cannot – and need not – be simply discounted and subtracted from the information. The case-studies tell us not only about Brabanders, Hollanders, Jews, or gypsies involved in crime, however, but also about the customs, language, names, gender relations, and family patterns obtaining in the wider cultural communities to which they belonged. This is why the next chapters may also be regarded as micro-historical essays dealing with the historical anthropology of marginal groups: indigenous vagrant Hollanders and Brabanders, and poor immigrants from the southern Netherlands, England, Wales, Scotland, Ireland, and Germany in Part II; gypsies and east European Jews in Part III; and Brabanders, immigrant Walloons, Jews, and ethnically mixed itinerant groups of the later eighteenth century in Part IV. Again, though, the aim is not to generalize: we are not discussing 'the' Jews, 'the' Brabanders, 'the' vagrant population of the Netherlands, or 'the' gypsies.

Images

The case-studies expose the many differences between these groups as well as their similarities – as seems fitting when discussing people who may well have been surprised to find themselves put together in the same category by the judicial authorities, and who may, moreover, have disliked each other as much as they were in their turn feared and despised by established Dutch society. One of the purposes of this study is to discover whether they had anything at all in common apart from their involvement in illegal activities. This brings us to the third theme: images and representations of crime, which can never be completely separated from the 'facts', however much we might want them to be, and however far we might go in distinguishing between the two when examining the criminal records.

In its most concrete and elementary form this is 'only' a matter of a critical use of historical sources; seen from a more abstract, analytical point of view, it affects the whole issue of relations between historical 'facts' and their representations. I shall not go into this problem and all its philosophical ramifications: suffice it to say that, whatever the relation of the criminal records to 'historical reality', we should at least try to distinguish between the judges' opinions and their effect on representations of crimes and criminals on the one hand and the actual deeds and people on the other. It is to this middle range between elementary source criticism and philosophical abstraction that I referred when stating that it might be dangerous to follow too closely in the footsteps of the early modern Dutch courts. Most of the risks and consequences of seeing and hearing through the eyes and ears of the judicial authorities do not need to be dwelt on here. They have been discussed by historians like Douglas Hay, J. M. Beattie, Geoffrey Parker, Peter Burke, Carlo Ginzburg, and Natalie Zemon Davis, all of whom have made imaginative and judicious use of legal records.[9] Three points, however, deserve some attention.

First, what cannot be avoided when looking through the eyes of the judicial authorities – as we have to – is partial blindness. If a bailiff was not told about a crime, did not discover it, refused to see it, or was paid not to notice it, this offence simply does not exist for us either. This in itself may be frustrating, but the real danger lies in not recognizing the blindness. We need not concern ourselves with the well-known 'dark figure' problem it creates (which has given rise to most sophisticated and useless debates on amounts and quantities of unregistered and therefore unknown crimes), since this study does not discuss quantitative aspects of crime. Secondly, the dangers become more serious if we fail to recognize that the blindness does not always affect the same areas. While presenting an apparently straightforward and even 'objective' registration of illegal activities, criminal records by their very nature only present those cases that were defined as crimes at the time. Perceptions and definitions of crime change and shift, without the judicial authorities necessarily telling us about it. The sixteenth-century 'reversal' of attitudes towards begging and vagrancy is a relatively familiar example. Changing prosecution policies with regard to prostitution is another. As it turns out, such shifts did not occur with respect to the offences discussed here. During the seventeenth and eighteenth centuries they were always considered important enough to be registered, investigated, and prosecuted – if, that is, they were brought to the attention of the judicial authorities.

Thirdly, even if we recognize that 'crime' is not a fixed category but a shifting moral concept defined by those in power – a concept, moreover, which also serves as an instrument of control – the viewpoints of the authorities still structure our information in other, more insidious ways. Criminal records, and in particular the verbatim reports of interrogations, create an effect of immediacy and straightforwardness. This impression is not completely false, and yet it cannot be trusted. All the questions asked by prosecutors, all the evidence presented, and all the terms (even the most apparently neutral ones) used by them to describe the defendants and their activities are intricately and inextricably bound up with their image of the people they were dealing with. This is not a matter of individual prejudices or of opinions held by only a few prosecutors or judges. The present study is based on the records of more than three hundred courts. Notions of crime and images of the perpetrators of illegal acts which emerge from these records therefore reflect collective representations and stereotypes shared by the judicial authorities and, in all likelihood, since many of them were nothing but well-to-do, respectable middle-class Dutchmen, by most established Dutch people.

It would be simplistic, then, to believe that we can ever gain direct access to the defendants. The only opinions and points of view that we can observe directly are those of the prosecutors, interrogators, and judges. Yet, to some extent, we do get to know the people on the other side of the bench. It is the measure of this extent that should be determined more precisely here. Seen from this perspective, the present study may be regarded as an exploration of the possibilities, limits, and limitations of the criminal records. The only way to make such an exploration is to try to come to grips with the stereotypical images and notions of crime and criminals held by the judicial authorities. Only by obtaining detailed knowledge of their opinions and prejudices will it be possible to use the criminal records and at the same time distinguish between the bias of the authorities, the suspects' understandable interest in presenting themselves as favourably as possible, and the latter's actual behaviour and way of life. That we can do so at all is, of course, only because we are not dealing with fiction, whether in the sense of fantasy or of cases fabricated by the courts. A court's liberty in its presentation of a criminal case was constricted both by its own procedural rules and by the inventiveness of the defendants.

It is no coincidence that this theme of image and presentation is discussed only in the concluding chapter, which demonstrates how criminal cases were structured by the courts' stereotypes, while at the same time giving rise to them. By enhancing and spreading a stigmatizing image the criminal proceedings themselves helped to exclude, marginalize, and control groups whose very position as members of Dutch society was doubtful and insecure. Whereas all the preceding case-studies deal with particular groups and individuals and should reveal the enormous diversity of the world of crime and marginality, the final chapter shows how the judicial authorities tried to reduce this variety (by means of stereotypical notions) to an indistinct, homogeneous mass of frightful and revolting outsiders. To a large extent they have been successful: after all, much historical (and modern) criminology could be discarded if we stopped believing the courts' representations and concluded that there is no other link between people committing crimes than the definition of their acts as illegal by lawmakers and prosecutors. The final chapter raises the question of whether we should not have started doing so long ago.

Besides attempting to reclaim at least some marginal groups from their peripheral position in historiography, I hope to show that organized crime cannot be studied separately from the social structure and customs of the groups involved – as if crime were a totally discrete section of their existence, or as if illegal activities could only be understood by classifying them as abnormal behaviour. Nor can we investigate organized crime and social marginality without looking at the norms, beliefs, and concepts of those in power. Such acts of setting apart, excluding, and reducing only repeat the suppressive and marginalizing acts of the early modern authorities in a different sphere. Since both crime and marginality pertain directly to the central values of established society, this may be one more reason why the study of peripheral phenomena and marginal groups need not necessarily lead to marginal insights.

2
Confronting the Authorities

In the Dutch Republic, as in most parts of early modern Europe, the world looked different when seen from the perspective of an outsider. To start with, all outsiders shared a low status as well as an adverse legal position. Many, perhaps even most of their contacts with dominant groups in their society involved unequal confrontations, determined by the idiom of public order and criminal law. Within their own world nearly all of them were cognizant of the major division between towns and countryside, between urban and rural organized crime. It is these aspects of life as an outsider, as a member of a marginal group, which will be explored in this chapter. In so far as it is possible we will try to do so by looking through the eyes of the defendants. How much did they know about the people and institutions they were up against, the authorities? What did they know of criminal law, legal procedure, punishment, or the organization of criminal justice? Did they develop special strategies in trying to cope with legal disadvantages? To what extent and how did they demarcate the world of organized crime: who were 'we' and who were 'they' in their terms, and was there any clear distinction between, for instance, amateurs and professionals? Did the people concerned regard themselves as 'the underworld'? And how exactly should we envisage the distinction between town and countryside in terms of criminal organization?

The notion of a homogeneous Dutch society hangs on the social and legal gap which separated established, respected Dutch people from the generally mobile and despised marginal groups. As in many other European countries, this distinction reflected differences not only in economic opportunities and social position but also in legal status. Before the French Revolution legal equality was, after all, a foreign and disputable notion. As far as civil rights were concerned, various factors determined a person's place in the Dutch legal hierarchy. White and wealthy Protestant men who were born in families with urban citizenship found themselves at the top. Nearly all of them enjoyed full civil rights; they could hold public office and claim extensive protection when involved in criminal proceedings. They were followed by other Christians – most of them Roman Catholics – who lacked, at least formally, the right to hold office. The same applied to wealthy and established Jews, whose urban citizenship, however, was not hereditary. (The economic activities of all Jews were restricted by extensive regulations.) Finally, many Dutch Christians who had a fixed abode none the less did not qualify for the position of fully-fledged citizens (mostly on financial grounds). A man's position in this fine-meshed classificatory system was thus determined by religion as well as social position and fixed domicile. All women followed the legal status of their fathers or husbands but lacked some of their rights.

Legally, these social categories differed only in terms of civil rights. It is at the very point separating those with fixed domicile from those without that we find the borderline between people with a relatively protected position as regards criminal law and those who were invariably treated harshly by criminal justice. This major distinction was incorporated in the great legal codes which were proclaimed by the Habsburg rulers Charles V and Philip II during the sixteenth century and were not abolished in the Dutch Revolt. (Until the reforms of the period 1795–1809 the Constitutio Criminalis Carolina and the Criminal Ordonnances continued to form the basis of criminal law in the Dutch Republic, but they were supplemented by local and provincial placards, by edicts of the Estates General, and last but not least by customary, unwritten law.)[1] The distinction should be seen in the context of the numerous new legal and administrative rules issued against beggars, vagrants, and 'idle poor' in many European countries at this time. Established and respected inhabitants of a jurisdiction could not be arrested unless the bailiff had been granted permission by the local court to do so, and approval was only forthcoming if there was a large amount of evidence. Mobile suspects, on the contrary, were arrested much more readily. They were invariably remanded in custody. Permission to use torture required fewer formalities, and they were commonly tried by 'extraordinary' procedure. Only in very exceptional cases could they claim the much less common 'ordinary' procedure reserved for respected inhabitants, which included the right to a counsel for the defence. 'Ordinary' proceedings obviously took more time, involved a more complicated registration, and were much more expensive.[2] We will shortly see what 'extraordinary' criminal procedure entailed and how the defendants dealt with it. Courts attached less importance to evidence provided by an itinerant person than to the testimony of an established individual. Itinerant suspects were rarely condemned to the payment of fines, not only because they were almost invariably poor but also, it seems, because physical punishment (flogging, branding, imprisonment, or banishment) was considered an appropriate way of dealing with people who managed to elude most forms of social control. The legal position of gypsies – who were denoted as *Heijdens* (heathen) at the time – compared unfavourably even with other itinerants, for their way of life itself was formally defined as punishable by law. As will be shown in more detail later, Dutch official policy *vis-à-vis* gypsies during the years 1695 to 1730 can be characterized only as organized persecution.

Non-established members of the urban and rural lower classes found themselves barred from certain civil rights and could claim little protection in criminal matters. If they suffered from illness or were indigent, they were not reckoned among the poor who deserved church or town assistance. The only way to prove that they were not undeserving, infamous, or dangerous was to find a permanent address and give up travelling. Naturally, few of them were able to do so – and perhaps even fewer were willing – since their jobs as rural labourers, street sellers, rural pedlars, musicians, and so on were predicated on mobility. Why itinerancy was so harshly penalized in early modern European society is easy to understand. Mobile people were relatively impervious to social control by neighbours, relatives, church councils, and other local institutions, and in the virtual absence of police or comparable bodies such forms of control formed the main underpinning of public order.

Legal distinctions and sanctions thus compensated for administrative and judicial weakness. How strong in reality was the position of the judicial authorities? On the one hand, early modern criminal justice on the continent has been portrayed as a cruel and arbitrary system which inflicted horrendous forms of torture on innocent and unsuspecting inhabitants with a total disregard for the legal rules. On the other hand, there exists an image of an absentee government which cared very little for its respectable citizens and was powerless to protect them against the attacks of mercenaries, robbers, and the like. As usual, both images are gross exaggerations. Administration and justice in the Dutch Republic were indeed characterized by an enormous degree of fragmentation (see Appendix). In the province of Holland alone, for example, more than two hundred first-instance courts – each with its own medium-sized, small, or even minuscule territory – had full competence in criminal cases. Local bailiffs and court members often jealously guarded their independence, though they were frequently willing to cooperate and exchange prisoners or witnesses. Means of communication did not exceed the speed of a horse or a barge, and in the absence of fingerprinting techniques and photographs it was extremely difficult to establish someone's identity with any degree of certainty. But postal services in the northern Netherlands were comparatively fast and efficient, and the various courts kept each other informed. Torture did exist and was regularly used, but it was subject to fairly stringent rules which were – judging from the criminal records – only infrequently disregarded. What is more, the defendants themselves knew as much.

Criminal Proceedings

Let us see what happened when a person was arrested on suspicion of burglary and of belonging to a band of vagrants. As pointed out earlier, a bailiff and his assistants could arrest a vagrant more easily than a respected local inhabitant, but all arrests had to be endorsed by the court, which consisted of a varying number of aldermen (*schepenen*). (Consent was often given afterwards, however, in the case of vagrants.) Generally speaking, the first interrogation took place within a few hours of the suspect's being apprehended. Initial questions dealt with identification: the defendant's name, place of birth, age, sex, domicile, marriage, occupation, and sometimes parents, wives, husbands, and children. Next followed questions about the alleged offences. Apart from identification, the principal aim of interrogation was to obtain a confession, not to expose motive (a more general interest in motive only began to develop during the second half of the eighteenth century), or analyse the structure of the group to which the suspect had belonged, or even to uncover crimes he or she had committed in other jurisdictions. The parochialism which accompanied judicial and administrative fragmentation usually precluded any real curiosity about the composition of thieves' networks or patterns of criminal activity. Besides, the high costs of detention did not encourage repeated or lengthy interrogations.

This lack of interest was generally mutual. Defendants who had been arrested on minor charges, such as 'simple' theft, often confessed immediately, or during the second or third interrogation, which took place within three to at most fourteen days. The same applied to first offenders and very young suspects, all of whom must have known that punishment would be fairly light: they were usually banished or detained for some months, and perhaps flogged. Many professional thieves and burglars seem to have regarded even more serious forms of punishment – such as combinations of flogging, banishment, branding, and confinement in the house of correction – as an occupational hazard. These defendants (both men and women) rarely bothered to deny the bailiff's charges, and criminal proceedings lasted only a few days or at most two weeks. The courts wanted nothing but a quick and therefore cheap procedure. The defendants mostly concurred: as long as they were caught, they might as well get it over with as quickly as possible.

The situation changed drastically when more was at stake: life or long-term imprisonment for the defendants, serious threats to public order and safety for the authorities. Such was the case in nearly all criminal proceedings against members of professional gangs suspected of armed robbery and violence, especially if they belonged to ethnic groups; in proceedings against men or women with more than one previous conviction; and, occasionally, when first offenders had been involved in series of burglaries as well as crimes of violence. Confession was still extremely important and it continued to form one of the main purposes of interrogation, but it was no longer enough (see, for instance, the case of Herry Moses in Chapter 6). In fact, bailiffs and courts often took a surprising amount of trouble in order to establish all the details. They were not prepared to believe just anything, even if it might have saved them a good deal of time and effort to do so. If a suspect's statements were full of discrepancies, if defendants contradicted each other, or if evidence turned up that did not fit previous confessions, bailiffs usually checked the stories by comparing them with other available evidence. The costs entailed by a protracted period of detention were no longer considered prohibitive. Prosecutors were more inclined to ask for the assistance of their colleagues in other jurisdictions – for instance, by having them interrogate their detainees anew – and much trouble was taken to establish a suspect's identity. In such cases the courts also showed more interest in relations between band members, their criminal careers, and previous convictions. Consequently, criminal proceedings might drag on for months and even years.

A good example of the care taken by a court to establish a suspect's identity is the case of a robber nicknamed the Glory of Holland (Roem van Holland). In September 1718 the local court of Buren in Gelderland wrote to the Hof van Gelre concerning the vagrant Johannes Petersz, alias the Glory of Holland. Peters had admitted to beating up a constable and also confessed to a rape and some other acts of violence. Both his victims and his accomplices accused Glory, as he was usually called, of participating in a number of armed robberies and burglaries in farmhouses and rural churches; during one of these a farmer's son had been murdered. In spite of being tortured twice, the prisoner continued to deny these allegations. The local bailiff nevertheless demanded a capital sentence. At this stage the Hof van Gelre was asked for advice. It suggested sentencing Peters to flogging, branding, and twenty-five years in the house of correction instead, purely on account of the crimes he had admitted. The court's extensive research and correspondence had revealed that the nickname Glory was carried by two or possibly three more vagrants; furthermore, witnesses did not fully agree on his personal description. Therefore his involvement in the robberies, burglaries, and murder could not be established beyond doubt. The local court heeded only part of this advice. It sentenced Peters to death by hanging, but without referring to the 'second' list of crimes. On the morning of his execution Peters admitted to these crimes as well.[3]

Glory's case illustrates not only the care taken by the courts but also some of the ways in which defendants made use of particular weaknesses of the judiciary. Besides denying the alleged crimes, many defendants tried to raise doubts about their own identity. They protested, maintained that they were innocent passers-by, or tried to convince the court that they were indeed members of a vagrant group but carried different names and had, of course, never participated in any thefts. Some gave no explanation at all but stubbornly denied being the person they were said to be. Such stratagems took very different forms from one cultural group to another, but nearly all defendants tried to create confusion about identity. Interestingly enough, hardly any of them claimed to have an alibi. (Could this be because identity was much more difficult to establish than presence – or absence – in a society in which it was impossible to become invisible, either by disappearing into urban crowds or by hiding in forests, deserts, and other wildernesses?)

Defendants were often left in the dark as regards details of procedure and the exact nature of the evidence against them. Unlike modern defendants, they had no right to legal assistance. The whole setting of a criminal interrogation, where matters of liberty and even of life or death were at stake, was characterized by huge disparities in the means available to the two parties facing each other. Yet it would be a mistake to regard a criminal interrogation as anything other than a confrontation. Some defendants were obviously more proficient in the art of selectively imparting and withholding information than others. A few even became experts in dealing with interrogators and skilfully tried to minimize the risks of the situation.

Defendants often attempted to reduce punishment by suggesting extenuating circumstances, such as pregnancy, youth, simplicity, temporary insanity, or acting under duress. In 1722 a fifteen-year-old boy confessed to a number of petty thefts and a few burglaries in farmhouses. His accomplices were banished from the province of Holland for ten to twenty years, but the boy himself was sentenced to only a few days of detention. He had managed to convince the court that he had been kidnapped by his companions and forced to join in the burglaries.[4] Others tried to excuse their illegal activities by references to the bad example of parents and friends, broken homes, a bad education, and, of course, indigence. Poverty was particularly often mentioned as both reason and excuse for involvement in criminal activities. It seems to have been the kind of 'explanation' the courts expected, though it did not usually induce them to lessen punishment.

In these serious cases suspects frequently tried to mislead their interrogators by confessing to only part of their illegal activities and remaining silent about those which, according to their expectations, might result in a death sentence. For Stoffel van Reenen capital punishment had become unavoidable, but even then further indignities could be avoided by a judicious timing of confessions. In 1668 Stoffel was sentenced to death by hanging on account of several burglaries and armed robberies involving maltreatment of the victims. On the morning of his execution he admitted to quite a few more armed robberies, during one of which fire had been used to torture a man. The victim had died afterwards, and Stoffel would certainly have been broken on the wheel if he had confessed to this particular crime before being sentenced.[5]

Defendants thus knew not only which factors would be regarded as extenuating but also which ones might be better kept in the dark. The particular setting and conditions of an illegal act influenced the penalty that was going to be imposed. Had it been committed at night, by a group, by armed men, and had violence been threatened or actually used? Instead of a flat denial of involvement, a judicious rendering of the circumstances might lead to lesser punishment. Defendants tried to hide any traces of previous convictions, knowledge of which would certainly induce the court to impose heavier penalties. Most of them simply hoped that the court would not discover an earlier sentence – a not unreasonable expectation considering the territorial fragmentation of criminal justice and the slowness of communications. Some defendants took more drastic measures and had the marks of branding on their shoulders cut out or removed by quicklime. As a result judicial authorities began to distrust all scars on shoulders. On the whole the courts frequently managed to gather information about previous convictions from all over the Dutch Republic.

The care taken by prosecutors and courts is perhaps all the more impressive if it is remembered that they regarded most vagrant suspects as a lower and lesser sort of people, and that the means available to the judiciary were limited indeed. The case of 34-year-old Jacobus Hermansz, an itinerant pedlar and quack from Austrian Flanders who regularly visited Zeeland, is not exceptional. In 1723 Jacobus was arrested in Amsterdam, sent on to Zeeland, and confronted with the victim of one of his alleged robberies; he persistently denied everything.

The bailiff demanded either torture or a capital sentence, but the local court refused both and decided to release the suspect because of inconclusive evidence.[6] Obviously, legal mistakes were made, then as now, and it seems likely that a number of defendants were victimized by prosecutors who were too lazy, too ignorant, or too prejudiced to give them a fair trial. But there was no question of a systematic miscarriage of justice. Whatever the modern opinion about the legal rules and practices of the *ancien régime* – and particularly about legal inequality, the use of judicial torture, and the undeniable harshness of punishment – prosecutors and judges in the Dutch Republic did on the whole remain well within those rules. They did not construct fictitious cases against suspects; nor did they systematically invent illegal acts, indulge in extra-legal mass persecutions, or use different standards in judging the evidence.[7] From the ways in which defendants dealt with interrogation and detention we may infer that they positively counted on their opponents' adherence to the rules.

In some criminal cases which dealt with crimes whose penalty was corporal punishment in public neither a considerable amount of circumstantial evidence nor repeated interrogations and confrontations with witnesses were enough to induce a confession. Under those circumstances – and only those – judicial torture might be applied. (Formal rules prescribed the order and duration of each degree of torture, starting with thumbscrews and ending with the *palei*, or rack. Very little is known about its application in practice; the criminal records offer extremely fragmented and scanty information.) Again, nearly every defendant seems to have been aware of the regulations governing torture and of the legal restriction which determined that a sentence of public corporal punishment could only be imposed if the defendant had confessed.[8] At least one man thought he could outsmart the judicial authorities. In 1798 a member of the Great Dutch Band (1790–9), the son of an Amsterdam house painter, was arrested just a few weeks after torture had been officially abolished. He pointed out to the court at Amsterdam that he could not be sentenced to death unless they succeeded in obtaining his confession, which would not be forthcoming since he could not be tortured. He did not realize, however, that a death sentence no longer required a confession, and was eventually sentenced to death.[9]

Bailiffs could by no means apply torture immediately if a confession was not forthcoming: they required formal permission from the court and a written recommendation by two impartial jurists. A consideration of the costs may have been an even more serious cause of delay. Torture could be applied by the executioner only in the presence of several court members and a doctor. All these people had to be paid substantial fees

– and we have not yet begun to calculate the costs of maintaining the prisoner.

When a defendant had confirmed the already considerable amount of evidence by his or her confession, the bailiff (in his role of public prosecutor) presented a written summary of the case to the court, demanding a final sentence and suggesting a particular form of punishment. Often the penalty decided upon by the court in its final sentence was less severe. Even before they were caught, most defendants knew exactly which type of punishment they might expect. Andries Orville, for example, a member of the Zwartmakers Band which committed armed robberies in Gelderland during the 1690s, declared 'that he knows that he will have to die now' and 'that he would have to die even if he was as heavy in gold as he is in the flesh . . . and that he is willing to die if it would be tomorrow morning'.[10] Most band members had had ample opportunity to learn about penalties. As has been pointed out by several scholars, the varied types of public punishment in use on the Continent during the *ancien régime* formed a consistent visual code which could be 'read' by a partly illiterate public. The punishments were plainly intended to show which particular crimes had been committed and frequently mirrored or symbolized offences.'[11] Public executions were often attended by the accomplices of the men and women on the scaffold. Orville himself had been present at the executions of two of his colleagues. Convicts and spectators did not just passively consume such messages but blended them with their own beliefs and fears. Orville expounded his personal ideas on punishment and redemption when he learned that he was going to be executed:

> Says he does want to be tortured. Asked why, he says 'to do penance and for his sins'. Says 'he prefers dying to being sent to the East Indies' [which he, not the court, regarded as an alternative punishment] . . . and says that he would not like to go to the East Indies or to some other foreign place overseas, because if he were to perish there he would be suffocated in his sins, and therefore would prefer to die repentant on the orders of the court and would certainly go to heaven if he was punished for his sins by the court.[12]

Punishments were harsh, not only according to modern standards. They were intended as such, aiming at deterrence by giving a horrible, degrading, and extremely public example. The usual, 'lighter' forms of punishment included banishment, flogging, branding, and short periods of detention in the house of correction. Capital punishment was regularly imposed when murder or violent robbery had been committed, or when the number of previous offences and convictions had reached a critical margin. Those involved in crimes combining burglary or robbery with assault, manslaughter, or murder ran the risk of aggravated capital punishment: being broken on the wheel. If the defendants had used little or no violence but had a number of previous convictions, they were often sentenced to death by hanging. In slightly less serious cases they were punished by the *poena proxima mortis*: flogging and branding with the hangman's rope around the neck, followed by a combination of long-term imprisonment and subsequent banishment. Decapitation – the most honourable form of capital punishment – was generally reserved for the perpetrators of manslaughter, especially if they belonged to the 'respectable' part of the population. Because it served as an important means of communication, this code of punishment hardly changed in the course of the seventeenth and eighteenth centuries.

It is important not to forget that a large majority of the criminal cases discussed here did not end in death sentences. If they had, the many references to numerous previous convictions would be incomprehensible. Trijn Jans from Bremen, alias Trijn Blue-thread (Blaeugaren), is a case in point. She was born around 1630 and her 'criminal' career spanned at least thirty-five years. Trijn sometimes earned a living as a casual rural labourer and servant. She also begged and participated in a number of vagrant bands which committed thefts and a few large-scale burglaries and robberies. Between 1655 and 1688 she was convicted at least seventeen times (including six times at Amsterdam, two at Hoorn, and four at Alkmaar). Punishment generally consisted of flogging and banishment; she was occasionally sent to the house of correction for a few years.[13]

Even a long-standing involvement in much more serious crimes might result in a death sentence only after a number of years and several convictions. The history of the vagrant Jan Willems, alias Jan Fixbe, from Amsterdam shows as much. Between 1663 and 1667 he had been sent five times to the house of correction by the courts of Amsterdam and Utrecht; he was also flogged twice, at Leiden and Rotterdam. In 1667 the court of Haarlem sentenced Jan Fixbe to branding, flogging and twenty-five years' banishment. Within a year he was caught again at Delft, and this time the court had him whipped, branded twice, and banished once more for the duration of twenty years on account of his participation in a number of armed robberies. This was his ninth conviction; by that time he was just twenty years old.[14]

When defendants were sentenced to terms of detention in the house of correction, their unequal contest with the authorities continued in a different form. Their behaviour during provisional custody and afterwards in the house of correction and their frequent escapes indicate that convicts were generally well informed about local prison rules, the various means of gaining access to imprisoned colleagues, and the habits of warders. In rural districts suspects were often detained provisionally in the local inn or the bailiff's own house before being transferred to a provincial town. Even there 'prison' usually meant a few rooms or cells in the basement of the town hall. These could certainly be locked and barred, but had not been constructed to resist saws, files, chisels, knives, and especially fire. None of these local prisons could compare with the huge Gevangenpoort (serving as house of detention for the Hof van Holland, the provincial court) at The Hague with its thick walls, heavy doors, and professional staff. Even there communication between detainees was perfectly possible. During the 1790s, for instance, shared card-games, meals, and drinking were sometimes allowed at the Gevangenpoort. Inmates as well as warders and women coming in to clean and do the laundry took part in this conviviality.[15] In smaller towns detainees were provided with food and clothes by friends and relatives during regular, sometimes daily visits. This helped to keep the costs of detention down, but it also provided ample opportunity for smuggling weapons and tools into the building and for the exchange of sundry bits of information.

It was a two-way system, of course: those inside could warn their colleagues who were still at large; those outside in their turn offered moral support and exerted pressure on the inmates not to confess. In the course of April and May 1805 nineteen-year-old Harmen Hendriks Wijnands – a member of the Zwartjesgoed, a band involved in violent robbery and murder (see also Chapter 8) – was visited almost daily by his mother at the Gravensteen prison at Leiden. She brought food but also tried to keep her son from confessing, as Harmen mentioned to a spy who shared his cell. His mother ran a considerable risk during these visits: both she and her husband had been among the most important members of the band. When Harmen eventually began to talk, his parents were arrested and later sentenced to death.[16] In many other cases, however, similar visits were followed by a collective escape.[17]

Early modern criminal justice in the Netherlands was not so much a matter, then, of crimes being invented by persecuting authorities as of certain categories of people being more liable to prosecution and persecution than others. These people possessed a highly specific and generally accurate knowledge of their opponents' procedure. It was pragmatic knowledge, which covered a restricted – though crucial – section of criminal prosecution dealing with territorial fragmentation, identification, evidence, torture, confession, and punishment. This knowledge gave at least some bargaining power to defendants who were placed at an enormous disadvantage by current social and legal rules, who had no right to a formal defence, who had very little else to support them, and whose 'petty' illegal activities (such as begging and vagrancy) were immediately subsumed under the category of serious crime and regarded as aggravating circumstances, while their serious crimes were punished very harshly indeed.

Up Against Whom?

Clearly a confrontation with Dutch criminal justice held serious risks for itinerant defendants: risks created and aggravated by an adverse legal position, which more than balanced their relative independence from social control. But they also had some advantages, into which we should inquire more closely. By looking at the major weaknesses of their opponents we may learn how it was possible for thieves, burglars, and robbers to operate more or less successfully for any length of time at all. Having already glanced at the problems surrounding identification, we will now turn to aspects of judicial organization, starting from a division which was crucial to both parties: the distinction between town and countryside. Let us begin with the side of law and order.

Bailiffs and their assistants could hardly be said to constitute a police force in any modern sense of the term. In a big city like Amsterdam (175,000 to 200,000 inhabitants) the principal public prosecutor could at least rely on several deputies, various official assistants, and a fairly large number of nightwatchmen. In contrast, the two or three assistants of a bailiff in a provincial town should be regarded as his part-time personal staff rather than as 'civil servants'. Many of them had other jobs and duties as well, which were often more important in terms of both income and status. Compared with the countryside, however, this amounted to considerable 'state presence'. Town walls, gates, and other similar boundary markers symbolically and effectively helped to keep out dangers, thus denoting a perceived contrast between 'safe' towns and a 'dangerous' countryside. Until the final years of the eighteenth century the city gates of Amsterdam, for instance, were locked every evening, while iron barriers were lowered into the canals to prevent strangers from entering the town in this way. Urban crime rates may in fact have been higher than rural ones,[18] and quite a few thieves had developed their own methods of circumventing such barriers, but the sense of insecurity which was certainly much stronger in the countryside was not completely unfounded. There was (and is), after all, an important qualitative difference between the everday urban risks posed by having pockets picked, burglary, drunken brawls, or stabbings in alleys and the even more threatening, but much less frequent dangers of life in the open countryside. Rural inhabitants might be attacked at night by a dozen or so armed and masked men who ransacked farmhouses and did not hesitate to maltreat or even torture and kill the inhabitants.

Both the authorities and the general public were well aware of the difference. A sentence of 1620 denotes some thefts and burglaries as particularly serious because they had been committed in the open countryside, 'where people are less able to defend themselves against thieves and violence than in enclosed towns'.[19] The situation had hardly changed by the beginning of the eighteenth century. In 1700 the court of Bergen op Zoom in western Brabant stated that theft committed in the countryside, 'where there is no more protection than the law itself', is a worse crime than theft committed in a town.[20] Nearly another hundred years later, in 1798, the minister of justice urgently discussed matters of public safety with the local authorities in South Holland because an increasing number of robberies and the presence of vagrant bands had created something close to panic among the inhabitants of the countryside near Rotterdam.[21] At night rural inhabitants were supposed to protect themselves; during periods of unrest and military disturbance most villages organized nightly patrols. If necessary, the local militia was called upon. These militias consisted of generally unwilling local artisans and farmers who had to leave their work, use the few available weapons as best as they could, and rely if need be on their farm utensils to ward off men who might be armed and on horseback. The same militia men were also required to assist in the so-called *Generale Jagten* (literally 'general hunts') organized during certain periods by the provincial authorities to get rid of the many vagrants, either by arresting them or by driving them away into neighbouring jurisdictions and provinces.[22]

Under normal conditions the bailiff's assistants took care of most of the day-to-day business of public order and safety, and as long as they were dealing with 'local' affairs, their small numbers seem to have been sufficient. Bailiffs and constables were generally well informed about local conflicts and potential offenders, for the social and geographical distance between the judicial authorities and 'the population' was relatively small. As soon as outsiders and, in particular, large groups of mobile and even armed 'strangers' were involved, the situation changed. The executive powers of bailiffs (in their role as head of police) were seriously hampered by the territorial delimitation and fragmentation of first-instance jurisdiction: unless they had been given formal permission to do so by their colleagues, bailiffs could not track down – let alone arrest – suspects outside their own territory. Restrained by territorial boundaries and confronted by 'mobile criminals', bailiffs were forced to cooperate, whether by joining forces, exchanging information, and allowing their prisoners to be transported to another town for confrontation or by extradition. None of these forms of cooperation was institutionalized, however, and prosecutors generally continued to jealously guard the autonomy of their jurisdictions.

Some of the complicated logistics necessitated by the fragmented organization of criminal justice are illustrated by a report of the confrontation between Andries Orville and some of his accomplices on 11 June 1694. The men had been arrested in several different jurisdictions in the province of Gelderland:

> When the provincial court of Utrecht, upon the formal request of the bailiffs of Amersfoort and Rheenen, had permitted a certain territory to be used for the confrontation of their [Amersfoort's and Rheenen's] prisoners as well as those detained by the court of Lienden and some others, all of these persons gathered today at Doorn – which location had been chosen and approved by all of the courts and bailiffs concerned, but *without in any way encroaching upon or 'prejudicing' any court's privileges and competence* [my italic].[23]

Matters of competence were even more important, if possible, at a provincial level. In the Netherlands in the seventeenth and eighteenth centuries a neighbouring province was as good as a foreign country. Relations might be warmer between a Dutch province (Gelderland, for instance) and adjacent German territory (belonging to Prussia) than between two Dutch provinces. Until the beginning of the eighteenth century no formal arrangements existed between any of these provinces concerning extradition of prisoners, cooperation in tracking down suspects, and so on. The bilateral treaties of 1709 between Holland and Utrecht, and between Holland and Gelderland – which regulated, among other things, the pursuit of vagrants in their respective border areas – were followed by just one more such agreement during the rest of the eighteenth century, between Holland and Utrecht in 1725. It is no coincidence, by the way, that the treaty of 1725 was concluded only because of the grave view taken by various authorities of the dangers posed by extremely mobile gypsy bands. Even in 1799 *Generale Jagten* against vagrants and beggars in Gelderland and Brabant were still arranged as the occasion arose. Only the French-inspired reforms of the years after 1800 brought about major changes in this situation (see Zwaardemaker 1939 and van Weel 1989).

The use of banishment as a form of punishment exemplifies this general lack of concern about other provinces in general and other jurisdictions in particular. During the seventeenth century and most of the eighteenth century persons convicted in Holland and Zeeland on account of lesser offences were simply banished from the jurisdiction in question, while perpetrators of serious crimes were banished from the whole territory of these two provinces. Gelderland and Utrecht had a similar policy. In Brabant the relevant unit remained even smaller for a long time, probably reflecting its rather piecemeal integration in the Dutch Republic during much of the seventeenth century. There, convicts were banished from *Stad en Meijerij* (town and surrounding rural district) of 's Hertogenbosch, or from town and barony of Breda. After the 1760s banishment concerned the whole of the *Generaliteitslanden* (Brabant, Limburg, and Dutch Flanders). Nowhere in these parts of the Dutch Republic between the 1650s and the late eighteenth century did the size of the relevant moral community exceed the province. Until the reforms of King Louis Napoleon in 1806–9 national integration did not become effective in this respect. By that time serious offenders were banished from the whole of the northern Netherlands; during the brief period of annexation by France (1810–12/13) they even had to remove themselves from the whole of the French empire. Banishment policy thus reflects the strength of Dutch juridical and administrative particularism as well as the slow process of political and administrative integration.

Rural bands profited in many ways from these characteristic shortcomings of their opponents' organization. Naturally, imperfect co-operation on the part of the authorities made it easier to avoid arrest – either individually or as a group – as long as one remained on the move. It also caused delays in criminal proceedings, as we saw in the case of Andries Orville, which improved the chances of an escape from detention. Besides, some forms of punishment – banishment in particular – were ill suited to deterring defendants who had a low social status to begin with and were already used to an itinerant way of life. Unlike most established defendants, they did not stand to lose most of their social and professional contacts. Bands benefited more indirectly as well. To some extent they based their *modus operandi* on the territorial demarcation of jurisdictions. Many bands showed a marked preference for border areas, and gypsy bands in particular used to establish their encampments right on the frontiers of jurisdictions. The houses of many rural fences and other local assistants could be found on the periphery of villages and jurisdictions. Several bands even tended to concentrate their burglaries and robberies in provincial border areas. Members of these groups were well aware both of the territorial delimitation of a bailiff's powers and of the precise location of such administrative and legal boundaries.

The structure of the criminal world – the organization of crime – presents a striking and hardly fortuitous parallel with the basic urban/rural distinction in the maintenance of public order, in 'state presence'. It does not really matter whether the division between groups operating in an urban setting and those active in rural domains simply reflected the organization of criminal justice (and thus the fairly exact knowledge prevailing among thieves, robbers, and burglars of their opponents' organization) or denoted a more basic urban/rural contrast underlying both criminal and judicial organization. Nor do we, at present, need to go into the important differences between the various rural bands in their relations with towns. The main point is that there was such a division within the world of crime at all. We will take a closer look at this partition, both because differences between urban and rural crime help us to focus on the main characteristics of the rural bands which form, after all, our principal subject and to find out more about internal demarcations within organized crime, about the distinctions thieves and robbers themselves made.

Urban Organized Crime

The significance of an urban/rural distinction in the world of crime is all the more striking since contrasts between town and countryside were probably less pronounced in the northern Netherlands than in many other European countries. Besides, hardly any rural band in the Dutch Republic lacked connections with urban life, and most of the groups which operated in the densely populated and urbanized province of Holland definitely relied on urban ties. Yet a separate category of typically urban organized crime should be distinguished, comprising a wide range of activities and patterns of organization. To this world belonged confidence tricksters, gangs of card-sharps and gamesters operating on the barges which maintained regular services between the Dutch towns, wide-ranging networks of cutpurses and pickpockets, groups of thieves and burglars who specialized in the theft of jewels, silver, or porcelain, burglars who stole large quantities of white lead, coffee, textiles, and other valuable merchandise from urban warehouses, sneak-thieves, circles of shoplifters, small groups of burglars who specialized in prising open shutters and windows, burglars who used ladders and entered houses through the attics, petty thieves who tried their hand at anything, and finally street robbers who assaulted passers-by at night and stole their money and watches under threat of murder.

Many of these men knew each other. All of them relied on a wider urban 'criminal infrastructure', both for information and for the sale of stolen goods. They all belonged to the Dutch urban underworld which, unlike the underworld of Paris or London, was not so much a local as an interurban phenomenon.[24] If only for this special feature, urban organized crime in the Dutch Republic deserves a separate study, dealing with patterns of organization and the urban geography of crime as well as jargon, ritual, names, and in particular the problem of 'criminal subcultures'.[25] Characteristically, urban thieves and burglars rarely if ever were to be found outside the big towns of the western part of the Dutch Republic. The countryside was largely irrelevant to them, not only in a professional sense but, it seems, in every other respect as well. These men lived in towns; most of them rented rooms or boarded at cheap lodging-houses. They spent their hours of leisure in towns, drinking in pubs, visiting fairs, working, fighting, and showing off. Most of their legitimate jobs were connected to the urban economy – very few of them, for instance, ever worked as casual rural labourers – and their main, illegal business was exclusively urban. In short, their whole orientation was urban.

This restriction to cities does not, however, imply a lack of mobility. Most urban burglars and thieves operated in several towns in the area now called the Randstad: the region enclosed by Amsterdam, Rotterdam, The Hague, and Utrecht, which has always formed the most densely populated part of the Netherlands. Like the other inhabitants of this region, men and women involved in criminal activities made use of the existing infrastructure and the excellent means of transport. It was not at all unusual for them to take the morning barge from Amsterdam to Haarlem, say, spend an afternoon there with some friends in a pub, burgle one or two houses in the evening, and leave next morning for Delft or The Hague. They often remained in one town for a number of weeks or even months before going on to the next. Amsterdam and Rotterdam formed the main bases for their expeditions. Accordingly, urban thieves of any professional standing who operated in only one city are almost impossible to find in the Dutch criminal records. Most thieves had a long list of previous convictions by town courts all over Holland. A few even operated internationally, like Cesar Cambalot and Jacques Richan. Both were born around 1635 in the southern Netherlands and had served in the Spanish armies. By 1659–60 they had committed a large number of exclusively urban burglaries in Amsterdam, Rotterdam, The Hague, Zwolle, Antwerp, Brussels, Liège, and several other towns; they were sentenced to be whipped, branded, and banished at Rotterdam.[26] Others extended their activities even further, to the coastal towns of northern Germany such as Hamburg and Bremen.

Urban thieves differed from their rural counterparts not only in their confinement to one domain but also in their patterns of organization. Large, interurban networks comprising various types of thieves and burglars as well as their fences, tavern-keepers, and informers were typical. Within these loose-knit networks – which might include as many as fifty or eighty people – smaller groups of thieves can be distinguished who actually committed the thefts. The composition of the groups shifted continually according to various circumstances: who was available (that is, interested, in town, and not in prison), who had certain technical skills, who might be relied upon for information about the house or the expected booty, and so on. Urban thieves were often recruited for a particular job or a series of jobs in one town.

Andries Wissenhagen and his companions belonged to such networks during the 1650s. Wissenhagen, who came from Berlin, was involved in various kinds of illegal activities all over the western half of the Dutch Republic. He lived for most of the year at Amsterdam, but regularly visited Rotterdam, The Hague, Delft, and a few more Dutch towns. Wissenhagen and this associates spent much of their time in taverns frequented by a mixed company of sailors, former soldiers, artisans, and unskilled labourers. They met at these pubs partly in order to plan series of sneak-thefts and burglaries. In 1653–4 Wissenhagen committed a number of burglaries together with Piet van Leiden, alias Piet Pair of Shoes (Paer Schoenen), and Hollow-eyed (Holoogh) Hendrik. In the course of a few weeks they broke into several houses and shops in Amsterdam, The Hague, and Leiden, stealing silver, money, clothes, and small pieces of furniture. These were sold to their regular fences. During the same period each of the men was also involved in thefts with different sets of companions.[27]

As well as the restriction to urban territory, the numerous interurban connections, and the organizational pattern of overlapping networks, three more distinctive characteristics of urban organized crime in the Netherlands should be mentioned. First, there seems to have been a fairly high degree of specialization. Pickpockets rarely joined in a burglary, jewel thieves seldom turned to stealing large quantities of merchandise from warehouses, and thieves who regularly employed certain instruments (such as a fretsaw) rarely altered their techniques. During the 1680s a group of three men had developed the following elaborate method. The most experienced thief, Isaac Lopes de Luna from Livorno, was disguised as the tutor of a young baron, who was played by the second thief; the third man, Willem van Meckenum from Brussels, pretended to be his valet. They presented themselves on the doorstep of a rich merchant's house in Amsterdam, but left again after a few minutes upon their 'discovery' that they had been directed to the wrong house. In the meantime one of them had managed to obtain a wax imprint of the front door key. A few weeks later – generally on a Sunday morning when the inhabitants had gone to church – the same three men entered the house by the front door and removed a large quantity of merchandise from the basement. On one occasion they stole a few thousand pairs of (silk?) stockings, valued at roughly 8,000 to

9,000 guilders. Some of their booty was illegally exported to England and sold there.[28]

Secondly, the number of men actually involved in the execution of a theft or burglary rarely exceeded five or six. Silence and speed (both in entering a house and in getting away in case of an alarm) were of prime importance. The presence of a large group invited discovery and impeded mobility in the narrow urban streets. The small size of these groups as well as their typically changing composition may well have contributed to the third characteristic: the comparative lack of hierarchy in urban groups of thieves and the near absence of 'leading' figures. Of course, there was a difference between newcomers and experienced thieves. But thieves who had reached a prominent status were usually known for their individual skills, numerous previous convictions, and wide range of experience rather than for their authority as captains. (In some groups of thieves, innkeepers and fences acted as coordinators. I have found no one, however, with a position comparable to the eighteenth-century 'thief-taker general' Jonathan Wild in London.)

Cornelis Jansz van Swieten was a figure of some stature. During the 1680s he belonged to the same circles as Isaac Lopes de Luna and another well-known burglar and street robber, Abraham Jansse Genaer, alias Pistols (Poffertjes) Bram.[29] Van Swieten was better known as De Achtkanten Boer, which might be rendered as 'the square peasant' (in the sense of blunt and straightforward), though this does no real justice to the pun of *Achtkant* (eight cornered) as a superlative of *Vierkant* (square). Together with his colleagues the Achtkanten Boer burgled the town houses of wealthy patricians and merchants, stealing large amounts of money, jewellery, silverware, and other valuables. A comment by one of his associates – Willem van Meckenum – illustrates the magnitude of their activities. He described his share in the booty as '*not more* than 350 guilders': the rough equivalent of a year's wages for a skilled shipwright.[30] The Achtkanten Boer was famous not only among his fellow thieves and burglars but even among ordinary country folk all over the Dutch Republic. As much is evident both from nineteenth-century folk-tales and from the behaviour of a local civil servant in the extreme north of the province of Holland at a time when the Achtkanten Boer was still at large. The man (a beadle) was discovered running around at night in the woods near his village shouting, 'I am the Achtkanten Boer and I will set fire to the whole village.'[31]

Preliminary research indicates that the extent of these urban networks fluctuated markedly, but their structure appears to have remained largely unchanged during the seventeenth and eighteenth centuries. The overlapping networks to which most urban thieves in the Netherlands belonged formed neither a single, centralized criminal organization nor a haphazard assortment of local criminal circuits operating separately. Together they constituted 'the Dutch urban underworld', precisely because of their interconnections and overlaps. When we use the term 'underworld' here to include both the principal actors (the actual perpetrators of criminal offences) and their supporting cast – in short, all those who formed the infrastructure of organized crime (cf. McIntosh 1975, pp. 18–27) – it raises the question of whether the division between urban and rural underworlds constituted a social and cultural boundary as well as a demarcation in terms of organization and expertise.

The answer – if we may rely on the evidence provided by the biographies of band members who operated in the countryside of Holland, within 5 to 50 kilometres of big towns such as Amsterdam or Rotterdam – is that it did not. Many rural thieves in this area came from urban lower-class backgrounds and continually visited towns, looked for jobs in towns, lived there for part of the year, and kept up their connections with members of the urban underworld – without, that is, shifting their professional territory to the urban domain. It was the urban thieves who showed an almost complete lack of interest in setting foot outside a town, not the other way around.

Demarcations

In terms of organization and territory, then, urban and rural underworlds of the northern Netherlands should be distinguished, though not separated. In social and cultural terms, by contrast, 'we' incorporated both urban and rural thieves and their associates. It is by no means easy to discover where the boundaries of the world of crime lay. Who were the outsiders of these underworlds? Who found themselves at its margins? Again, we should distinguish between a cultural and social perspective on the one hand and an approach which regards underworlds mainly in terms of professional organization on the other.

With regard to the former, there are definite indications that the world of crime did not form an independent 'subculture' at all. First, defendants never spoke of themselves in general terms as belonging to 'the underworld' but as members of a particular band or ethnic or regional group; each of these had its own boundaries and thus its own outsiders. The character and importance of these mutual distinctions and divisions will become evident in the following chapters. Secondly, there is a conspicuous absence of generally recognized and practised rites of passage, in particular of rituals of admission to 'the underworld', whereas several individual bands had their own ceremonies. Thirdly, it is hard to believe that the norms and values revealed in the implicit rules of exclusion observed by both urban and rural bands were not shared by a much larger segment of early modern Dutch society. The emphasis on life in public – the crucial importance of sociability – forms a good example.

It is worth noting that all the tales told by thieves and robbers are social tales: about groups of people who committed thefts together, about pairs of thieves who negotiated sales of stolen goods with dealers, about groups of men and women travelling and spending their time in pubs together. It is too easy to say that this is only to be expected from people who belonged to groups. Nor does it seem likely that all defendants systematically refrained from mentioning 'private' spheres or moments. By far the larger part of the lives of these people was, in fact, spent in public: on urban streets and country roads, in pubs and workshops, in the barns and stables of farmhouses, at work in the fields and at fairs, and in cheap lodging-houses. Privacy appears to have been both rare and undesirable. In these circumstances it certainly becomes easier to understand why the defendants seldom referred – and then only in negative terms – to members of their profession who habitually worked, travelled, and lived alone. To wish to be on one's own must have been regarded as odd, and probably as dangerous, since a preference for privacy implied a desire to be free not only from the conveniences of sociability but also from its controlling side. Perhaps it was a sign of eccentricity to have such wishes in this type of society. (The whole concept of privacy may well have been a foreign or different one in early modern European society.) In so far as it valued sociability for reasons of control and safety, the 'underworld' displays a remarkable similarity to its more respected counterpart.

Not every burglar, thief, robber, pickpocket, or confidence trickster who used to act single-handedly was reckoned to be one of the 'loners'. Most of these thieves operated in towns, were highly specialized in certain types of theft, and relied on a wide circle of assistants. They definitely belonged to the urban underworld in a social sense, as is exemplified by Engelbrecht Stroo (Straw) from Hamburg. While working as a domestic cook at The Hague, he stole a large amount of money and valuables from his master. During the period 1656–8 he became a professional urban burglar who specialized in sneak-theft from the houses of wealthy noblemen and diplomats (such as the Polish ambassador) at The Hague. Stroo invited assistance only if a specific job required it, yet he was well known among the thieves and fences who made up the local criminal circuit. In 1658 Stroo was arrested and condemned by the Hof van Holland on account of a large theft of diamonds; a few years later he was sent to the Amsterdam house of correction, but he broke out after a short while. By 1663 he had changed both his *modus operandi* and his way of life by joining a large network of 'most famous thieves' who operated mainly in the countryside of the provinces of Holland and Utrecht. He was eventually arrested again and sentenced to death at Leiden.[32]

In the countryside very few thieves and burglars worked alone. Unlike most of their urban counterparts, who were generally at the top of their profession, solitary rural thieves were outsiders in a dual sense. They had lost contact both with established rural society and with the regular vagrant groups. Soldiers and sailors who had recently left their company or ship appear to have been particularly vulnerable in this respect. Some of them eventually settled down, re-joined the army, or managed to form new ties with a group of vagrants. A few were arrested before very long, perhaps for lack of support. Others were unable or unwilling to belong to a group for any length of time. Peter Bessems from Meer in Limburg, for instance, had been a soldier from the age of fifteen; previously he had worked as a spinner and pig herd, and when necessary, he had begged. In 1723 Bessems, then in his late twenties, murdered a fellow soldier after the two of them had stolen some food and clothes. Four years later he briefly joined forces with two soldiers and committed an armed robbery in German territory. On their journey back to their garrison town in western Brabant the three men decided to kill the first person they met on the road. Accordingly, they murdered and robbed a tinker and buried his dead body. Bessems left the army some time afterwards, re-joined, and left again. He lived for some years at The Hague, worked as a sailor, and finally returned to Brabant, where he begged and sold pencils. Almost twenty years after his second murder he was arrested in Brabant and executed.[33] Bessems was not unusual among solitary rural burglars and robbers. These men were known for their often extremely erratic and arbitrary violence, which in its turn may well have contributed to their social isolation.[34]

In at least some cultural respects, then, criminal circles can hardly be distinguished from a much larger, lower-class segment of Dutch society. They did not reveal an explicit sense of belonging together and forming a separate 'underworld'. None the less professional contacts between members of different bands and networks (to which we will return in more detail in Chapters 7 and 8) point to an implicit recognition of belonging to the same sphere. This acknowledgement seems to have rested at least partly on a shared appreciation of the differences between professionals and amateurs – to use anachronistic terms once more. These differences are not as easily determined as Beattie and McIntosh, for example, appear to think. Beattie, following McIntosh, speaks of '"professional" criminals in the straightforward and limited sense that they were fully dependent, for the time being, on crime for their income'

(1986, pp. 256–7). McIntosh points out that

> because professional crime is a relatively distinct occupational sphere, it has its own patterning and continuity, whereas amateur activities, being only part-time, are much more influenced by a variety of circumstances, often peculiar to the individual criminal. Professional crime is thus distinguished not by its scale, or degree of turpitude or efficiency, but by its organisational differentiation from other activities . . . So professional crime is more uniform, in the sense that criminals of the same type are all in the same boat, as full-timers who have nothing much else to fall back on. (1975, p. 12).

Very few professional thieves, burglars, or robbers active in the early modern Netherlands would have agreed. Neither McIntosh's emphasis on full-time involvement in crime nor Beattie's criterion of total dependence on crime for an income would have made sense in their world. During that period very few people were employed full time in any kind of occupation, and this was certainly true of even the most professional burglars and robbers in the Netherlands. Instead, it looks as if professionals in crime recognized each other by patterns of organization, styles of operating, specialization and expertise, training by older and more experienced thieves, ties of kinship and marriage with people involved in similar activities, reputation among other thieves, nicknames, and occasionally by their use of jargon. Nearly all of these characteristics were predicated on a long-term involvement in illegal activities.

Most groups of amateurs, on the other hand, were only infrequently involved in criminal activities. In 1751 a small group of local crabbers at Axel in Dutch Flanders broke into a warehouse and stole some barrels of brandy. Several of these men had been smuggling regularly; theft was their new, ill-fated venture. Soon after their burglary in the warehouse they were caught in the act of robbing a chicken coop and arrested by other local inhabitants.[35] The many poor urban families who took to stealing food and firewood from the market gardens during periods of dearth, such as the mid-1740s, the early 1770s, and the 1790s, were even less familiar with the world of crime. Whereas certain types of cattle theft and the stealing of large quantities of lead (which were likewise linked with periods of war and scarcity) were mostly committed for commercial reasons, food and firewood were usually stolen to be used by the thieves themselves.[36] Amateurs generally lacked expertise, as well as routine, specialization, connections, and efficient organization. As a consequence they chose the wrong places to rob, did not check whether they could get away when discovered, and did not know how to get rid of stolen goods safely. (This is not to say, of course, that all professional thieves were really good at their jobs; quite a few members of rural bands went about their illegal business in a careless way, bungled simple burglaries, and got themselves arrested because of not taking the most elementary precautions.)

Contacts between groups of amateur thieves and professionals were scarce, and they never cooperated. The small number of groups of amateurs who became professional thieves or robbers indicates the extent of the gap, though one or two bread- and fruit-stealing, 'family groups' did make the transition.[37] Bands of plundering soldiers form another borderline case. Military requisitioning and pillaging were often hard to distinguish from armed robbery. In 1676, for instance, thirty-four soldiers from the garrison of the Flemish town of Damme (then part of the Spanish Netherlands) crossed the border into Dutch territory. They were looking for trouble and found it, as could be expected, at a local inn where they beat up the innkeeper and plundered the house.[38] In the province of Holland groups of soldiers were generally smaller, but formed just as much of a threat to the rural population. Three cavalrymen and one of their non-commissioned officers (all of them billeted in villages near Alkmaar) forced their way into a farmhouse in the summer of 1747. They tortured a woman and her children, and plundered the house. Their names were known to the court of Alkmaar and a high reward was offered in case of their capture, but they seem to have escaped arrest.[39] When caught, soldiers frequently claimed to have been sent out on a foraging expedition with instructions not to be too particular about the rules. As long as their commanders backed them up, very few civil courts were in a position to challenge their statements.

Similarities in their methods however, did not automatically lead to contact and collaboration between soldiers and rural bands. As will be shown in Chapter 4, the transition from military plundering to professional robbery required time, mainly to develop a particular mode of operating and forge connections with local assistants and dealers. Expertise in military techniques and familiarity with military organization models certainly helped, but a rural band without access to fences, reliable innkeepers, or informers did not survive for long.

Viewed as a whole, it would be a considerable exaggeration to designate the world of crime in the Dutch Republic as a separate subculture. Besides their illegal professional activities, thieves, burglars, and robbers – whether belonging to urban or rural circuits – appear to have shared notions of sociability and professionalism; they certainly recognized a common adversary in the shape of the judicial authorities, of whose organization and procedures they had considerable working knowledge. They did not, though, regard themselves as members of one 'underworld'. Nor did they even share a common thieves' language, rituals of admission or exclusion, patterns of mobility or recruitment, religion, family or gender relations, occupations, and so on. It is to these topics and thus to the cultural variety of rural organized crime that we will turn in the following case-studies.

Part II

Warfare and Banditry

3

Post-war Bands: Holland and Zeeland, 1615–1720

The image of undisturbed prosperity and peaceful, well-ordered existence presented by so many seventeenth-century Dutch paintings and drawings tells only part of the story.The seventeenth century was, after all, not only a 'golden age' but also a period of warfare. The final phase of the 'Opstand' – the Dutch Revolt against Habsburg Spain – ended only in 1648. In the Dutch heartland of Holland and Zeeland fighting of any consequence was largely limited to the years before the Twelve-years was concluded in 1609. Both provinces, however, continued to be substantially involved in financing and organizing the big military campaigns undertaken after 1621 to (re)capture Brabant from the Spanish. Together Holland and Zeeland bore about 70 per cent of the total costs of the Dutch armies, while their towns served as the main naval bases, mustering places, and supply centres for the upkeep of both army and navy. Besides, the Spanish armies came extremely close. The resumption of warfare after the expiry of the truce in 1621 had been marked by Stadholder Frederik Hendrik's famous siege of 's Hertogenbosch (1629) and his march along the Maas river to recapture Maastricht (1632). Retaliating, Spanish troops crossed the provinces of Gelderland and Utrecht and reached the town of Amersfoort, only about 40 kilometres from Amsterdam. They did not succeed in pushing on, and during the final decades of the Dutch Revolt parts of Brabant that had hardly ever been 'Dutch' before were gradually joined to the Dutch state. For a large part of Brabant the Peace of Münster of 1648 formed the beginning of territorial unity and integration in the Dutch Republic.

Douglas Hay and J. M. Beattie have convincingly demonstrated the links between warfare and fluctuations in property crime in seventeenth- and eighteenth-century England (see Hay 1982, pp. 135–46, and Beattie 1986, pp. 199–264; cf. Beattie 1974, pp. 93–5). It would be hard to imagine that the Dutch Revolt – which dominated so much of the first half of the seventeenth century, and to a large extent determined the territorial shape of the Dutch Republic – would not have had an impact on the incidence and structure of Dutch rural crime. But did connections between warfare and organized property crime in the Netherlands conform to the English pattern? In England the actual amount of property crime dropped dramatically during each period of warfare between 1660 and the late eighteenth century, only to rise again sharply just after each war, and to remain at a relatively high level in peacetime. This applied to all forms of property crime, but the post-war increase in serious offences, such as highway robbery, burglary, and horse theft, was even more pronounced than in petty theft and simple larceny (Hay 1982, pp. 143–4).

In England the absence of tens of thousands of young, unskilled, and often unemployed or underemployed working-class men largely accounted for the wartime decrease. Paraphrasing contemporary commentators, Beattie describes how 'The peace brought back to England large numbers of disreputable men who had spent several years being further brutalized by service in the armed forces, without any provision being made for their re-entry in the work force' (1986, p. 226). Hay too points to the massive demobilization of soldiers and sailors who, 'whatever their previous histories, once paid off necessarily became vagrants fated to a labour-market that was chronically over-supplied, especially later in the [eighteenth] century' (1982, p. 142).

The Dutch Republic was not an island, however. Continental wars were fought on or close to its territory, so that warfare in these parts did not necessarily mean the absence of numerous young men. It seems unlikely, all the same, that the demobilization of large numbers of soldiers and sailors would have had a completely different impact.[1] The northern Netherlands had in fact to contend twice with large numbers of discharged soldiers in the course of the seventeenth century: during the first years of the Twelve-years Truce (1609–12) and again during the years after the conclusion of the Peace of Münster in 1648. The numbers of discharged soldiers must have been particularly high in the 1650s and 1660s, for it was not only the Spanish and Dutch who reduced their armies: the Thirty Years War had ended, and mercenaries of Scottish, Polish, Swiss, Irish, French, Dutch, and German origin took to the road. Not a few of them ended up in Holland.

The Dutch criminal records provide examples of both Dutch and foreign ex-soldiers who tried to find work as sailors, casual labourers, or retail traders. Some joined a new company; a few made use of their artisan training as shoemakers, cobblers, weavers and spinners, ropers, manufacturers of pipes, masons, or carpenters; many just wandered from one town or village to another, without exactly knowing where to go. They had few skills except for their experience in the use of violence, and they rarely had more than a small amount of money. Some of these men had been involved in property crime before they joined the army. They cannot have had any difficulties in finding new companions and accomplices among this crowd of poor, jobless, and often homeless ex-soldiers and sailors. Thomas Bentley, a 52-year-old Englishman, was one of them. He had served as a corporal with the *waardgelders* (local militia men) at Rotterdam. After his dismissal, in 1648, he joined two German burglars who had been operating for some years in the provinces of Utrecht and Holland. Bentley was caught fairly soon, in 1649. The court of his 'own' town, Rotterdam, sentenced him to flogging, branding, and twelve years' banishment.[2]

The criminal records of most first-instance courts in Holland and Zeeland do indeed show the expected post-war increase in the amount of prosecuted property crime: not only during the decades after the Peace of Münster but equally, though less markedly, during the earlier period of the Twelve-years Truce. Few towns and even fewer rural jurisdictions in Holland and Zeeland possess continuous series of criminal sentences starting before the 1620s (unbroken series may be found in Delft, Schoonhoven, Den Briel, Zierikzee, and Goes), but every one of these presents the same pattern. A 'busy' period, which began around 1610 and lasted for the whole of the Twelve-years Truce (1609–21) as well as the next ten years, was succeeded by a rather 'quieter' phase between about 1635 and 1650. For the period after 1650 more evidence is available. Again, both urban and rural court records show a noticeable rise in the number of prosecuted property crimes – an increase which usually started in 1652.

Neither the size of the groups operating during the 1610s and 1620s nor the scope of their activities should be exaggerated. The small band of Stephen Tougoet provides a good example. It operated between 1613 and 1615 in parts of Zeeland and the environs of Rotterdam and Dordrecht. Five to seven men in their twenties were involved, most of whom seem to have begun stealing in Zeeland in the course of 1612–13. They frequently used ladders to climb into the upper windows of farmhouses; sometimes they dug a small tunnel underneath the threshold of the front door. Tougoet and his companions were interested mainly in small amounts of ready money and in clothes, which they sold or pawned. Although armed with rapiers and knives, these men tended to avoid confrontations with the inhabitants of the houses they robbed.[3]

Tougoet's group was among the more professional bands of this period, but in other respects it hardly differed from the many vagrant groups of beggars arrested during these years. Even if the records had not mentioned their native country, the names of Tougoet and his companions – though slightly disguised by Dutch spelling – would have betrayed their origins. Stephen Tougoet, alias Stephen Barton, and his associates Thomas Joons, Philips Herdy, Willem Joumen, Dirk Wels, and Jan Gerington had crossed the Channel to serve in the Dutch armies. Many other men from England, Ireland, Wales, and Scotland had made the same journey: attracted by the armies, by the prospect of work in the textile industries of the towns in Holland, or perhaps repelled by a distinctly intolerant religious policy in England. (The predominance of the English, Scots, Welsh, and Irish among those arrested for combined vagrancy and theft all over Holland and Zeeland during this period is surprising. There may be still other reasons why they came to Holland in such large numbers.) Whatever their motives or careers, many of these men found themselves out of work and money after the conclusion of the truce. They begged, roamed the countryside of Holland, and were frequently arrested by the local courts and usually banished from the jurisdictions concerned.[4]

After about 1630 the number of English-speaking vagrants diminishes rapidly in the remaining records. By that time a more general decrease of prosecutions on account of serious property crimes seems to have set in which continued all through the period 1635–50. The years 1650–2 formed another turning-point. From that time onwards many new groups of thieves and burglars began to appear in the criminal records of Holland and Zeeland, and bands proliferated in this area between 1652 and 1668. To discover a pattern in Brabant is more difficult. It took several decades for local administration in this region to 'recover' from the extremely unsettled political and military situation of the 1630s and 1640s. Even during the 1660s and 1670s the continuing subordinate political position of Brabant as well as attempts by the Protestant north to stamp out Roman Catholicism did little to stimulate local inhabitants to make a supreme effort in the performance of their civic and administrative duties. As a consequence the criminal records for most parts of Brabant are extremely fragmentary until the 1680s or 1690s. (The criminal records of Breda and the surrounding barony, which form an unbroken series from the 1620s until the end of the eighteenth century, are a notable exception.)

To establish that an expected upsurge of organized property crime did indeed occur during the 1650s and 1660s is hardly exciting. We may further investigate the connection between warfare and organized crime by looking in more detail at some of the groups involved. Who were these people? Were all of them discharged or deserted soldiers? Did they have any previous experience in crime, or were most of them newcomers to the business? What was the relevance of military models to the organization of their exploits, and should we in fact regard their bands as 'military bands'?

The Band of Hees

Two bands are especially interesting: the Band of Hees (1654–61) and the Band of Stoffel van Reenen (1663–9). Both operated all over Holland as well as in parts of Utrecht, Zeeland, and Gelderland. Members of each band had belonged to smaller groups during the first half of the 1650s, and some of them were simultaneously involved with other bands.

In a sentence pronounced in Leiden during the final year of the Band of Hees's activities the court of Rijnland described its robberies as 'the most important violence, housebreaking, and theft that has been heard of for a long time'.[5] The Band of Hees formed a large network of rural thieves, burglars, and their relatives and assistants. Between about 1655 and 1661 sentences were pronounced by numerous courts in the western part of the Dutch Republic against at least seventy-five men and women; several dozens more were named as accomplices.[6] Those involved toured the Dutch countryside in pairs or small groups of two or three men and their wives or mistresses. Quite often men and women travelled separately, meeting every few weeks at a fair, an inn, or another well-known location. (Children below the age of fourteen are never mentioned; perhaps they were boarded out.) The itineraries of these small groups covered all of Holland, Zeeland, and Utrecht as well as parts of Gelderland. The whole network as such could never be seen together, and gatherings of more than six to eight men occurred only shortly before the armed robberies. Such meetings took place at the houses of trusted innkeepers and fences: 'where they had their *rendezvous*-place'.[7] The most important of these men – the person who acted as a kind of 'patron' of the band – was Mees Rutgers, alias Father (Vader) Mees, who lived at the hamlet of Hees near Soest, not far from Utrecht. (Because of his pivotal role, I have named the network after the hamlet where he lived.)

Sentences pronounced against Father Mees himself, his wife, the innkeeper Egbert Kool and his wife, and another innkeeper and fence – all of them living at Hees – make abundantly clear that this hamlet was for some years a 'robbers' den' as well as a clearing house for large quantitites of stolen goods.[8] As one of the women, Magdaleen van Schoonhoven, put it, all band members were 'provided for at Hees by a man called Mees who has two dogs, and as soon as these make a noise they [the band members] come out into the open armed with pistols; as soon as they arrive Mees sends to Amersfoort for beer and food'.[9] Together the above-mentioned inhabitants of Hees probably made up almost the whole population of this most conveniently placed hamlet. It lies on the borderline between sandy terrain covered with heathland and woods, and the clay area along the river Eem with its flat and open meadows. Dunes and woods provided the necessary protective cover. Farms located on the richer soil of the Eem valley could be robbed. But the chief attraction of Hees may well have been its proximity to the main thoroughfare connecting the town of Amersfoort – a gateway to Gelderland and the eastern provinces – with Utrecht and Amsterdam, the Randstad.

Councils were regularly held at Hees to discuss and plan future robberies. Band members hid their booty in the haystacks and barns of this hamlet, and they often returned there from their expeditions very late at night or in the early morning. According to Magdaleen van Schoonhoven, it was at Father Mees's house that an intriguing ceremony took place. In the presence of Mees, his wife, and at least five more band members, including Magdaleen herself, nine men were formally accorded military ranks: Marinus Jansz became *commandeur*, Booy was given the rank of *kapitein*, Willem Kool became *lieutenant*, Abraham Kuijteman was named *vaandrager* or *vaandrig* (ensign), Huijbert, alias Lucifer, was *sergeant*, Frans Thijsse was appointed *corporaal*, and Jan den Blauwen became *adelborst* (naval cadet). To complete this interesting compound of military ranks, the band appointed its own *beul* (executioner), a task given to Herman the German (de Mof).[10]

It does look, then, as if the familiar ranks of army and navy provided a model, which could be freely adapted and used to express and confirm the band's hierarchy. (Magdaleen's statement is not corroborated by reports from other band members, and no one else refers to military ranks. At least five of the men she named, however, had prominent roles during the burglaries and robberies.) It is noteworthy that this formal endorsement of its hierarchy coincided with the extension of the band's field of operations into the eastern part of the Dutch Republic. During its first phase (around 1654 to 1657) the Band of Hees's activities had been 'limited' to parts of Zeeland and the southern section of South Holland. Between 1656 and 1659 they moved slightly to central South Holland, the environs of Amsterdam, and parts of North Holland. After 1657 and until its demise in 1661 expeditions to the eastern province of Overijssel and part of Gelderland were added to the usual burglaries and thefts in South Holland. It was at the beginning of this final phase that band members selected Hees as the meeting place where they regularly halted, ate, drank, gambled, and rested on their way to their prospective burglaries in the east or on their way back to Holland.

The origins of the band members may throw some light upon this gradual shift from South Holland to the north and the subsequent extension to the east. Most of them were born in the area where they operated: they came from towns and villages in South Holland, such as Delft, Schoonhoven, Alphen aan den Rijn, Den Briel, Benthuizen, Gouda, and Rotterdam. Others were born in Dutch Brabant, the north-eastern provinces, or adjacent German territory; a few had come from France. The only important group of 'foreigners' in the band was from the southern Netherlands, but they were foreigners merely in a strictly formal sense. Huge numbers of immigrants from the southern Netherlands had, after all, reached the western part of the northern Netherlands in the fairly recent past (especially between 1580 and 1609). Warfare, the devastation of the countryside in Spanish Brabant and Flanders, and the blockade of Antwerp had driven both well-to-do merchants and poor rural inhabitants to the north. During most of the seventeenth century immigrants from the southern Netherlands continued to arrive – though in less massive numbers. By 1622 a majority of the total population of Leiden was of 'Belgian' origin; certain quarters of Amsterdam were mainly inhabited by Flemings and Walloons (see van Deursen 1977, pp. 53–70; cf. Schöffer et al. 1985, pp. 172–8). Members of the Band of Hees who were born in the southern Netherlands had clearly followed a familiar pattern of migration: rather than travel straight from Antwerp or Ypres to Gouda, Leiden, or Amsterdam, they slowly 'drifted ' north via Zeeland and the islands south of Rotterdam to the environs of Amsterdam, to North Holland, and finally to Utrecht, Gelderland, and Overijssel.

To some extent territorial expansion went hand in hand with increasing magnitude and seriousness of the band's criminal activities. Before 1657–8 band members had generally concerned themselves with picking pockets, shoplifting, and breaking into barns and farmhouses. They stole mainly clothes and money, and avoided using violence: when discovered during a burglary, the thieves fled. On Whit Sunday 1658 Jan the Nightingale (de Nachtegaal), Piet the Leper (de Lasarus), and Michiel the Girl ('t Meijsje) were busy removing a bag which contained about 900 guilders worth of silverware, besides clothes, linen, and cash, from a farm in the province of Utrecht when the inhabitants woke up. The thieves quickly sneaked out of the house, hid their booty under a hazel tree, and fled to the unsheltered polders, running fast and jumping across ditches and weirs. They were chased by the farmer and several neighbours. Even so two of the men managed to get away. Only Piet the Leper – 'being tired, saying I can't go any further, and jumping into a dry ditch where he tried to hide himself' – was discovered and arrested. That same evening he managed to escape from the prison at Gouda.[11]

After 1658 members of the Band of Hees continued to commit many types of non-violent theft and burglary. During expeditions ranging from the border area of Utrecht and South Holland to the eastern parts of Overijssel and Gelderland, though, they seemed far less inclined to avoid confrontations. In November 1660 five of the most prominent band members broke into a farmhouse not far from Hilversum. They entered through one of the upper windows, looked for the occupants, trussed up the farmer, and locked him and his wife and children into the cellar. They stole a considerable amount of money and silverware.[12] The increasing boldness of the robbers had also been noticeable when they attacked a house and inn belonging to the bailiff of the town of Kampen in Overijssel in the summer of 1658. Some of the inhabitants had recently died of the plague, and the original plan had been to wait until the few remaining ones had gone to bed. But when the innkeeper had not retired by ten o'clock, Michiel the Girl and a certain Piet van Luxemburg tried to break through a window anyway. The innkeeper heard them and attempted to chase the burglars away, brandishing a firelock and a sword. Thereupon Piet took out his pistol and tried to shoot the man. He just missed, singeing the man's trousers and hitting his dog. The burglars finally gave up.[13]

So far most of the available evidence about the Band of Hees points to a gradual process of professionalization: the band extended its area of operations and at the same time broadened its range of activities. The emphasis shifted very slowly from petty theft and sneaking into houses to housebreaking and armed robbery. The loose-knit network began to coalesce and – if Magdaleen's story is true – differences in status and expertise between the leading band members were formalized and expressed in a military-style hierarchy. Any such process implies that we are dealing here with relative 'newcomers' rather than with men and women who resumed their criminal activities after a few years' absence during the wars.

There were, nevertheless, a few band members whose personal histories suggest a long-standing involvement in organized crime. Flat or Coarse (Platte) Thijs, for instance, was the son of Sleepy (Slaperige) Thijs, who had been known in his time as the terror of North Holland. After a twenty-year career in theft, burglary, and violent extortion Sleepy Thijs had been hanged at Hoorn in 1652.[14] The father of Cely Claes (mistress of Commander Marinus Jansz) seems to have been almost equally famous: according to Magdaleen van Schoonhoven, this Claes the Walloon (de Wael), a professional burglar, was hanged at Gouda in 1660.[15] A few others were familiar with 'traditional' criminal lore, which may likewise indicate long experience. A woman nicknamed Brazilian Mary – who by 1661 had been the mistress of nearly every important band member – spoke of 'breaking and stealing with her *volk*' (that is, folk, people, with the connotation of a separate group) during an early spell of detention in 1657. Four years later she went on to declare that they put a dead man's hand 'on' the fire during a burglary in order to prevent the inhabitants from waking up.[16] This custom was known to several other groups of thieves and burglars. Whether they actually put it into practice, believed in it, or instead regarded it as part of trade lore does not really matter here. It is enough that this practice was apparently spoken of as an ordinary precautionary measure.[17]

In every other respect, however, information regarding the Band of Hees indicates a fairly recent – post-war – involvement in serious property crime and, as we have seen, a process of gradual professionalization. As much is evident from the patterns of recidivism, the social background of band members, and their attitudes towards the use of violence. By 1659 or 1660 male or female band members without several previous convictions were hard to find. Jan Davidtsz, alias Jan Balff, for example, must have begun his criminal career almost before he was twelve years old. By 1660, when he was seventeen, he had been sentenced at least six times. Herman the German, mentioned earlier, was convicted five times in quick succession between about 1656 and 1659. Strikingly, almost none of their convictions dated back before 1653.

Several band members came from working-class or artisan families who had fallen upon hard times: among the fathers of band members were a baker, a tailor, and a glazier. The records offer some striking tales about running away from home at fourteen, getting involved with 'bad company' at roughly the same age, or being raised in an orphanage and having to provide for oneself at an early age. Some of the women had been married to men who had died or disappeared during the wars; several husbands who did return – in particular the disabled ones – proved unable to support their wives and children. All band members belonged to the poorest segment of society, but only a few came from vagrant families with a tradition in crime; the biographies of the majority reflect the more recent downward mobility of working-class and artisan families.

Members of the Band of Hees regarded toughness and a readiness to use violence as a sign of being real, professional criminals. After a whipping and branding on the scaffold in January 1659 Jan Bruijn was asked by members of the public whether he was going to behave better in the future. He answered that 'he would improve like sour beer on draught', meaning that he would go from bad to worse, and went on to say that 'now was not the time to mend his ways'; he would start by stealing some stockings 'and then behave in a way that would shake gallows and wheels'.[18]

Very little violence was actually used against outsiders, but it seems to have served as an idiom through which status, hierarchy, and discipline within the band could be expressed and confirmed. Some statements intimate a direct link between physical strength, endurance, and status: 'That Booy is one of the principal band members and a match for five men'; Commander 'Marinus, who has more marks of branding than anyone else, and accordingly the first vote'.[19] The possibility that frequent references to the use of violence were part of 'impression management' within the band in no way detracts from the seriousness of their threats – fights among the men occasionally ended in the death of one of them. Nor was violence an exclusively male affair. Commander Marinus cut open the cheek of another man's mistress; on a different occasion he would have strangled a female band member suspected of betrayal if the stocking he was using had not snapped; and together with Booy he threatened to cut out Magdaleen van Schoonhoven's tongue if she did not stop talking about confidential matters; instead, they beat her up using sticks. (Considering Magdaleen's subsequent detailed statements about the band during her detention at Schoonhoven, Marinus had good reason to worry.)[20]

Much of this talk about violence none the less sounds as if band members were trying to prove to themselves and others that they were real 'tough guys'. Once more a brief remark by Magdaleen van Schoonhoven is revealing. She says Booy, an older thief, is 'tough and teaches others to be tough, and has taught this to Marinus and Herman the German'.[21] Apparently they had needed instruction. It was the older, influential band members who explicitly set the limits to the amount of violence considered acceptable. In the course of the evening of 14 February, 1659, for instance, three men carrying big travelling bags knocked on the door of Father Mees's hut at Hees and asked for directions. Apart from Mees, at least five band members were present in the hut. Marinus – perhaps wanting to show off – said, 'Why don't we knock them down in the [nearby] dunes and see what is inside the bags? Nobody will know.' The others refused and Willem Kool (who was hanged two years later at Leiden) said; 'You shall not do that, we are thieves, let us not become murderers.' Father Mees supported Kool, though not for any humanitarian reasons, saying, 'Children, if you want to shoot them, don't do so near my front door, for it would cost me my life, but if you want to do it, wait until they have gone a little way into the dunes, then I can say I did not know about it.'[22]

Father Mees did not call them 'Children' for nothing. The bragging of Jan Bruijn, the fact that Herman the German and Marinus had needed lessons in toughness from Booy, the running away from home, the lack of convictions before 1653, the gradual extension of the band's territory, the more audacious character of its exploits, the demarcation of a hierarchy as epitomized by the conferring of military ranks, and of course the role of Father Mees himself – all of these aspects fit together and make sense if we consider the ages of the band members. Even by the time of their last known (and sometimes final) sentences – between 1659 and 1661 – hardly any of the men were older than twenty-three; most were still in their teens. Clearly they cannot have been older then twelve or thirteen when they first joined the small groups of vagrants and beggars which had formed the roots of the Band of Hees. (The women were rather older: in their twenties or thirties by the end of the 1650s.) In 1648, by the end of the Dutch Revolt, these men had been only eight to twelve years old. In view of their age it is hardly surprising that references to service in the armies are almost completely lacking. Rather than a post-war band of discharged soldiers we have found a band of children and teenagers which developed into a full-blown criminal network.

Evidence about the other networks of the 1650s is much more fragmentary, but it looks as if the Band of Hees epitomizes a more general post-war process of gradual professionalization and the growth of close-knit, hierarchical bands out of loose-knit vagrant networks. The same development – including the extension of their field of operations from South Holland to the north and the east – occurred in the group of Engeltje Simons and Piet Kaalkop during the same period. It can also be traced in the association of Gillis Crabbe, Arnoult Fransz, and their companions (1650–4), and in the band of David Maes and Gerrit Jongejager (1654–5). In each of these groups we find some experienced and older thieves. But there seems to have been no return *en masse* of 'pre-war' professional criminals who took up their trade again. Like the Band of Hees, these groups consisted largely of men and women from poor working-class, artisan, and vagrant families. Their regional background was the same, and in the little we know of their occupations unskilled activities predominate. They were generally born in the province of Holland or in the southern Netherlands. Many intermittently worked as casual rural labourers or performed odd jobs on farms; some went from door to door singing songs and selling pipes, buttons, and haberdashery. A few had worked as cobblers and some were spinners and weavers. The women had been servants, seamstresses, or washerwomen.[23] The insignificant role of former sailors and soldiers is again striking, and ages – though somewhat higher than in the Band of Hees – were still fairly low.

Neither the Band of Hees nor the other bands operating in Holland and Zeeland during the 1650s can be designated 'military bands'. They were part of a post-war increase of criminal activity, however, and as such these bands formed a war-related as well as a post-war phenomenon. As Hay and Beattie have not failed to point out, wars did not affect only the soldiers themselves. Besides the return of unskilled men to the labour market, a considerable reduction in the strength of the armies also entailed a slackening of orders. Workshops, mills, trading companies, merchants, and transport businesses, which used to supply food, clothes, boots, horses, and every other imaginable item needed for the upkeep of the armies, lost part of their business. As a consequence jobs in the army and in the supply industries – that is, careers open to new generations of young unskilled men – might be blocked for a number of years. Such was the situation that eight- to twelve-year-old children from poor families had to deal with around 1650. Naturally, not all of them became involved in crime. But for many of those who lacked professional training and had grown used to life 'on the road' – whether as runaway orphans, as members of vagrant families, or as immigrants who had taken a long time to travel from the southern Netherlands to the north – the option of joining other vagrants and forming a band must have been appealing.

The Band of Stoffel van Reenen

The history of Stoffel van Reenen's band (1663–9) shows that professionalization and the formation of more closely knit hierarchical bands did not stop with the demise of the Band of Hees around 1661.[24] Like its predecessor, Stoffel van Reenen's group was known as the *alderfameuste* (most famous) band of its time. Several of his companions were former members of the Band of Hees, and during the 1650s Stoffel himself had been closely associated with Magdaleen van Schoonhoven and at least five or six other members of that band. Among them were prominent thieves such as Jan Davidtsz, alias Jan Balff, and Tall (Lange) Claes van Polsbroeck, who became a central figure in Stoffel's band.

Resemblances between the two bands are striking. Stoffel's group operated in the same area: South Holland, parts of Zeeland, North Holland, Utrecht, and Gelderland. It committed roughly the same range of illegal activities (from picking pockets and stealing laundry to burglary and armed robbery). Band members came from the same social and regional background, and only a few of them had served in the armies; former textile workers from the southern Netherlands were rather more prominent in Stoffel's group than in the Band of Hees. Most members of Stoffel's band belonged to the same generation as the men involved in the Band of Hees, and nearly all of them were too young to have participated in any military activities before 1650. By the mid-1660s, when they had joined Stoffel's band, they were naturally slightly older and much more experienced than their colleagues of the earlier Band of Hees: most had reached their mid- or late twenties. Except for a few newcomers, all of them had been convicted before.

Stoffel's band was much smaller than the Band of Hees and lacked any kind of formalized hierarchy – perhaps because it was a rather close-knit group. In the Band of Hees people had worked together with continually changing sets of colleagues. Stoffel's group consisted of forty men and women at most, fifteen to twenty of whom may be regarded as regulars. These 'core' members constantly named each other as their principal accomplices. Among them we find Little (Cleijn) Jacob, an itinerant chair-mender from Leiden,[25] and Dirck Fredericksz, alias the Stork (de Oijevaar) or the Distressed Fowl (het Kommerhoen), a former wool comber and spinner from Utrecht. The first of Dirck's arrests dated back to the time when he was twelve or thirteen years old and his father had him detained on account of petty theft. On his release Dirck started stealing again; he was arrested and sentenced at Utrecht once more, and departed for the East Indies. He returned, however, and thereafter joined Stoffel van Reenen's band. By the time of his final sentence in 1669 Dirck had committed numerous burglaries and burnt down a farmhouse.[26] Stoffel van Reenen himself, of course, also belonged to this 'hard core' of respected, prominent, and experienced band members. During the late 1650s he and his brother Dirck Hendricks van Reenen had belonged to a band which partly overlapped with the Band of Hees; in 1657 both had been arrested and sentenced at Alkmaar to long periods of imprisonment. Stoffel was released in the spring of 1664; by Easter he had resumed his former activities with a partly new set of companions.[27]

'Hard' core does not seem to be an exaggerated qualification if we examine two of the robberies committed by these men. In February 1666 Stoffel van Reenen, Claes van Polsbroeck, and two more band members made a hole in the roof of a farmhouse and inn to the east of Amersfoort. Finding themselves in the bedroom, they immediately proceeded to beat and tie up the farmer and his wife. The farmer's old mother was dragged naked from her bed, where the robbers found some money hidden in the straw mattress. After threatening to cut the throats of their victims and set fire to the house, Stoffel and his companions searched cupboards, chests, beds, and so on. They finally left in the course of the night, taking money as well as clothes and linen. The four men spent the next few days travelling to the small village of Langerak in the border area of Utrecht and South Holland, where they had planned their next robbery. During the night of 6 March 1666 they broke into the house of Maarten Schats, a jurist. Discovering their victim in hiding under a table, they threw a noose around his neck, dragged him out, trussed him up, threw him down on the floor, and severely kicked and beat him. They refused to believe Schats when he told them that he kept very little cash in the house, and began to torture him. Having made a big fire in the front part of the house, they 'horribly burnt and scorched him on both sides; also put his feet close to the fire', threatening to burn down his house with him inside. The robbers had to leave without obtaining any more money. Schats died three days later.[28]

These two robberies belong to a different category from the usual activities of Stoffel's group and even from the most violent enterprises of the Band of Hees. Here, violence was an integral part of the proceedings. It had been planned – the men had brought sticks and knives – and the robbers did not hesitate to torture and maltreat their victims in the most brutal way. Whereas most members of Stoffel's band, just like those of the Band of Hees, tended to avoid confrontations, the 'hard core' was both prepared and willing to use force. Judging from their deliberate use of torture, their familiarity with violence cannot have sprung up overnight. It may be a coincidence that several 'core' members were born outside the province of Holland (in Utrecht and Gelderland), but there was nothing accidental about the geography of the two violent robberies. Both took place in the border area of Utrecht and Holland. Like the Band of Hees, Stoffel and his companions confined their most brutal activities to areas outside the Randstad. They were not the only ones to do so.

In several respects Stoffel van Reenen's band followed in the footsteps of the networks of the 1650s. It represented a third phase in the development of the post-war bands. The loose-knit networks of the early 1650s had begun to coalesce during the late 1650s, resulting in slightly more 'structured' bands with the beginning of a hierarchy. By the mid-1660s smaller, close-knit bands had formed in which a 'hard core' of experienced burglars and robbers set the tone. Rather than by a formal hierarchy of commanders and corporals, the smaller bands were 'controlled' by this set of more or less equally prominent men. During the early 1650s the networks had consisted mainly of very young men and only slightly older women, who were doing their best to become accomplished thieves. By the late 1660s the cores of the close-knit bands consisted of the survivors from that period: men with fifteen years of experience in organized crime who did not shy away from the use of violence.

Post-war Patterns

The question remains whether the specific configuration of the 1650s and 1660s represents a more general post-war pattern, which might be traced in eighteenth-century as well as seventeenth-century post-war phases. Only one eighteenth-century period properly qualifies for comparative purposes: the years following the War of the Spanish Succession (1702–14). Actual fighting mostly took place outside the territory of the Dutch Republic, as had been the case during the 1630s and 1640s. But the war – unlike most other eighteenth-century European wars – entailed a major Dutch war effort and a notable increase in the size of the Dutch army for a number of years. The army had already been maintained at considerable strength during the 1690s due to the permanent threat of French expansionist policy. After the end of the war, in 1715, the costs of keeping a huge army in the southern Netherlands (100,000 to 200,000 men) and a high contribution towards the upkeep of an 'allied' fleet caused the near-bankruptcy of the Dutch state. Priority was given to cutting down those costs, and in 1717 it was agreed to reduce the total size of the Dutch army to 32,000 men (Schöffer et al. 1985, pp. 273ff).

All over Holland and Zeeland the similarities between the prosecution patterns for serious property crime during the two periods 1630–60 and 1700–25 are unmistakable. Again there was a phase of relative 'quiet' during the years of warfare (1702–14).[29] Again the first post-war decade proved to be extremely 'busy'. The type of bands that sprang up was quite different, though. Instead of the extensive, loose-knit networks of vagrant beggars and young inexperienced thieves which had been so conspicuous in the 1650s, we find smaller, closer-knit, and generally well-organized bands during the years 1714–25. Some had a real captain; a few had a distinct hierarchy. Most of them engaged in a variety of rural thefts, burglaries, and armed robberies. One or two even specialized in armed robbery. Within a period of about fifteen years after the end of the War of the Spanish Succession many such bands were active in the countryside of Holland and Zeeland. To name only the most important ones: the Jaco Band (1715–17), the Band of Gerrit the Cow (de Koe) (1714–17); the association of the Glory of Holland (de Roem van Holland) and Kees Seven-deaths (Sevendood) (1714–23); the small band of Jacob the Leper (de Lasarus) (1720–3);

and the bands of Dirk Odendaal, the Glory of Holland Junior (1723–30), and Lambooy (1725–8).

The bands of both Gerrit the Cow and Jaco were based in Amsterdam, but operated almost exclusively in the countryside. Gerrit Claaszn Rubon, alias the Cow, a German in his late twenties, played a leading role in a band which in many respects resembled Stoffel van Reenen's group of almost fifty years before. The band comprised about twenty-five to thirty-five vagrant men and women, most of whom were the same age as Gerrit or slightly older. They often met in small parties in Amsterdam to discuss and plan new thefts and burglaries all over Holland and in the border area of Holland and Utrecht. There were a few former sailors among them, and some band members had been convicted before. Although Gerrit and two or three of his colleagues committed at least one murder and robbery, the band as a rule did not use any violence during the burglaries.[30]

Members of the Jaco Band spent even more of their time in Amsterdam.[31] All their robberies were carried out at rural dwellings, however, and their expeditions ranged from the environs of Amsterdam and Haarlem to areas as far apart as the countryside near Gouda (South Holland), the environs of Utrecht, and the north-eastern provinces of Friesland, Groningen, and Overijssel. If necessary, the men rented carts or a boat in order to reach the houses they wanted to rob and to transport the stolen goods. These consisted mainly of money, silverware, jewellery, linen, and other valuables. The band was usually well informed and the value of their booty regularly exceeded 500 to 1,000 guilders. Once or twice it even amounted to several thousand guilders – a fortune at the time. Unlike the Band of Gerrit the Cow, Jaco's group used or threatened to use violence during almost every robbery. They rammed open doors, brandished pistols, knives, and clubs, shot at the inhabitants, beat, kicked, tied up, and occasionally raped their victims. They murdered at least two of them. In July 1716 six band members noisily broke into a farmhouse to the east of Alkmaar. Once inside the robbers started to shoot at the owners and some of their rural labourers, who defended themselves with knives and scythes. The robbers had to retreat, but again forced their way inside, chasing the occupants and shooting at them. They beat up and killed a farm-hand and threw his dead body into a muddy ditch.[32]

These violent and spectacular expeditions, in the course of which the robbers seized exceptionally large amounts of cash and valuables, were carried out by a comparatively small group of twenty to twenty-five people in all. The band as a whole lacked a clear hierarchy, but Jaco – or rather Jacob Frederik Muller, a professional thief in his late twenties – was its undisputed leader. There were no young or inexperienced thieves to be found in this group: all the men were over twenty, and mainly between twenty-five and thirty-five. Barent Voorenhage, a 46-year-old sailor and former coppersmith from Amsterdam, was probably the oldest member. He was well known among urban thieves and burglars, and had been arrested at least six times since 1695.

It looks as if Jaco hand-picked his accomplices from among a circuit of friends, fellow countrymen, and their colleagues and relatives. Many of them came from northern Germany – like Jaco himself – or from the north-eastern part of the Dutch Republic. The others were born in Amsterdam. All of them belonged to the Amsterdam underworld, maintained close relations with professional urban thieves and burglars, and spent much of their time in two quarters of the town known as more or less disreputable lower-class areas: the Jordaan and the area near the Zeedijk. The early eighteenth-century Jordaan may perhaps be compared with the rookeries of London during the same period (on the Jordaan see Dijkhuis 1937–9; cf. George 1985, Chesney 1972, McMullan 1982, and Thompson & Yeo 1971). It formed a maze of narrow streets, alleys, and backyards, in which countless working-class families lived. Many of its inhabitants worked or passed their days at the numerous small artisans' workshops, pawnshops, semi-legal taverns, lodging-houses, and counters where anything could be bought or sold. All through the seventeenth and eighteenth centuries professional thieves and burglars from any part of the Dutch Republic came to the Jordaan to sell their booty to the fences of the Franse pad (French path) and various other alleys at the centre of this quarter.

During the immediate post-war years, a time when the urban underworld of Holland itself appears to have been particularly active, the urban-based bands of Jaco and Gerrit de Koe were especially prominent. Other, more rurally oriented groups should not be underestimated. Like the post-war bands of the 1650s and 1660s, they comprised a mixture of Hollanders and immigrants, almost none of whom were either newcomers or unskilled thieves. In these groups – as in the Jaco Band – the immigrant segment consisted not of people from the southern Netherlands (whose absence is striking) but of men from northern Germany and the north-eastern part of the Dutch Republic. Most of them had already been living in Holland for a few years by the time they became members of the bands. Several mention the years 1712–15 as the beginning of their vagrant way of life. By the late 1720s and early 1730s some of their sons and nephews were joining the bands, just as the Glory of Holland Junior was following in his father's footsteps. By that time a second post-war generation was coming alongside the first.

Taking all post-war bands of the period 1715–30 together, it looks as if three intersecting social categories 'supplied' nearly all band members: the itinerant poor; professional soldiers and sailors; and former artisans. The majority belonged by birth to the first category: people who spent a large part of the year on the road and earned a living by a combination of peddling, mending chairs, grinding knives, tinkering, performing at fairs and parties, and begging. Some of the men had spent a year or two in the army, or on a trip to the East Indies. The second category, professional soldiers or sailors and their immediate relatives, made up a far smaller section. Relatives – in particular sons, sisters, and widows – may have joined the bands before the soldiers or sailors themselves. During interrogation band members quite frequently refer to fathers, uncles, husbands, and brothers who had disappeared or died during the wars, who had returned unfit for work, or who had simply been away for years on end, leaving their families without income. The third category – which was second in size – consisted mainly of former ropers, masons, painters, sawing-mill hands, coppersmiths, cloth shearers, and other textile workers. Some of them may have been independent craftsmen, but most appear to have worked as labourers in the artisan or small industrial establishments of Amsterdam and the provincial towns of Holland. They, of course, had been the first to lose their jobs when demand contracted during the post-war depression.

Prosecution patterns concerning serious property crime in the countryside of Holland and Zeeland fitted the 'Hay–Beattie model' rather closely. During the two relevant post-war periods (1650–70 and 1715–30) prosecutions rapidly increased, just as they did in England. Armed bands and groups of rural thieves and burglars, which had been much less noticeable during periods of warfare, proliferated almost as soon as peace had been concluded. As in England, this upsurge of organized rural property crime was no brief, transitional phenomenon. On the contrary, bands which had sprung up shortly after the wars often continued to operate for at least three to five years, and periods of five to eight years were no exception. Occasionally the overlapping membership of two successive groups as well as the participation of men belonging to two different generations of one family points to the even less transient character of such bands.

Rather unexpectedly, post-war bands active in Holland and Zeeland proved to include very few deserted or discharged soldiers, and military models of organization appear to have had little appeal. The seventeenth-century bands differed, however, in some important respects from their counterparts of the years 1715–30. The former started out as extensive loose-knit networks of predominantly young and relatively inexperienced thieves. They gradually developed into closer-knit, hierarchical, and professional bands. The bands of the late 1710s and the 1720s were smaller, better organized, and more professional from the start. Obviously, not all their members were veteran burglars who had just returned from the army or navy, but former soldiers and sailors – some of them with a previous career in crime – were slightly more prominent in these eighteenth-century bands. Both the rapidity with which such groups organized themselves and the leading position of certain experienced burglars and robbers (who were plainly familiar with urban as well as rural criminal infrastructures) suggest that we are not dealing here with 'newcomers' to the business of property crime.

Considering the lack of military ranks and hierarchy in every band except possibly the Band of Hees, and taking into account the not even remotely influential role of former soldiers, we can hardly call these groups military bands. The situation in Brabant, which had a much more immediate experience of warfare, was quite different.

4

'Foreign Soldiers': Military Bands in Brabant, 1690–1720

Warfare in Brabant was by no means limited to the final phase of the Dutch Revolt. Fighting took place on or very close to the territory of this province in the course of the 1670s, 1690s to 1710s, 1740s, and 1790s. Consequently, the presence of all kinds of soldiers – whether they were deserters, had been discharged, or were still in active service – is much more noticeable in the criminal records of this region than in Holland, Zeeland, or Utrecht. Single soldiers, pairs, and small groups were frequently involved in petty theft, extortion, knifings, and related offences.

In the course of the winter of 1740–1 two middle-aged deserters, who were born in the same village in Bohemia and lived at Breda in the western half of Brabant, committed a series of thefts in the countryside surrounding this town. They were later joined by a 52-year-old former soldier from one of the villages in this region. Together they broke into a farmhouse, stripped and strangled a widow, beat up her son, and plundered the house. All three men were sentenced to death.[1] The same fate awaited two young Hungarian soldiers who had been attached to several European armies as boot-makers and hussars. The first, Joseph Koetsera (aged twenty-nine), had served in the Prussian, French, and various Italian armies; he had deserted at least three times. In September 1747, when the French had invaded parts of Brabant during the War of the Austrian Succession, the two men travelled on horseback through Brabant, along with a companion who did not yet have a horse. They decided to stop and plunder the post-chaise from Maastricht to 's Hertogenbosch, positioned themselves on both sides of the road, drew their pistols, and waited for the post-chaise to appear. All went according to plan: they robbed the passengers (four army officers and the parish priest of a nearby village), took one of the horses, and travelled on –

only to steal four more horses on their way through eastern Brabant, and to get caught in Gelderland.[2]

Of course, these were no military bands, but the examples make clear what irregular military presence in the countryside meant at the time, and illustrate some of the side-effects of the European wars. Nearly all such small groups of soldiers were active *during* periods of warfare. In Holland and Zeeland we find them in 1670–2, 1699–1702, 1706–7, and again during the French revolutionary period. In Brabant they were particularly active in 1670–1, 1693, 1695, 1698–1702, 1707–8, 1709–13, 1747–9, and during the 1790s. As far as the province of Brabant is concerned, the most important of these small groups are to be found between 1690 and 1715. This was also the period when two of the most impressive bands that have operated in the Dutch Republic committed large-scale armed robberies and extortion in the countryside of Brabant and Gelderland: the Zwartmakers (Blackeners) and the Moskovieters (Moscovians). These bands not only acted within a short period of each other – Zwartmakers between 1692 and 1699, Moskovieters from about 1706 to 1708 – but were also 'close' in a geographical sense. Each concentrated its main activities in Dutch Brabant. Besides the whole of western Dutch Brabant, the Moskovieters covered the Land of Heusden (on the northern border of Brabant, then still belonging to Holland) and parts of the area between the rivers Maas and Rhine. The larger Zwartmakers Band operated all over Dutch Brabant as well as in the German Land of Ravenstein to the east and in a large section of Spanish Brabant to the south; an almost independent branch of the Zwartmakers operated in Gelderland and Utrecht. A third and rather smaller band formed around the Van Exaerde brothers belonged to the same period and area: in the course of 1712 and 1713 it was active in western Brabant, roughly between Antwerp, Breda, and Dordrecht (see Figure 1).

Are these, at last, the expected 'military bands'? Did large bands like the Zwartmakers evolve from the small groups of soldiers touring the countryside of Brabant at the time? And, if so, did this process resemble the merging of the numerous vagrant (but non-military) post-war groups of the 1650s in Holland? Were the Zwartmakers, Moskovieters, and van Exaerde bands by any chance identical with the famous stereotypical bands of 'foreign mercenaries' that have regularly been blamed for many kinds of disturbances of peace and order in the countryside of the early modern Netherlands?

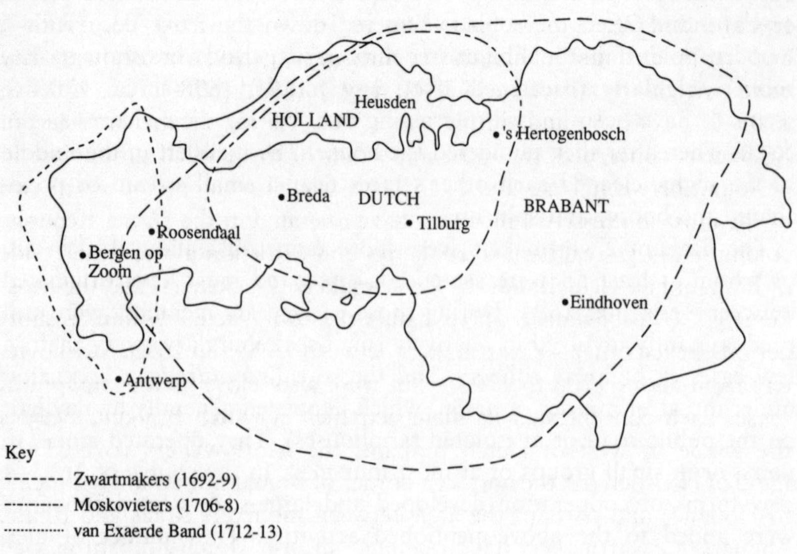

Figure 1 Brabant

Zwartmakers

Between the autumn of 1693 and the end of 1700 at least 69 men and women belonging to the Brabant and Gelderland branches of the Zwartmakers were convicted by courts as far apart as Brussels, Amsterdam, 's Hertogenbosch, Arnhem, and The Hague; 48 of them were sentenced to death. In all, as many as 160 people may have been involved in the two branches, which operated independently and whose membership only rarely overlapped.[3]

The Gelderland branch was the smaller one: it comprised about 40 to 50 people altogether, 16 of whom were convicted. Its big exploits date from the years 1692–3. Until the late autumn of 1693 these men committed a series of well-organized, large-scale armed robberies directed at isolated farmhouses, inns, and the houses of rural officials, many of which were located near small towns and villages along the right bank of the Rhine. (This was the southern border area of Gelderland. They robbed houses near, for instance, Amerongen, Renkum, and Wijk bij Duurstede.) Generally, ten to twenty men met late at night at some distance from the house they were going to rob. They blackened their faces – using soot, gunpowder, or the fat from a frying pan – approached the house, and posted sentries. All of them carried pistols or bayonets. Often the robbers battered down the front door with a wooden pole. If the inhabitants tried to resist, they were shot at. The robbers regularly threatened arson and murder, but actual violence seems to have been limited to trussing and locking their victims in the cellar. Thereafter they plundered the house. The men left in the middle of the night, cleaned each other's faces near a small stream or pond, shared the booty, and split up.

The Brabant Zwartmakers were more numerous: about 110 in all, of whom at least 53 were sentenced. The band must have originated between 1691 and 1694. During those early years members were still predominantly involved in relatively small-scale burglary, petty theft, a few cases of highway robbery, and the so-called *afdreijgen* (extortion under threat of murder or arson, which happened generally by daylight on the public road or at isolated farmhouses). They operated alone, in pairs, or in small groups of at most four men. In the course of 1693–4 new forms of cooperation developed and large-scale armed robberies were added to the above-mentioned activities. The number of men participating in the expeditions increased, and especially between the spring of 1694 and December 1695 the Zwartmakers committed numerous armed robberies all over Dutch Brabant and adjacent Spanish and German territory: from the western area near Dordrecht to the Peel district in the east, and from the German Ravenstein in the north-east near the river Maas to villages far to the south in Spanish Brabant and the Land of Liège. As with the Gelderland branch, these extensive activities were cut short by a series of arrests. During a long 'aftermath' (between 1696 and 1700), however, small groups of former members resumed the burglaries, petty theft, and extortion of the years 1691–4.

The big expeditions of the Brabant Zwartmakers followed much the same pattern as those in Gelderland. Here too a member of men met near the farmhouse, mill, or inn they had chosen, blackened their faces, posted sentries, and battered down the front door. The groups of men actively involved in the robberies may have been slightly smaller, between six and fifteen. The main difference between the two branches lay in their use of violence. The Brabant Zwartmakers not only threatened, but actually perpetrated murder, arson, and torture. (They sometimes made particularly detailed and horrifying threats: to haul a woman up the chimney, or to scorch a farmer's face with burning bushes of straw.) Some of their victims were killed outright, such as a clog-maker who was shot when Zwartmakers broke into his house at Best in 1694. A few died afterwards. In January 1695 three blackened men entered the bedroom of a sixty-year-old farmer and threatened to shoot him in the belly unless he told them where his money was hidden. He refused and was beaten with an axe while his seventy-year-old wife was struck down and pulled by her hair into the cellar. The man still denied having any money, whereupon the robbers began to torture him by dropping hot candle grease on his face and genitals. A few months later Zwartmakers forced their way into a farmhouse near Eindhoven. They tied up the farmer, his sister, a farm-hand, a servant-girl, and a child, and they tortured the farmer's sister by using the lock of a pistol as thumbscrew. Before leaving, the bandits almost invariably warned their victims not to attempt to free themselves before daybreak, follow them, or report the crime.[4]

The men's threats had to be taken very seriously indeed – first, because the robbers had shown themselves prepared to use violence and, secondly, because there was almost nobody who could protect the inhabitants of isolated houses in the countryside of Brabant. In his case against the Zwartmaker Willem Teunissen the chief bailiff (*hoogschout*) of 's Hertogenbosch described the situation in 1694: 'it is deplorable that country folk cannot rest in their beds at night, and even by day do not remain unmolested'.[5] Placards issued by the Estates General in 1691 and 1693 sharply rebuked both first-instance courts and local constables for their negligence in taking down depositions, inspecting the scene of crime, and prosecuting the perpetrators. As the placard of 28 April 1691 points out:

> witnesses who live at some hours' distance from the Criminal Court are very difficult and slow in coming to the court, and when they have arrived – discovering that their costs are not paid – they become unwilling to testify; yes, cited witnesses frequently conceal the truth against their conscience and better judgement because they fear the delinquents, their patrons, friends, and adherents, or just because of a wrong inclination to excuse the malefactors. (Groot Placaet-boeck 1705, p. 505)

Referring to a placard issued by the Estates General on 31 January 1695 (see ibid., p. 510) – which must have been at least partly inspired by the Zwartmakers – the above-mentioned bailiff stated 'that an honest man hardly dares sleep in his bed, especially those who have testified against the vagabonds'.[6] During their heyday the Zwartmakers terrorized the rural population of Brabant. For a long time their name remained a generic term for all kinds of armed robbers.

The Zwartmakers did not attempt to pass themselves off as regular soldiers, nor did their victims regard them as such. Asked to describe the robbers, the sixty-year-old farmer who had been tortured said that 'he was unable to identify them or point them out except that they were certainly no soldiers but rather belonged among the vagrants who were going around the countryside'.[7] Yet in many respects they had been strongly influenced by the military. The band members' obvious familiarity with various types of guns points to their experience as soldiers. (One of the leading figures in the Brabant branch was said to always carry one or two pocket pistols and a carbine.) Frequent references to bayonets and flintlocks strengthen this impression, as do certain tactical aspects of their expeditions, such as the posting of sentries, their systematic way of plundering houses, and their routine of extortion which resembled army requisitioning. The principal signs of military influence, though, are to be found in their organization and in the way members referred to themselves.

There was a clear order of command before, during, and after the expeditions. 'Red [Roijen] Jan gave the orders and pointed out where each man had to post himself'; or 'during every expedition Hendrick van Bergeijck has been known as the Chief (*Cheff*) or Commander (*Commandant*)'; and 'Hendrick was an even higher Captain of this company than Jacobus van der Slossen who was broken on the wheel at Ravensteijn'.[8] In Brabant each segment of the band seems to have had its own commander. These men regularly met to plan new exploits: 'he [Jan Spoormans, a rural carter and carpenter] and the Captain of the Zwartmakers and murderers, Hendrick van Bergeijck, as well as the other leaders of that Band, that is to say Jan Bartels van Peer, Green [Groenen] Thomas, and Red Jan, have held regular murder councils at his house'.[9] Laurens Thijssen, an itinerant musician who was always accompanied by two dogs, acted as the principal commander of the Gelderland branch. One band member recalled that 'Laurens had made him swear an oath with these words, "that the Devil would come and fetch him or tear his limbs apart if they did not keep faith with each other", and that he has sworn this oath together with all the others'.[10] Those in command were invariably designated as 'captains', and their principal subordinates were likewise referred to in terms of military rank: Captain or Lieutenant Hendrick van Bergeijck, Sergeant Pier Cuttepom, Corporal Guilliam Stoeldraaijer. Members of each branch described their band as a 'company' and spoke of joining it as if it had been an official military unit. One of them even called Anthony Cornelisz van Dijck, alias Lichten Toon, 'an accomplice or rather a soldier of the famous captain of those thieves that are called Zwartmakers'.[11]

A number of Zwartmakers – especially in the Brabant branch – had served as soldiers in various armies. One had been in garrison at

Antwerp; another had joined the Spanish cavalry in the southern Netherlands; yet another carried a Spanish army pass; two had served in the French armies; a few were described by their accomplices as deserters; and at least two were still in active service (they were convicted and sentenced to death by military courts at Brussels and The Hague respectively). In 1693 one member of the Gelderland branch joined some Dutch troops in garrison at Coevorden. Travelling all over Gelderland, he combined his activities as a band member with his duties as recruiting officer, and he may have been recruiting for both his companies. It is likely that several more band members served as soldiers at some point in their lives. The courts were not particularly interested in this aspect of their background, however, and the actual number of former soldiers in the Zwartmakers bands can only be guessed at.

A 'military band' the Zwartmakers certainly were – because of their hierarchy, the way they described themselves, their organization in separate segments or 'companies', the planning and method of their expeditions, and their relatively close links with the armies. But were they the stereotypical plundering bands of foreign mercenaries mentioned earlier? If so, band members would have been outsiders – if not real foreigners, then at least men who did not belong in the region. Where did they come from?

In fact, the Zwartmakers were exactly the opposite of foreigners. A large majority of the members of the Gelderland branch were born in Gelderland, Holland, or Utrecht. A few came from Wallonia, Germany, or the Flemish-speaking parts of the southern Netherlands. All the men had lived in Gelderland for a number of years before becoming involved in the band. To most of the Gelderland Zwartmakers the sandy area in central Gelderland known as the Veluwe, which bordered on the river Rhine to the south, was their home base. They knew it as well as anyone and called it *het hoge land* (the high land). Although nearly all these men spent most of their time in the region, they were none the less outsiders: none of them belonged to the established and respected part of the rural population. Among the band members and their relatives were quite a few former constables (many rural constables were part-time, underpaid personal assistants of the bailiff). A large number of the others had worked as artisans, but had lost their jobs and their homes. Now they toured the region as pedlars, chair-menders, cobblers, chimney-sweeps, fiddlers, or beggars. They almost all spent the larger part of the year on the road.

Jan van Velsen, alias Jantje van Emmenes, is a good example. He was born in 1661 at Leiden, where some of his relatives earned a living as textile workers. He learned the trade of cobbler, toured Holland, enlisted in the French army, and subsequently joined a group of vagrants and thieves. In 1686 he stabbed a vagrant beggar, who died afterwards; Jan was arrested and banished from the province of Holland. Having spent some three years of his banishment in England, he returned to the Netherlands and resumed his work as an itinerant cobbler. During the early 1690s he travelled all over Holland and Zeeland. At about the same time he progressed from petty theft to burglary. Jantje van Emmenes probably met some of his future colleagues on his trips through Gelderland. As beggars or fiddlers they used to attend the funeral meals traditionally held by the farmers of the Veluwe. In the course of the 1690s these ceremonial occasions even came to serve as regular meeting places where Zwartmakers passed on information and plans for new expeditions and future meetings.[12]

The Brabant branch of the Zwartmakers included, if possible, even fewer foreigners. Its links with the region were extremely close, and most members had grown up there. The border area of Dutch and Spanish Brabant was at the core of their field of operations. Each of the three different segments within the Brabant branch 'controlled' its own district and was connected to a cluster of families based in villages of their particular area. Of central importance to the north-eastern part of Brabant was the van Beugen family (see Table 1). Almost every member of this family was born at Berghem, a village to the east of Oss, which itself was located east of the provincial capital 's Hertogenbosch. Together with several associates – among them Jacobus van der Slossen, who was born and executed in the neighbouring Land of Ravenstein – the van Beugens spent most of their lives in this area; the majority met a violent death. By no means all the men had a fixed domicile: they served in the armies, worked as pedlars, carters, or casual rural labourers; they begged, extorted the rural population, and toured the whole of Brabant. But their base remained the village of Berghem; their wives, children, and elderly parents generally lived in or near the village.

To the south and west – in the border area of Dutch and Spanish Brabant – we find two more extended families at the core of sections of the Zwartmakers band. One of these was especially active in the area between Antwerp and Breda. Captain Hendrick van Bergeijck and some of his relatives (see Table 2) spent most of their time in the neighbourhood of Antwerp. Since the childhood of Hendrick and his brother Jacob (an almost equally important leader of the band) the van Bergeijck family had paid regular visits to an inn called Het Vuijl Hemd (The dirty shirt), just outside the town of Antwerp. The inn was kept by a local widow, Catlijn Verheijden, alias Kee Vuijlhemd, whose former husbands had been mayor and churchwarden of a nearby village. It became an important meeting place for the band: a safe locality to keep

Table 1 The van Beugen family

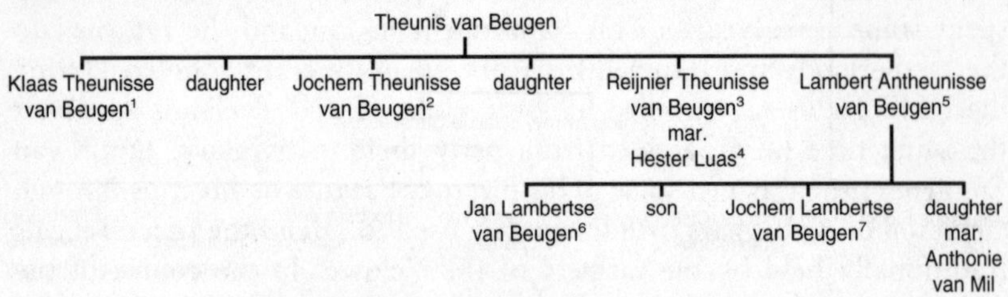

[1] Joined the French army after a prize had been put on his head. Shot and killed at Gemert.

[2] Served in the Dutch army. Sentenced and executed by a court martial at The Hague, probably before July 1697.

[3] Alias Reijnier Montal. Born at Berghem, 1649. Soldier. Fled to South Holland around 1695, lived at Zoeterwoude in a house called De Frisschen Romer, and worked as a market gardener. Sentenced by the court of Rijnland; broken on the wheel at Leiden, 30 July 1697.

[4] Born in 1650. Widow of Dirk Maasakker, who had no connection with the Zwartmakers and was hanged at Grave in 1687.

[5] Lived at Berghem. Possibly ex-soldier. Hanged at s' Hertogenbosch, 3 August 1695.

[6] Lived at Berghem. Probably executed at 's Hertogenbosch around 1690.

[7] Lived at Berghem. Arrested by soliders from Megen, but freed from prison by his relatives. Later (1692–5) drowned when he tried to escape arrest by soldiers near Megen.

appointments, sleep, feast, hide the booty, and so on. Except for begging and intermittent service in the armies, none of the van Bergeijcks seems to have had any occupation. Ordinarily they looked more like vagrants and beggars than the respectable tradesmen as whom Kee Vuijlhemd preferred to pass them off. Yet, if we may believe one of their accomplices, at the height of their great expeditions Hendrick van Bergeijck had his 'pockets full of gold' and he ordered 'costly meals to be served at inns'.[13] The Bergeijck cluster in south-western Brabant and the third section of the band, which was at home in the environs of Eindhoven and in Spanish territory further to the south, frequently worked together during expeditions. Jan Bartels van Peer acted as the principal captain of this third segment. He too was assisted by local inhabitants living in hamlets not far from Eindhoven, such as the carter and carpenter Jan Spoormans, mentioned earlier, and a certain Cornelis van Mierlo. Both played an important role as informers, fences, and carters, while their houses were safe meeting places.

No branch of the Zwartmakers, then, consisted of foreign mercenaries. Quite a few of the members had indeed been soldiers, but they were certainly not foreigners. Members of the Gelderland branch were closely tied to the Veluwe, while nearly all the Brabant Zwartmakers had spent

Table 2 The van Bergeijck family

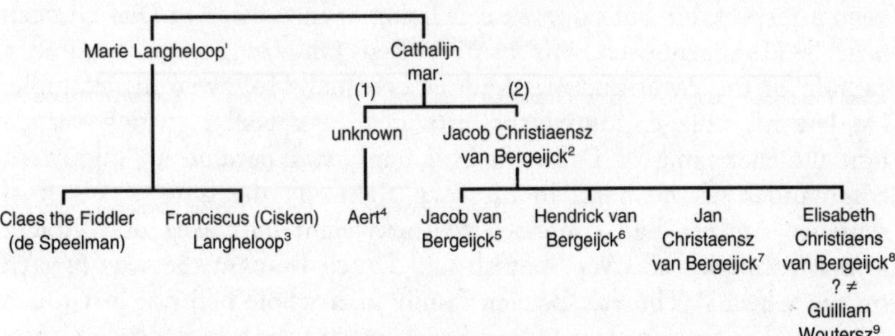

[1] Probably born in the southern Netherlands. Vagrant.
[2] Probably one of the initiators of the Brabant Zwartmakers. Ex-soldier. Hanged at 's Hertogenbosch, 11 January 1698.
[3] Alias François Waterloo or Sus the Hare (de Haes), or Sus the Furrier (de Peltenaar). Born in the southern Netherlands. Possibly furrier, skinner, or poacher. Hanged at 's Hertogenbosch, 24 September 1696.
[4] Half-brother of the younger generation of Bergeijcks. May possibly by Aert Heijligers, who later lived with Anna, alias the Old Magpie (d'Oude Exter); both she and their son, Little John (Cleijn Jantje), were later involved in the Moskovieter Band.
[5] Probably ex-soldier. Ambushed together with his brother Hendrick by some of his fellow Zwartmakers. Shot, and finally beaten to death by them, between December 1695 and October 1696.
[6] Principal commander of the Brabant Zwartmakers.
[7] Born at Meerhout, north-east of Antwerp. Ex-soldier; in garrison near Antwerp. Hanged at Antwerp, 30 December 1695.
[8] Vagrant and beggar. Probably lived with Guilliam Woutersz. Hanged at Brussels, 12 April 1696.
[9] Alias Guilliam the Dog (de Hond) or Guilliam Stoeldraaijer (?chair-mender or wood turner). Foundling at Antwerp. Cobbler's apprentice, shepherd, ex-soldier, and vagrant. Previous sentence (June 1695) at 's Hertogenbosch. Hanged at Geel, 24 January 1696.

most of their lives in the area where they committed their armed robberies. Even their family names betray as much: van Mierlo, van Hoogloon, and van Bergeijck refer to villages in the region. Although rooted in local rural society, many Zwartmakers in Brabant were on the brink of being outsiders. Some had already crossed the borderline and made the transition to a life of nearly permanent itinerancy, just like their colleagues in Gelderland. Many still had female relatives or elderly parents in some Brabant village with whom they could stay, but their links with respectable rural society had become tenuous to say the least. Loss of work, increasing destitution, and the gradual disintegration of ties to local society – the fading of a sense of belonging – set the pattern of many band members' lives.

Until the late 1680s Andries Nauwersz van Breugel, for example, had been a respectable but poor weaver living at the village of Den Dungen near 's Hertogenbosch. His brother Red Jan van Breugel became a captain of the Zwartmakers; Andries eventually followed his example. He left his village, toured the province as a pedlar (which earned him the nickname of Dries the Ragman), and became an important commander of the band in his own right. By the time of his final sentence Andries had confessed to thirty-eight burglaries and violent armed robberies all over Spanish and Dutch Brabant; he was broken on the wheel.[14] The van Beugen family as a whole had not lost touch with local society in their village Berghem, but the van Beugens clearly belonged to a marginal section of its population. They had a reputation for violence. In 1688–9, long before the Zwartmakers began to operate as a band, Lambert van Beugen and two of his sons were involved in a serious shooting incident at the market in nearby Megen. Another time, a third son of Lambert was arrested by the military (probably on account of theft), and his father organized an expedition of at least ten to twelve kinsmen and neighbours to 'free our Jochem from the prison at Megen'.[15]

Military service must have played an important part in the process of dissolving local ties. 'The most brutalizing employment of the century', as Hay describes it, 'a life which it was widely agreed unsuited men [used] to civilian routine' (1982, p. 142), can only have increased their readiness to employ violence, even if it also accustomed them to army discipline. Knifings were a normal part of village life in both Brabant and Holland, but firearms were not so readily available and their handling required some training. Most of the Zwartmakers knew how to use flintlocks, pistols, and carbines, but they also employed knives, bayonets, and wooden clubs when they tortured and killed during their expeditions. Even when not committing robberies their violence was hardly more restrained. In 1694 one of the van Beugens shot and killed a man who had called him a 'Swartmaker' in public. Before the bands had even formed Green Thomas had been present at the murder of a young beggar by one of his companions. The father of the captain Jan Bartels van Peer had been murdered in 1681, and in 1694 Jan himself shot and killed his own brother during a drunken fight. Around 1695–6 the principal commanders of the Brabant Zwartmakers, Hendrick van Bergeijck and his brother Jacob, were ambushed by some of their fellow (and rival?) Zwartmakers. Hendrick managed to escape but Jacob was shot. When their attackers discovered that he was not yet quite dead, they returned and beat him to death with the butts of their rifles.

So besides being military bands, the Zwartmakers were distinctly regional bands which recruited new members from among the population of the areas where they operated. Their success was predicated upon local knowledge and local ties. (It is worth noting that the home regions of the two branches – the Veluwe and the borderland of Spanish and Dutch Brabant, the so-called Kempen – were, like so many other military recruitment areas in Europe, traditionally poor regions which offered few alternative ways of earning a living.) The special character of the Zwartmakers lay in the combination of mobility (a semi-itinerant way of life), marginality in terms of social position (they belonged to poor families with a low status, some of whom were both despised and feared), and the importance of family and kinship ties. Many band members had only recently made the transition from belonging to one of the rural communities in Brabant to being outsiders. Individually, this must have been a painful experience, meaning poverty or even destitution, loss of position, and probably rejection by friends, relatives, and former neighbours. Seen from a different perspective, this process of gradual uprooting from the local community to a large extent removed them from its concomitant social control.

Moskovieters and the van Exaerde Band

Within seven years of the demise of the Zwartmakers the rather smaller band of the Moskovieters had begun to commit armed robberies in the western half of Brabant (1706–8). At least thirty-eight people – twenty-eight men and ten women – belonged to this band: twenty-three of them were sentenced by first-instance courts in Brabant. Twelve men were executed; one man died in prison of a leg wound sustained when he was captured.[16] In many respects their expeditions continued ordinary military practice. Band members regularly operated on horseback. At lonely places in the middle of woods or heathlands a small group of Moskovieters would stop carters and other travellers. Drawn pistols in hand, they forced their victims to surrender money and valuables, or just left them, taking horses and loaded wagons with them. More rarely they attacked farmhouses and rural inns at night. They trussed up the inhabitants and plundered the house. The bailiff of Breda summarized their activities: 'the so-called Muskovieters – have been despoiling and robbing the possessions of people all over the area in their houses and on the public roads'.[17]

Weapons, violent solutions to internal disputes, and military ranks were at least as important among the Moskovieters as they had been in the Zwartmakers Band. Two men were shot and killed during internal fights 'about the point of rank, or being the principal commander'. This command was held by Willem Christiaense (aged twenty-three) from Ghent, known as Captain Willem. He was assisted by several lieutenants and by a sixteen- or seventeen-year-old boy, nicknamed Prince William. Nearly every band member had served in one or more European armies. Hendrick Wighmans (aged thirty-two), alias Savage Henry (Heintje Woeste), for instance, had enlisted in at least four different companies, including a French one. When asked in which army they served, these men always referred to the commanders of their companies and only rarely mentioned the country for which they were supposed to be fighting. In fact, they were not fighting for any country at all and did not entertain even the vague notion of serving a king or state (let alone the modern idea of identifying with a nation). They were mercenaries; their first loyalty (or enmity, for that matter) was towards their immediate commander. To them – and many of their contemporaries – there was nothing reprehensible about serving in the armies of several different states in quick succession. But to take the republican equivalent of the King's shilling from one company, never show up, and join another, only to desert again immediately and join a third or fourth one – a common practice among members of the Moskovieters Band – was regarded as a very serious offence indeed at the time.

The name 'Moskovieters' is said to derive from a Polish or Russian mercenary company which had fought under the Duke of Marlborough during the War of the Spanish Succession.[18] Many band members had apparently once belonged to this company. Whether or not such a company ever existed, the birthplaces of band members point to less exotic regions. Only two of them can properly be regarded as 'foreigners': Prince William was born in Holland and Savage Henry came from Hanoverian territory. Every other person among the thirty-eight known to us was born in Dutch or Spanish Brabant. The similarities between Moskovieters and Zwartmakers do not end there. Ties between the Moskovieters and specific local communities in Brabant may have been slightly less strong, but detailed knowledge of the region and reliance on local assistants were at least as important to their operations. Two of these accomplices lived in or near Tilburg: Arien Huysmans, a weaver and innkeeper, who regularly hid part of the booty in his house and transported it in his cart and Strong (Stercke) Herman, who provided safe lodgings at Tilburg

Geographically as well as socially the Moskovieters, like the Zwartmakers, belonged to the fringe of local rural society in Brabant. The personal history of Goyaert van den Boom, alias Goijken Wannelappers (tinker), illustrates how rural poverty, military service, and increasing social marginalization went hand in hand. Goijken Wannelappers was born in 1676 at Geel in Spanish Brabant; his sister lived on the Dutch side of the border. Goijken enlisted in the Spanish armies, probably during the War of the Spanish Succession, and afterwards joined the Moskovieters. He escaped the trials of 1707–8, but was arrested nearly twenty years later, in 1727, for threatening arson. As he told the court, he had spent most of his life – both before, during, and after his activities as a Moskovieter – working as a casual rural labourer in the summers and begging in the barony of Breda and the environs of Tilburg and Eindhoven during the winters. In the meantime he had enlisted twice again, in German and French companies. In 1727 Goijken still spoke of 'his regiment' and told his interrogators he planned to re-join it, even though he had deserted more than ten years before. His statements provide one of the very rare clues to the reasons why such men might get involved with a robber band. A former employer, probably a farmer, testified that Goijken had left his house about twenty years ago to join the Moskovieters, who could be found almost daily at the house of their local assistant Huysmans. At the time the employer had spoken harshly to Goijken, saying, 'What do you want with those vagabonds?' whereupon Goijken answered, 'Life is better with those people, for they don't have to work . . . Now I can work when I want to; now I am my own boss.'[19]

The van Exaerde Band was considerably smaller than either the Zwartmakers or Moskovieters. Nine band members were sentenced (seven of them to capital punishment) by the courts of Rotterdam and Putte, a small village in western Brabant; four women were detained and probably banished without formal sentence at Rotterdam; sixteen more band members and assistants figure in interrogations.[20] The main robberies were committed by a group of nine to twelve band members, among them the brothers Cornelis and Anthonie van Exaerde. These men attacked and robbed a number of big isolated farms in the countryside of western Brabant and on the island of Tholen (Zeeland). They rammed in front doors and regularly beat, tied up, and shot at their victims, some of whom they tortured by putting them near the fire. They murdered at least two of them.

Being small, the van Exaerde Band did not use military ranks, but most of the men had served in one or more armies (Dutch, Spanish, or French). Military experience marked their operations, which often resembled requisition expeditions. Again, like the Zwartmakers and Moskovieters, these were local men and women. All of them were born in the rather limited area of their main operations and most of them came from either Antwerp or a cluster of three or four villages lying close together between Antwerp and Bergen op Zoom – almost on the Spanish–Dutch border. They too had local assistants: an innkeeper called Black (Swarte) Piet, who acted as their main informant, besides providing food and lodging, and a woman, Barbel de Clercq, at Bergen op Zoom who bought stolen goods. (Barbel begged while pretending to be a leper. Her first husband had been hanged; the second one was broken on the wheel.)[21] As in the other military bands, women took no active part in the robberies, but assisted by looking for information, and transporting and selling the stolen goods. Some of the women worked as rural labourers during the summers, touring western Brabant like the men, but travelling separately. Detailed knowledge of the region and familiarity with each other's patterns of work, itineraries, and regular rural employers enabled them to split up, work for a number of weeks or even months on different farms, and find each other again within a few days.

Like the Zwartmakers and Moskovieters, members of the van Exaerde Band were not just local people, however. They belonged to the local fringe of poor and disreputable inhabitants. Some were drop-outs, such as Peter Adriaens, a young man from Ekeren near Antwerp. He told the court that he had left his place of birth 'so that his friends need not be ashamed'.[22] Hardly any band member had learned a trade. When they were not actively serving as soldiers, they begged, bought and sold old clothes and scrap, skinned dead animals, and occasionally worked as shepherds or rural labourers. Most of them had a history of violent behaviour, including knife-fights at fairs, extortion at gunpoint, highway robbery, stabbing, and intimidation. By the time they joined the band their links with the local communities of western Brabant had become extremely tenuous. The few remaining ties must have been severed when they maltreated and robbed local farmers who had given them temporary jobs. Some of these farmers recognized their attackers as former employees. One said to Cornelis van Exaerde, 'Did I deserve this for giving your dead mother one of my own shirts to be buried in?'. Cornelis answered, 'That doesn't help you; you've got it coming anyway.'[23]

Generally, we do not know whether or not a band would have changed its patterns of activity if transferred to a quite different region, but the van Exaerde Band provides a rare example of such a transfer. After Cornelis van Exaerde and some of his accomplices had been arrested, tried, and executed in western Brabant in the autumn of 1713, some of the remaining band members attempted to shift their activities to South Holland, in particular the environs of Rotterdam and The Hague. This endeavour was not successful: their robberies failed and most of the members were soon arrested and tried. In western Brabant the band had often attacked farmhouses with which they were familiar because of their work as rural labourers. There they had committed 'classic' armed robberies involving much violence and noise. In the area between The Hague and Rotterdam these men were out of their depth.

They obviously appreciated that a different region required different tactics, ceased to plan large-scale expeditions or carry guns, and realized that noisy attacks would not be feasible in this area. But they had not yet acquired a criminal style suited to Holland. In the course of one night four of them tried to break into five farmhouses in succession. They were obviously aware that their usual 'technique' of more or less openly approaching the houses and battering down their front doors would attract rather too much attention in this densely populated area, but they had not developed a new method. So, the same men, who had confidently plundered large farms in Brabant and had not hesitated to terrorize, torture, and kill their inhabitants, were scared off in Holland, by the barking of a dog at the first house, by a woman crying, 'Thieves, thieves' at the second, and by a man opening his bedroom window at the third. The robbers returned that same night to Rotterdam without having stolen anything, only to be arrested within the next few days.[24]

Military Bands and Local Ties

In Brabant we thus find a pattern of war-related organized crime completely unlike that in Holland, Zeeland, or indeed England. There we had found *post-war* bands, consisting of loose-knit companies and average-sized networks, which rarely included more than about fifty people. Their geographical background was diverse: most band members (in particular the women) were born in Holland or Zeeland, but there was always an important contingent of recent immigrants, usually from the southern Netherlands or Germany. Marked hierarchies or military ranks were rare. Male and female members toured the countryside in small groups and met at rural inns or, at certain times, in town. Most of them were full-time vagrants, itinerant pedlars, rural labourers, or former artisans; some had worked as sailors, but military experience (and thus the use of firearms during robberies) was rare; only a few men had served in the armies for any length of time. Except for a small number of trusted rural innkeepers and urban fences, band members lacked contacts with the local rural population.

The *wartime* military bands of Brabant could hardly have been more different. They were active only during periods of warfare, never afterwards, prospering especially between 1690 and 1715. From that time onwards no military groups other than the small parties of soldiers discussed at the beginning of this chapter operated in either Brabant, Holland, or Zeeland. (As will be discussed in Chapter 8, real military bands did not even return during the French revolutionary period.) The military bands of Brabant operated like military companies and used weapons which very few civilians could handle. They might comprise as many as 150 or even more than 200 people, though not all military bands were big. Military hierarchies and ranks were quite common, as was a military style of operating – on horseback, putting out sentries, and so on. The bands consisted predominantly of men with years of military experience, and, perhaps most importantly, their very existence and success were dependent upon their ties with the established local rural population, to which the band members themselves had once belonged. For this is one of the most surprising characteristics of Dutch military banditry: it is extremely difficult to find any real foreigners among the members of these bands. Foreign mercenaries especially are almost completely absent, as are deserters of foreign abstraction. It seems as if only one particular section of all former soldiers managed to join or form military bands in the Netherlands: that is, those soldiers who were or had been local inhabitants as well. (The number of outsiders – that is, men born outside the area of operations – may have been lower in the military bands than in any other type of band.)

It was, however, just one category of local people who joined the bands. The two major military bands – Zwartmakers and Moskovieters – consisted of poor rural inhabitants at the fringe of local society, who had been further uprooted by military service. The personal histories of the van Exaerde members confirm the pattern and show the same tell-tale characteristics: local or regional background and concomitant knowledge of the area; individual (and occasionally family) histories of poverty and downward social mobility; limited professional training resulting in a lack of economic opportunities and recourse to begging, casual jobs on the fringe of the rural economy, and military service; growing familiarity with army discipline and the use of violence; a semi-itinerant way of life and a slipping away from local social control; increasing marginalization and a loosening – though not a complete rupture – of ties with the local community. Although some of the women were vagrants too, most of them led more settled lives than the men. It was they who provided crucial assistance, such as information, food, and shelter, and links with other local inhabitants. Above all, they helped to maintain solidarity in families that otherwise might easily have fallen apart.

The character of the local ties deserves further specification. There is no evidence of any solidarity between members of these military bands and the 'respectable', established part of the local population. On the contrary: they robbed the local population itself. For their more spectacular armed robberies bands usually selected wealthy or at least well-to-do victims among local farmers, shopkeepers, and notables. Yet by no means all their victims were rich. They robbed poor and elderly people just as much as wealthy farmers. The Zwartmakers did not hesitate to break the windows of a farmhouse with the butts of their guns and shoot at random into the house until the front door was opened. They scorched feet, dripped hot candle grease on elderly victims, and used their pistols as thumbscrews – perhaps imitating judicial torture. They made no distinction between a farmer's money and the personal savings of his servants and farm-hands. Hence, delays in reporting crimes to the criminal courts and hesitations about testifying cannot be interpreted as signs of friendship and collusion between local inhabitants and band members. Besides, if such ties had existed, the state authorities would have been the first to show concern – especially in a region like Brabant, which was administered directly from The Hague because it was a politically and religiously insecure area. The delays and hesitations were due to fear. These bands terrorized the rural population of Brabant.

Zwartmakers, Moskovieters, and members of the van Exaerde Band were no social bandits, in Hobsbawm's sense of the term. They did not find support or protection among the rural population against an oppressive state, its representatives, or a powerful and distant elite (Hobsbawm 1981). The local ties they relied upon were limited to the lowest segment (in terms of income and status) of rural society – and not even to the whole of this part of the population. Yet, although their expeditions were not manifestations of social banditry, they may have expressed feelings of revenge and protest, besides serving the more immediate purpose of supplying booty. There was, after all, a wide social gap between the broad spectrum of respectable rural families on the one hand and the disreputable, generally poor, and often semi-itinerant local 'fringe' on the other.[25] Local solidarity existed mainly within these segments of rural society, not between them.

Small fragments of evidence indicate that at least some robberies were directly inspired by revenge, resentment, or 'class' enmity. Zwartmakers repeatedly chose to rob farmers who had refused to offer them food, drink, or a place to sleep in their barns. In the van Exaerde Band too personal antagonism between members and their former employers may have played a part. In more than one case, moreover, a Zwartmaker threatened to burn down the house of the president of a local criminal court who had convicted him some time before.[26] Even if there were no personal connections between victims and robbers, the robberies may still have been partly inspired by generalized resentment. The Moskovieter who said that he preferred to be his own boss, expressed a feeling of 'class' antagonism, which can also be traced in the statements of a member of the Gelderland branch of the Zwartmakers. Shortly before his execution Andries Orville evidently realized that the whole

Zwartmakers Band was finished. Thinking of what he was going to say to his wife during their last meeting, he declared that he 'realized that all those who wander around [as vagrants and robbers] have to die, and because of this she should earn her bread honestly'. At the same time he showed a kind of grim satisfaction about the terror they had caused, stating 'that the Swartmakers would not be eliminated for at least thirty years, because [the authorities] would tend to regard every person they caught as one of them, even though innocent'.[27]

Apart from these fragmentary statements, members of the military bands remained silent about any radical intentions, wishes, or purposes. They neither criticized the established order during interrogation nor complained about their situation or, for instance, about legal inequality. During interrogation defendants frequently named poverty as the main reason for their involvement in criminal activities – partly because most of them were indeed poor, partly because it was the kind of 'explanation' the courts expected. Yet even 'poverty' was almost never articulated as political subversion, condemnation of existing social conditions, denunciation of the elite, or just plain envy. Resentment did not lead to verbally articulate forms of social protest among this part of the population.[28] But perhaps it is extremely unreasonable to expect the defendants to express in words what they had already said in another language.

In this respect the military bands of Brabant were typical of all other bands, groups, and networks that have left traces in the criminal records of Holland, Zeeland, and Brabant. None of them can be regarded as a political or social protest movement in any but the most indirect way.[29] Nor does it appear as if resentment against the rich and powerful helped to forge a more general solidarity among the lower social strata. Cooperation among different circuits involved in organized crime did not develop until the second half of the eighteenth century, when the time of the military bands was long over and their place in Brabant had been taken by more loosely knit vagrant networks. But first we will take a look at a quite different segment of organized crime: ethnic bands.

Part III

Ethnicity

5

Gypsy Bands, 1695–1730

Discussing ethnic minorities in the Dutch Republic means speaking about Jews and gypsies. Both had a special legal status in the Netherlands, as in most other European countries, and both played a far more important role in organized rural crime than might be expected from their relatively small numbers. This part focuses on their bands, offences, and patterns of criminal organization. Did their special position as stigmatized minorities contribute to their involvement in organized crime? What exactly were their relations with Dutch society, and did these relations change? Did the men and women who became involved in 'ethnic bands' somehow detach themselves from their own respective backgrounds? – had they lost contact with the rest of gypsy or Jewish society or did they still belong?

Identification and Stigmatization

Even the simple designation of certain groups as gypsy bands immediately embroils us in the intricate problem of identification. How do we know that members of certain bands were gypsies? Contemporary authorities apparently had no problems in identifying gypsies and accordingly do not elaborate on their ways of distinguishing them. It seems likely that gypsies were easily recognized by their appearance and language. A rural court in North Holland describes three arrested gypsy women as 'in the shape and dress of Egyptians',[1] and the records frequently offer tantalizing indications, such as 'the usual frock of gypsies', besides references to a dark complexion and black or dark-brown hair. What this 'usual frock' consisted of, we do not know. We may, of course, turn to the few available contemporary pictures for more information, but their representation of gypsies can in no way be regarded as an uncomplicated portrayal of reality.[2] Many pictures show both men and women wearing wide cloaks, wraps, capes, and shawls. The women's dress included several wide skirts as well as head-shawls, and variously shaped turbans. The men's dress seems to have approached European fashions from a much earlier date; by the seventeenth century gypsy men mostly wore trousers, military-style hats, coats, and sometimes cloaks. Some nineteenth-century authors mention a preference for gaudy headgear, bright colours (especially red and yellow), stripes, and silver and gold embroidery. (see Dirks 1850, p. 14, whose discussion of gypsy appearance and dress of the past refers only to the sixteenth and nineteenth centuries). Very little of this is evident in their personal descriptions in the criminal records. At least one member of an eighteenth-century gypsy band wore a white coat, a blue cloak, and a bright-coloured waistcoat with silver trimmings.[3] Contemporary courts remarked rather more often on the poverty of their dress, the bare feet of women and children, and their generally dirty appearance; their dark skins were considered positively ugly.

Different appearances do not, in fact, help us identify gypsies in the judicial records. References to the use of a foreign language are rather more helpful. No standard name existed among non-gypsies for the language: in some rare cases the records call it Rommisceers or Rommischel, but far more often they speak of 'the *Heijdense* (heathen) language' or of a foreign language that was unlike any known dialect, and distinct from Yiddish and the ordinary thieves' languages. Occasionally bailiffs likened gypsy language to the noise produced by animals or to sounds that no one (that is, no ordinary, civilized person) could understand. Even such references to a special language are uncommon, however, and occur only in court cases against large bands which were considered important enough to be investigated in some detail. For smaller groups we have to make do with remarks like 'is a *Heijdinne* [heathen or gypsy woman] and also descended from generation upon generation of so-called heathens and vagrants'.[4]

Far more important for purposes of identification are personal names and the descriptive terms used by the authorities. The records never fail to mention the special, ethnic identity of gypsies. Sentences invariably speak of *Egyptenaars* (Egyptians) or *Heijdens*. The modern Dutch term *zigeuner* had not yet made its appearance, and the term *zigerinne* was used only once: in 1740 in the (German) area of Ravenstein in eastern Brabant. Whatever the precise etymology and meaning of the word *Heijdens* (see, among others, van Kappen 1965, pp. 99–109), it must have conveyed the impression that these people did not form part of the Christian world, of civilized human society. Gypsies themselves were well aware of this connotation. When Marcus Allemonde – a member of a large gypsy band involved in several murders and robberies – finally admitted to a certain offence, he added, 'Yes, and to be known under the name of *Heijden*, but to know very well that there is a God.'[5]

Usually the court's designation is borne out by the personal names of the defendants. Gypsy names, like the names of Jews, are unmistakable. First names and patronymics including diphthongs such as 'ei', 'ij', 'au', and 'ou' were particularly common among them: Reijnoud, Tiboud, Reijnier, Boudewijn, Valentijn, Ysbrantsz, Wijnand. Each of these names qualifies as a familiar (though not particularly common) Dutch name, but none was regularly used by non-gypsies during this period. A second category consisted of ordinary Dutch family names, such as Jansen, Engels, van den Berg, Kooiman, Evertse, and Philips. A third category comprised outlandish names which did not even resemble any known foreign naming pattern: Origlina, Aquatina, Geggele, Ergulius Hergalius, Alewijn Aardappel (potato – still a fairly exotic vegetable at the beginning of the eighteenth century), Claas D'Annenas (the pineapple), Lucretia, Urias Adams, Blommerantje, Pootje, Garneson, Montagne Ysbrants, Hannibal Haldewijl, Mosselo, Magdalone, Sansiranne, Cette Fuango, and Sandrina. It is the names in this category in particular that stand out among the others in the records and immediately register as being 'typically' gypsyish. When such exotic names occur in combination with the two first categories – as in Reijnoud Engels, alias Geggele – there is little reason to doubt that we are indeed dealing with gypsies.

All gypsies – women as well as men – used more than one name: Jan Berentse or Don Sjuan; Pieter Elleputten or Cette Fuango. At first sight it looks as if the exotic names were their 'real' names, while ordinary, Dutch-sounding names had been adopted as part of a protective cover. But why, in that case, did they not employ a much larger and random collection of Dutch names? Besides, would Dutch surnames have offered any cover to people who were apparently easily recognizable as strangers? It would seem, then, that the use of ordinary Dutch names was part of a more general practice of cultural borrowing by gypsies from the areas which they toured for some length of time. If so, we should at least hesitate to regard their Dutch names as less 'real' than their exotic ones.

The whole notion of a 'real' name thereby becomes problematic. Asked about the changing family names of her daughter – who was alternately called Sara Jans or Sara Jurriaans, and whose father's name was Louis Jurriaans – one mother explained that 'it was customary among them to add two titles [family names] to their [first] names'. The same woman's son used the family name of his godfather, and all members of this group had some other 'Dutch' and exotic names as well.[6] The case of the gypsy leader Garneson (about whom we will hear more shortly) points in the same direction. On his detention by the court of Rotterdam in 1714 Garneson called himself Sybrecht Jansz. Later he admitted that he was (also) called Garneson or Pieter Nonnee, but 'had quitted the name of Pieter because one of their people (called Pieter) had been shot and killed at Harderwijk by a certain Patriques [another gypsy], and it is customary among them when someone dies who carries the same first name as themselves to relinquish it'.[7] If he was telling the truth, the link between name and identity in gypsy society differed from the usual pattern in European society.[8] Among gypsies several names could certainly be used alternately – perhaps depending on circumstances or on personal relations with those present – without any of them being more or less 'real' than the others.

Apart from the meaning of names in gypsy society itself, there is also the practical use of names in their contacts with non-gypsies to consider, particularly with the judicial authorities. Earlier we saw that defendants from diverse cultural backgrounds tried to confuse the authorities by raising problems about identification. Each group, however, had its own ways of doing so. The number of different names presented by gypsy defendants tended to increase according to the length of time they had spent in detention and the number of interrogations. This also applied to their places of birth, ages, relatives, and activities. Such a proliferation of identities caused confusion, irritation, and occasionally even despair among the prosecutors. A sentence pronounced by the town court of Haarlem in 1740 illustrates this feeling of exasperation: every question calls forth new answers which do not match previous ones, and 'the longer they are interrogated, the more their responses present an incredible variety, the more they contradict themselves and each other, and the more they take recourse to notorious falsehoods and even impossibilities'.[9]

The presentation of continually changing names and identities might well be interpreted as the core of a defensive strategy deployed by a group which had no access to the usual protective cover of anonymity. By the late seventeenth century gypsies had been a stigmatized and occasionally even a persecuted minority for almost two hundred years. From the late fifteenth century onwards edicts barred gypsies from the German empire. Placards issued by the Dutch provinces during the first half of the sixteenth century proclaimed the same policy (see Dirks 1850 and L. Lucassen 1990, esp. pp. 22–3). Unlike any other group, it was their very presence – and not any offences which they might have committed – that put them within the range of criminal law in the first place. This position did not change until the end of the eighteenth century. So it is hardly surprising to find that gypsies had become specialists at concealment and evasion.

The special status of gypsies is clearly reflected in the terminology used by the Dutch courts. More frequently than other vagrant groups they were denoted by pejorative terms such as *troep* (troop), *rot* (gang), *gespuis* (scum, vermin), and even *gebroedsel* (brood).[10] To some extent the authorities put them on a par with animals or uncivilized creatures. In one case gypsies were described as 'vagrants and birds of prey or companies of the same'.[11] And they were regularly likened to a pest and a parasite of which society had to rid itself. A court in North Holland described a gypsy as 'feeding his lazy belly with the sweat and exertions of our rural inhabitants',[12] and placards as well as edicts issued by the various provincial estates and the Estates General used identical terms. A sentence pronounced against a twenty-year-old gypsy woman by the local court of Gorinchem in South Holland in 1754 adequately summarizes the official attitude: according to the court, she had 'conducted herself as a useless, dangerous, and harmful subject in civil society'.[13]

While official documents referred to gypsies in strongly insulting terms, popular attitudes varied. A rare example from Zeeland indicates that ordinary people shared these negative views to a certain degree. In 1718 a skipper or ferryman quarrelled with a gypsy about the use of his boat. He pulled the gypsy by his hair and pushed him off the boat. Later he defended his actions in court by saying 'that those *Heijdenen* are people without any quality [*qualiteijt*] or privilege [*vrijdom*], that they may be chased away and cast off at all times without thereby doing anything wrong ... and accordingly [he did] not owe a fine'.[14] The fact that he had to defend himself in court at all is, of course, worth noting. Now and then we also hear of conflicts between Dutch rural inhabitants and groups of gypsies camping near their villages. In one such case a farmer in North Holland reported being threatened with a knife by a gypsy who belonged to a group of about twenty. They had put up their tents near a water-mill, entered the miller's barn, and stolen some peat for their fires; they resisted and even stabbed some local constables who ordered them to leave.[15]

Mutual hostility and negative attitudes on the side of the local population formed only one part – and for most of the time not the largest part – of relations between gypsies and rural inhabitants in the Netherlands. Usually, individual contacts had a more impartial, businesslike, and sometimes even friendly character. Gypsies offered important and valued services to the rural population. Dutch villagers enjoyed the entertainment offered by gypsy families who performed as fiddlers and acrobats, showing off their trained dogs, goats, and monkeys. Gypsies told stories, brought news, and may have introduced new songs. The men repaired chairs, pots, pans, and farm utensils, going from one farm to another carrying their tinkers' tools. The women (as well as some of the men) sold pills, ointments, elixirs, and other medicines from door to door. Perhaps attracted by the magical formulas which added to the potency of the drugs, Dutch country folk readily bought their medicines. And although fortune-telling was officially regarded as 'unholy' business, many local people were fascinated and let gypsy women 'read their palms'.[16]

Naturally, an exchange of services does not necessarily imply or entail close relations, let alone a sense of equality. But besides outright fear and stigmatization there was indeed a good deal of kindness, interest, and sometimes intimacy and trust in these everyday contacts. People confided in gypsy women about troubles and illness afflicting both themselves and farm animals, and asked for their advice in matters of health and (future) happiness. In order to inspect the sick, gypsy women were allowed to enter parts of the house closed to almost anyone who was not a member of the family. And a gypsy woman who felt faint and sat down on the doorstep of a farmhouse could often count on being treated kindly and invited to drink some water or coffee in the kitchen – even though many rural inhabitants must have been aware that such a faint might well be the standard opening of an elaborate confidence trick, which involved treasures buried in the cellar, magical formulas, and jealous ghosts who had to be appeased by gold and silver. Again and again such episodes ended with a farmer and his wife losing hundreds or even thousands of guilders. In 1725, for example, a certain Yesabel Cornelis (aged twenty-six), who sold herbs from door to door, and her niece approached a gardener and his wife working on a gentleman's farm in North Holland. They told the couple that a sum of about 800 guilders lay buried in the cellar of the house. Some money was indeed 'discovered' under one of the tiles in the cellar, whereupon the women instructed the gardener to put all his valuables in a sack and bury them in the cellar 'where the ghost would play with them'. They promised to return the following day and dig up the treasure. Of course, nobody turned up and the valuables had gone.[17] That local people continued to invite gypsy women into their houses, in spite of the possible risks and in spite of the general reputation of gypsies, is the strongest possible evidence for a basically friendly popular attitude. It is important to keep in mind that such kindness and consideration applied to individual gypsies, to women and children, and perhaps to small family groups. They were not characteristic of popular relations with large groups of gypsies; in such encounters suspicion, fear, and dislike were rather more prominent – at least on one side, and perhaps on both.

Persecuting Policies

The question of whether gypsies have been singled out for harsh treatment by judicial and other authorities because of their actual behaviour has been raised more than once. Did a combination of vagrancy, trespassing, petty theft, and other 'minor illegal activities' – all of which have been regarded as characteristic of a gypsy way of life – somehow prompt a policy of brutal repression? If not, was their repression part of an autonomous policy of persecution by European states which were trying to gain control over more and more aspects of the lives of their inhabitants? This touches upon the problem raised at the beginning of this chapter: did the special position of gypsies as a stigmatized minority lead to their relatively prominent involvement in organized crime? It is directly affected by an issue which is particularly relevant in the case of gypsies: to what extent their striking presence in the criminal records reflects not so much their actual participation in crime but the notions of authorities who simply classified anything a gypsy did as crime. In other words, should we regard information about their illegal activities as a construct fabricated by fearful authorities?

There is no simple answer to any of these questions, for two reasons. First, a distinction should be made between gypsy involvement in vagrancy and petty theft (which may indeed be ranged under the heading of everyday activities) on the one hand and in burglary, robbery, or even murder and robbery (which can hardly be called part of their daily routine) on the other. Secondly, discrepancies between legal rules and actual prosecution could be considerable. Even after the formal proclamation of harsh measures during the late fifteenth and early sixteenth centuries the intensity of prosecution varied a great deal from one period to another.

All over the northern Netherlands formal proclamations issued by the nearly autonomous provinces follow the same pattern. After the sixteenth-century edicts some new measures were taken between 1614 and 1635. Then there was a pause – particularly in Holland, Zeeland, Brabant, and Utrecht – until January 1695, when the Estates General and several provincial estates issued placards announcing new and harsher measures against 'the large bands of gypsies travelling in these areas, carrying arms and threatening arson'. Gypsies arrested for the first time were to be whipped; the second time they could expect whipping and branding; the third time they might be hanged. Those among them who had been involved in violence (and those who resisted arrest) might be hanged outright. Between 1695 and 1730 several more edicts repeated and even added to the measures announced in 1695. In August 1725 the provincial estates of Holland renewed the 1695 resolution in every respect: gypsies were ordered to leave the territory of Holland immediately; when arrested for a second time they were to be whipped, branded, and put into the house of correction; and every gypsy who committed acts of violence, carried arms, or belonged to a group of more than six grown men might be hanged. By this time even provincial autonomy had been put partly aside in allowing prosecuting officers and bailiffs from one area to pursue and track down gypsies in the territory of a neighbouring province (see Dirks 1850, esp. pp. 138–57, and *Groot Placaet-boeck* 1705, pp. 509–10).

From the 1630s onwards – and perhaps even earlier – the number of criminal sentences against gypsies rises during periods of new legislation. This is less self-evident than it may seem. The old placards by themselves offered more than sufficient means to prosecute and punish harshly, but for long periods they were not applied rigorously. Apparently provincial estates and Estates General preferred to introduce new legislation at certain times instead of insisting on the full enforcement of existing proclamations. Rather than being used to stimulate an increasing number of arrests, new proclamations reflected the need for more effective (or at least harsher) legal means to deal with growing numbers of gypsies. A detailed inspection of the period 1680–1730 shows as much.

Before the 1680s gypsies appear infrequently in the criminal records of Holland, Zealand, and Brabant, and where they do it is generally as members of small family groups. From about 1675 the number of convicted gypsies begins to increase: some twenty years, that is, before the proclamations of 1695. (There may be a connection with the proclamation in 1682 of a royal decree affecting gypsies in France; see Asséo 1974, pp. 30–3.) At the beginning of this period most gypsies arrested in the Dutch Republic were born in France, Germany, or the southern Netherlands. They were only seldom accused of anything more serious than vagrancy, begging, petty theft, or swindle – usually fortune-telling and ringing the changes (*kilfen*). From the late 1680s, however, more gypsies said they were born in the northern Netherlands; larger bands began to figure among a still growing number of small family groups; and some gypsies were carrying out more serious offences.

In 1687 a group of about forty gypsy men, women, and children toured the Schermer polder in North Holland. The women had committed two burglaries in the area, stealing money, clothes, and textiles. The group as a whole begged and stole cats, ducks, chickens, and geese. They had entered and occupied an empty farmhouse, making three big fires inside the house (using stolen peat and brushwood), which, according to the local inhabitants, endangered the whole village. Most members of this group were born in Germany, France, or the southern Netherlands.[18] A second group of four men, four women, and four children was arrested at Amersfoort in the province of Utrecht in 1692. All of them came from the German territory of Berg. Some of the men had recently served as soldiers, and most had been arrested and punished before. During the late 1680s these gypsies had been travelling in Germany and the Dutch provinces of Gelderland, Overijssel, and Brabant. By 1692 they had joined a larger gypsy company (*compagnie*) commanded by Captain Symon, or 'in the gypsy language Samel'. Continuing their travels in small groups, they committed thefts and burglaries in Gelderland, Overijssel, Brabant, and Utrecht. The booty was shared according to a fixed rule: one third for the captain, two thirds for the others.[19]

The proclamation of the harsh edicts of 1695 should not be understood, then, as an autonomous change of policy, a course of action unconnected to the actual presence of gypsies in the Dutch Republic. It was an indication of the grave misgivings among both the established rural population and the authorities about the growing numbers of gypsies, the formation of larger and better organized bands, and their involvement in rather more serious offences. The sentences pronounced against gypsies point in the same direction. During the 1670s and 1680s punishment was relatively mild (banishment or whipping and banishment), even though harsher sanctions could have been imposed according to the law. Only from 1695 onwards did sentences tend to conform more closely to the penalties announced in the placards. It is worth noting, by the way, that shortly before 1695 gypsies still placed enough trust in the Dutch authorities to seek their protection against other gypsies in a case of internal strife. The band of Captain Samel asked for and got the assistance of a bailiff and his substitute in disarming another 'party' of gypsies.[20] For the period before 1700, then, we might as well believe the Dutch authorities when they justify their new measures by pointing to the increasing numbers of gypsies who were arriving in the Netherlands from neighbouring countries (see Dirks 1850, pp. 35–7; cf. van Kappen 1965, pp. 151–2). German and French prosecution policies confirm the Dutch contention: between 1650 and the end of the seventeenth century France and several German states took measures to prevent gypsies from staying for any length of time in the areas concerned.[21]

The international profusion of edicts not only reflected gypsy migrations but in its turn must have stimulated them. One 'wave' of migrations may have started around the middle of the seventeenth century in central Europe, continuing into France, Germany, and Poland. If so, it was probably linked to the conclusion of a period of major European warfare around the 1650s: first because the cessation of fighting opened up large parts of central and western Europe to the travels of gypsies and others: and secondly because authorities who had formerly been fully occupied by warfare and its attendant miseries were now free to address different aspects of public order and safety. The German and French edicts and proclamations of the 1650s to 1670s probably caused a secondary wave of gypsy migrations, which began to reach the Netherlands during the early 1670s and prompted the measures of the 1690s. A migratory pattern in which the main thrust was directed towards the north and north-west might help to explain why North Holland, more than any other part of the area discussed here, was the main region of gypsy activity during the 1690s.

Viewed as a whole, Dutch prosecuting policies between 1675 and 1700 cannot by themselves be held responsible for the increasing numbers of convicted gypsies. Before 1695 the Dutch courts did not boost gypsy criminality by simply declaring certain activities to be illegal; nor did prosecuting policies – as yet – stimulate or provoke illegal activities. Both the introduction of harsh new legislation in 1695 and the actual enforcement of severe punishments – which had been possible long before that time – followed and reflected changes in the presence and activities of gypsies in the Netherlands. The number of gypsies touring the Dutch Republic increased from the mid-1680s, probably as a consequence of changing migratory patterns in Europe in the course of the seventeenth century. Gypsy bands expanded and were carrying out serious offences. But these reactive policies also formed the opening stage in a process of escalation which gained momentum during the 1710s and by the late 1720s had ended in the nearly total disappearance of gypsies from the Dutch Republic. What exactly happened during these years?

Escalation: Gypsy Bands, 1690–1725

The formation of larger and better organized gypsy bands which can be observed in the Netherlands and in neighbouring territories between about 1690 and 1725 cannot be understood without reference to the legal measures which had originated in response to the immigration of more and larger groups of gypsies in the course of the 1680s and 1690s. In their turn the appearance and activities of the bands triggered new series of ever harsher legal measures all over north-western Europe. To mention only a few examples: Prussia issued new rules in 1709, 1710,

1715, 1717, 1724, 1725, and 1727, the province of Gelderland in the years 1698, 1699, 1704, 1705, 1714, and 1721 (see Dirks 1850, pp. 36, 50–5).

A closer look at the vicissitudes of Captain Samel's band and its most important successors reveals some of the conditions and effects of this process of escalation on the side of the gypsies. It was characterized not only by the alliance and association of extended gypsy 'families' but also by internal strife, rivalry, and fission. The history of Samel's group can be traced thanks to the exceptional (though brief and fragmentary) statements of Captain Garneson, Samel's son and successor, who was arrested and sentenced at Rotterdam in 1714, more than twenty years after the sentences pronounced against members of Samel's own band at Amersfoort in 1692. (Garneson's statements fit in with the handful of details supplied by the detainees at Amersfoort. He was one of the very few leading gypsies to provide information about 'inside' affairs to non-gypsies.) Returning for a moment to the 1690s, we find that Samel's company included about fifteen adult men; at least equal numbers of women and children should be added, but the group may well have been larger. Several members had joined the company for reasons of protection, mutual assistance, and more effective self-defence: all were looking for safety in numbers. Every man and woman swore allegiance to their captain, vowed 'to live and die with him', and promised to assist and defend him and each other. Members of Samel's company travelled all over Utrecht, Gelderland, South Holland, and parts of Brabant. They toured the countryside in groups of two or three men and women and a few children, but men and women might also travel separately. During these tours they sold pills, ointments, and other medicines. Band members also stole clothes, laundry from the fields, and small pieces of cloth from shops. Occasionally they broke into a farmhouse when the occupants were out. Like many other gypsies, the people in this group were experts at ringing the changes.

According to some band members, Samel was known as a 'commander of thieves, who demanded and received his portion of all stolen goods'. He was already a relatively old man by the 1690s. Around the turn of the century one of this sons, Garneson, took over the command of what was by then called the Band of the White Feather.[22] Garneson was born at Amersfoort in 1676; he had a sister, Rosijntje (Little raisin) or Digna, and a brother called Jacobus. Like many other gypsy men, he sold medicines, and he may have served in the army. Under the command of Garneson the White Feather company expanded until it had at least a hundred members (counting both men and women) who operated all over the Dutch Republic in more or less the same manner as Samel's group. Both bands used to build camps and arrange meeting places in areas which were not easily accessible, such as fens, moors, or dunes. Samel's band had often met in the so-called Rheense veenen (fens or moors in Gelderland). Garneson's group made camps of straw huts and tents in the fens near Leiden in the winter of 1711–12 and in the dunes along the coast of North Holland during 1712. Every year his company held a general assembly in May, which lasted for two or three days: 'they feast and enjoy themselves together, and everyone has to render account to the captain or chief of his company of what he has done in the meantime'.[23] At first these meetings took place near Doetinchem in Gelderland, later near Woudrichem not far from Gorinchem and Rotterdam. Every member of the band had to pay a portion of his or her legal and illegal earnings to the captain. In return the captain shared out money and new outfits.

Like most other members of gypsy bands active during the late 1690s and early 1700s, Garneson was arrested several times in the course of his captaincy and condemned to relatively light forms of punishment, such as whipping and banishment, on account of vagrancy and petty theft. These arrests do not seem to have impaired his position as commander, but between 1709 and 1711 Garneson was none the less deposed as leader of the Band of the White Feather by his lieutenant, Willem Jansz. Internal politics and 'clan' rivalry lay behind it. Willem Jansz was married to a sister of the chief commander (Alewijn Philips) of the second big gypsy company operating in the Dutch Republic at the time, the Band of the Black Feather. Jansz and his brother-in-law formed a coalition – perhaps in order to promote a union of the White and Black Feather bands against the third major gypsy company, the Band of the Red Feather. According to Garneson, the Red, White, and Black companies together comprised about seventy adult men, and roughly three hundred people in all. Statements by other gypsies who were arrested during these years likewise refer to three big gypsy companies. Garneson is the only person to mention a chief commander called Maxelaers, 'as good as an emperor', who travelled in Germany and was said to have 'at his command one thousand men on horseback'.[24]

Garneson was thus thrown out of the company of which his father had been the first commander. Some gypsies probably chose his side and he may even have started a new band, for in 1714 he was arrested together with several other gypsy men and women. By that time, however, he had already been living apart from his old band for about three years without regaining an influential position. As he put it himself, his former lieutenant, Willem Jansz, 'respects [*estimeert*] him in no way'. After his Rotterdam sentence in 1714 Garneson informed the judicial authorities about his former associates, which gained him a nine-year reduction from the imposed twenty years' imprisonment. He died in prison in 1717. In the meantime the Band of the White Feather carried on growing, and in the course of the late 1710s and early 1720s became the most important gypsy band to have operated in the Dutch Republic.

From 1710 onwards the operations of the White Feather company proceeded along the lines of the Samel and Garneson groups. Captains still commanded a fixed percentage of the booty. Members extended their tours all over the northern Netherlands and met regularly in various camps. The men carried on with their jobs as entertainers; they also repaired pots, pans, and farm utensils, and sold medicines. The women continued to tell fortunes, sell medicinal herbs, advise in cases of illness, and lay ghosts. Yet not everything remained the same. Violent clashes between groups of gypsies and rural inhabitants had been quite rare before the 1680s. Threats of arson and attacks upon local constables (who ran the risk of being beaten up with tent poles) were almost unheard of before the 1700s. By then irritations and feelings of hostility were expressed more and more openly – on both sides.[25] Expeditions too were becoming increasingly bold, and involved larger numbers of participants. In the past gypsy women had generally played a leading role in both petty theft and burglary. They still did so, but it was the men who began to undertake large-scale armed robberies in the decade from 1710.

The group of gypsies who had been using a camp-site near Haarlem (near the Bilderdammersaen not far from Aalsmeer in South Holland) since the autumn or early winter of 1719 forms a good example. Local inhabitants complained about the theft of ducks, geese, cats, fish (from the bow nets), peat, and brushwood. Some of the gypsies concerned had been convicted before in different parts of South and North Holland on account of similar offences. Before about 1710 the gypsies' activities would not have gone much further and relations between gypsies and non-gypsies might have remained distant and tense without reaching the stage of open hostilities. Now, there were several skirmishes with the local authorities. On 26 December 1719, for instance, when some constables approached the camp-site and ordered the gypsies to 'pull down their tents and rugs and lay down their sticks', one of the constables was beaten until he fell down. Members of the band were, moreover, committing organized burglary and even violent robbery. Official reactions, as might be expected, were severe.

Shortly before 19 January 1720 several young men belonging to this same group broke into a farmhouse in South Holland and stole a barrel of butter which they sold to a trusted innkeeper for a pint of gin and three guilders; the money was spent on bread, milk, and barley.[26] A few days later a local inhabitant discovered the same five men in the act of breaking into the house or yard of a local shipwright, and shouted,

'Thieves, thieves.' Thereupon one of the gypsies drew a gun and fired some shots into the building. Montagne Ysbrantsz, Ergulius Hergalius, Marcus Lucas, and Wynandus Engelse were arrested and sentenced to harsh punishments: double whipping and branding as well as lifelong banishment. Even so, the court of Rijnland had acted with relative lenience. It had explicitly ignored both the prosecuting bailiff and the placards. The former demanded and the latter prescribed hanging in a case of violent burglary by a group of gypsies, especially when some of them had been convicted before. A few years earlier the difference between actual and prescribed punishment might have been even greater. By 1720, however, escalation was well under way, and in a rare appeal case the Hof van Holland changed their sentences to hanging.[27]

Even at this time, when irritations and fear had slowly grown on both sides, when harsher laws had been proclaimed, and prosecution had become much more rigorous, we cannot yet speak of a coordinated policy of persecution. It was three armed robberies involving brutal violence against the victims that played a crucial role in bringing about such a policy. They triggered new and concerted measures of persecution, which eventually ended in full-scale gypsy 'hunts'. These robberies deeply shocked Dutch rural inhabitants and authorities alike, and must have confirmed their worst fears.

Around half past nine on the evening of Wednesday, 12 March 1721, five gypsy men – Marcus Allemonde, Cornelis Abener, Antichoon, Roeland, and Arnoldus Willemse or Mosselo – as well as one gypsy woman, Mellesine, and a Dutch itinerant quack left Amsterdam through the Haarlemmer Gate. They had hired a cart, and travelled via Haarlem to a hamlet called De Glip a few kilometres to the west of this town. On reaching the hamlet, Mellesine pointed out the house and local shop they were going to rob, and then retired to a nearby inn. Some time earlier Mellesine had found out how much money they could expect to find in the house; she had talked to the woman who lived there and promised to show her where she could find a treasure. Some of the men were posted as sentries near the front door. The others approached the back of the house. Two of the men knocked the woman down and strangled her with a rope found in her own shop; a dog which started howling was stabbed to death. The men took five big sacks of goods with them and also hundreds of guilders in cash. They walked to the inn where Mellesine was waiting for them, whistled for her, and quickly returned to Amsterdam. It was very late by then. The city gates were closed, but the whole group was able to enter the city by crossing the frozen canals. The stolen goods were carried to the house of Marcus Allemonde and divided. Each of the men received about sixty guilders in cash besides textiles, clothes, and some jewellery.[28]

All the gypsies involved in this murder and robbery belonged to a company of at least twenty which had been camping for some time near Amstelveen (close to Amsterdam). Three or more of them also participated in the second of the three armed robberies which caused so much agitation. During the night of 3 October 1721 eight gypsy men carrying pistols broke into the house of one Aart Tijmense near the village of Weesperkarspel east of Amsterdam. The men entered the house by smashing one of the windows and immediately started plundering, throwing valuables and money out of the window to be gathered by their waiting companions. They shot at and narrowly missed the farmer. Leaving soon after, they crossed the river Vecht in a farmer's barge. The robbers had been followed by local inhabitants, and fled to Amsterdam, where six of them were arrested. All were hanged at Weesp shortly afterwards.[29]

Both the men who took part in these two major robberies and the group of four condemned to death by the Hof van Holland belonged to branches of the by now even more extensive White Feather company.[30] Partly in response to the increasingly energetic persecution in the province of Holland, members of this company had begun to establish an encampment of straw huts and tents at the Zandschel (in gypsy language called the Cajol) between 's Gravenmoer and Loon op Zand to the north-west of 's Hertogenbosch. It formed a more permanent base than the transitory encampments mentioned before and was strategically situated in more than one respect. Because of its location just south of the big rivers, the encampment was almost beyond the reach of the provincial authorities of Holland. Because of its location right on the provincial boundary between Holland and Brabant, it was difficult to reach for the Brabant authorities as well. In this area, moreover, provincial and judicial boundaries coincided with an ecological border which divided sandy soils covered with brushwood, heather, and trees from the as yet undrained and waterlogged clay area south of the river Maas which was subject to intermittent flooding. Numerous small streams criss-crossed the clay soils, which were covered with grass and the tangled vegetation of marshlands. A mixed area, it was difficult to reach but provided dry and safe spots for tents and huts.[31]

Roughly between 1721 and 1725 the camp at the Zandschel served as a central base for the White Feather company: some families and small parties returned there after each trip, others stayed away for months on end or even for most of the year, continuing to make use of transitory camps in other provinces. While the main base had been shifted as far as possible beyond the reach of the judicial authorities, gypsy expeditions to Holland had by no means ceased. In fact, the company continued to concentrate its most important illegal activities in this provence. Concerted persecution was, however, beginning to have some effect on gypsy activities, as is shown by the case of Jan Pietersz, or Antremony. His activities represent a more general pattern of regional fluctuations in the company's operations. Antremony was born in 1705 near Amersfoort; many gypsies of this generation were born within the Dutch Republic. As a twelve-year-old boy he had been present at several burglaries and a church robbery some 20 kilometres east of Amsterdam. In 1718 Antremony was arrested and condemned to whipping and banishment, whereupon he departed for Brabant, one of the many band members who were looking for safer surroundings in a southward and eastward direction. Three years later he returned to Holland and joined a large group of gypsies camping near Kalslagen and Bilderdam, a marshy area in central South Holland. Antremony took part in some more thefts and burglaries, and was hanged in 1726 at Amsterdam.[32]

Nothing could have been more damaging than to admit having been present at the encampment near Kalslagen during 1724. Several leading members of the White Feather company – who could be found frequently at the Zandschel – spent most of this year and the following winter in South Holland, together with their families. All of them periodically stayed at the camp near Kalslagen. The women travelled all over Holland, begged, sold medicines, told fortunes, and so on. Most of the men regularly committed thefts and burglaries; for the rest of the time they engaged in their usual legal activities. Johannes Montagne Ysbrantsz, for instance, a 48-year-old Gypsy born in Friesland, sold *medikansanten* (medicine) from door to door and gave occasional performances together with his son and a trained monkey. During the daytime he travelled alone; at night he joined a larger group of gypsies, all of whom returned to the camp near Kalslagen at the end of a few days or weeks.

In February 1725 this particular segment of the Band of the White Feather committed the last and most violent of the three notorious armed robberies. Two months earlier, in December 1724, some of the men – among them Johannes Montagne Ysbrantsz, Droede Lubings, and Claas D'Annenas – had violently broken into a house not far from Rotterdam. They had stolen a huge amount of cash (about 2,300 guilders) besides some other valuables, and had subsequently moved their four big tents to the dunes to the west of Haarlem. During the night of 9 February about twelve gypsy men and two women participated in the robbery and double murder at the mill at Kalslagen. Again, a woman had explored the situation some time before, but the area as a whole must have been familiar enough to most of the men since the big summer encampment at the Bilderdam was only a few kilometres away from Kalslagen. Johannes Montagne Ysbrantsz, Roseboom

Fransse, his brother-in-law Mosselo or Johannes, Droede Lubings, Rossan Hoteij or Knolletje or Lansprans, Adolph Pieters, the women Griekhout and Wielke or Cross-eyed Griet, Stoffel Willems or Schopping, Johannes Karels, Reybelo, Don Sjuan or Jan Berentse, Mannetje or Orias, Hoevenaer or Schavallier, and Donis met in the course of the evening near the mill. Some of them had just come from Amsterdam, others from the direction of the encampment in the dunes. Six of the men stayed outside as sentries; the rest tried to enter the house. When the miller opened the door to see what was going on outside, Mosselo immediately fired two shots at him, and five or six gypsies burst into the house. None of the inhabitants seems to have offered any resistance. The miller was murdered first: he was brutally beaten, cut, stabbed, and kicked to death, and his body thrown outside into a muddy ditch. His sister – who was visiting – was treated similarly: her head was battered in, and an autopsy showed that she had been stabbed eleven times. The men then beat up the miller's wife. She was forced to hand over money and valuables. When the amount did not satisfy them, they started searching through chests, cupboards, and beds. They maltreated her once more, and only left her alone when they thought she was dead. Next the men proceeded to light a big fire inside the house, burning beds and other parts of the furniture. Roseboom Fransse and Knolletje picked up a child from its bed and threw it down on the floor near the fire; they may also have hurt the second child. Finally the men left, taking big sacks full of plunder with them.[33]

There is no need to quote extensively from the autopsy report to recognize that we are dealing here with violence far beyond the 'common' practice of burglars and robbers. Even the members of the military Brabant bands of the 1690s and 1700s who frequently tortured and maltreated their victims – and probably killed a much larger number of people than the gypsy bands – never proceeded in this way. Their victims mostly died during a shooting or a fight, or as a consequence of torture; outright and brutal murder which had been planned beforehand was pretty rare. The three violent gypsy robberies were totally different. Johannes Montagne Ysbrantsz described his state of mind during the murders, and said he could not recount how the miller's sister had died 'because of the rage [*drift*] which had taken hold of him at the time'.[34] It was this aspect in particular, the savagery and senseless character of the violence, that caused horrified reactions among rural inhabitants and local authorities alike.

Explanations for this type of brutality are hard to find. It should be borne in mind that by the mid-1720s the relations between gypsies and authorities had been becoming more and more antagonistic for nearly thirty years. It was not only certain gypsies who were prepared to use violence against their opponents: the same was true of the authorities. By this time they frequently imposed death penalties for crimes considered petty (or at least insufficiently serious to be thus punished) when committed by anyone else.[35] Both collectively and individually gypsies had experienced increasingly harsh treatment by the courts. The personal histories of some of the men involved in the Kalslagen murders epitomize the more general process of escalation, of petty crime followed by relatively lenient punishment, of violent confrontations between groups of gypsies and local inhabitants, of recidivism and stronger legal measures, and finally of collective and cruel violence followed by aggravated death penalties. The point may then have been reached when gypsies who planned a robbery and realized that death penalties would certainly await them if discovered were prepared to commit extremely brutal murders. Silencing witnesses had become a matter of life and death.

Taken together, then, the structure and development of the large gypsy bands of the early eighteenth century can by understood only in the context of this process of escalation which had been going on for at least thirty years by the mid-1720s. The Band of the White Feather had slowly grown from a small mutual defence association in the 1690s to an extensive interregional network in the 1720s. By that time it was organized in kin-based sections or clans, made use of several temporary encampments and a principal base at the Zandschel, and comprised perhaps as many as three hundred men, women, and children. During the same period planned thefts, organized and occasionally violent burglaries, and finally the extremely violent armed robberies – all of them executed mainly by men – were added to the regular repertory of illegal activities which in former times had largely been the domain of gypsy women.

Yet in many other respects little changed during these years. Family ties remained the principal basis for the organization of the company's sections, and most of the commanders were linked by ties of kinship. During the 1700s Garneson's lieutenant married the sister of the Black Feather's commander. Similarly, the sister of Alewijn Aardappel, chief commander of the White Feather company and ruler of the Zandschel encampment during the early 1720s, was married to his first lieutenant. As in Garneson's time, commanders continued to claim a considerable portion of both legal and illegal earnings. They returned some (or perhaps even most) of it in the form of personal munificence, feasts, and general largesse. Finally, Gypsy companies remained heavily dependent on indigenous innkeepers, informants, and fences (the last of which included several Jewish pawnbrokers). Since gypsies were more easily recognized than other groups involved in organized crime, the goods they offered for sale were immediately regarded as stolen goods, and the questions they asked raised suspicions. Accordingly, reliable brokers were amply rewarded by gypsy captains – at least once in a while. In the vicinity of the encampment at the Zandschel gypsies occasionally even returned stolen goods in order to prevent problems for their local assistants.

The concerted persecutions of the 1720s ended in the nearly complete disappearance of gypsies from the Dutch Republic by the early 1730s. Many had been arrested, executed, imprisoned, or banished. Others fled to safer areas in a reverse movement of their migrations of the period 1670–1700: first to southern and eastern parts of the Netherlands, then to neighbouring countries. After 1725–7 legislative activities directed at gypsies therefore came to a halt in the Netherlands. For the remaining part of the century only a few proclamations are known. In Holland, Zeeland, and Brabant no placards at all were issued against gypsies after 1730. This lack of legislative activity would seem to suggest they stayed away from the Dutch Republic for the rest of the century. As is shown in the next part, appearances may be deceptive.

6

Jewish Networks, 1690–1800

In 1735 Herry Moses, alias Abraham Mordechai or Hessel Markus, confessed to a crime he did not commit. According to his version of the story, he murdered a Roman Catholic priest in his house in the town of Weesp (some 20 kilometres east of Amsterdam) and robbed him of about 3,000 guilders. The murder and theft were real enough, and a less scrupulous court might have sentenced Moses to death on the strength of his confession alone. Adhering strictly to criminal procedure and confronted with some slight inconsistencies in Moses's confession, the court tried to obtain more information. Could Moses have murdered the priest, as he declared, when standing behind the bedstead? (There was no room for a man to stand there.) Was he lying when he denounced several Jews and a Christian as his accomplices in both the murder and a burglary at The Hague? His descriptions proved accurate enough to track down some of these men in different parts of the Netherlands and arrest them, but they denied any involvement in the crimes and told the court that they did not even know their accuser. Eventually they were released.

Herry Moses was interrogated a number of times during 1734 and most of 1735. Lengthy questioning yielded more detail and added more inconsistencies, but Moses continued to stand by his confession. The court, by now convinced of his innocence, saw no other solution than to torture him – not to obtain a confession, but to have him retract it. Moses still did not oblige. The case was finally sent to the provincial Hof van Holland, which shared the doubts of the local court. Finally, at the end of 1735, Herry Moses was sentenced to whipping, branding, and banishment for life from the provinces of Holland and Zeeland on account of his false accusations and his contempt for justice in general. Shortly before Herry's sentencing – after he had been in prison for well over a year – the priest's housekeeper and her husband confessed to having murdered the priest as well as the woman's first husband. Both of them were sentenced to death.

As might have been expected, Herry disappeared from sight after receiving his sentence, until, that is, September 1736. Passers-by caught him and his two accomplices in the act of attempting to strangle and rob a woman on a country road near Rotterdam. They arrived just in time to save the woman's life. Herry Moses was sentenced to death by the court of nearby Vlaardingen and hanged on 5 October 1736.[1]

Moses's case and the stories he told his judges are important in more than one respect. Court procedure shows that in criminal cases, Jews – unlike gypsies – were treated no differently from Christian suspects. (Civil law was another matter, as will be shown later on.) Courts were certainly not automatically convinced of the guilt of Jews, and Jews were not subject to special criminal legislation in the Dutch Republic.[2] Even when Moses was lying about names, places, and crimes – which he was not doing all the time – his tales were not totally preposterous. Moses's account of his crimes, way of life, companions, and journeys must have sounded plausible enough to his judges or else they would have spared themselves the considerable trouble and costs of verifying his statements and of tracking down his alleged associates. As his final arrest near Rotterdam shows, even his false confessions came close to the truth.

We may use his account, therefore, as a key to patterns of Jewish organized crime, to offences, associates, and types of organization – especially since his story agrees with the statements of dozens of Jews arrested and sentenced in the Netherlands between about 1690 and 1800. Eventually the confusing tales of Herry Moses may even throw some light on the issues raised at the beginning of this part: the prominence of stigmatized groups in organized crime, their relations with established society, and the connections between those who belonged to 'ethnic bands' and other members of the same minority groups.

Offences

Herry Moses and his Jewish associates committed numerous thefts and burglaries all over the Netherlands. In 1732, for instance, they broke into a house in the province of Brabant belonging to a sea captain who had gone to the East Indies. Shortly thereafter they stole a quantity of damask at Zwolle, in the eastern part of the Netherlands. In 1731–2 two of Herry's associates were hanged in Friesland for having committed robbery and murder. Herry soon found some new companions, and (after finishing his prison term at Weesp) the small group continued its illegal activities, which included picking pockets in various Dutch towns, stealing textiles and cash at fairs, shoplifting, breaking into the shops of tin-, silver-, and goldsmiths, robbing churches, and committing burglaries and robberies at farms and town houses.

In this survey of Moses's activities certain types of crime deserve special attention: picking pockets, the theft of textiles and gold or silver, and church robbery with its concomitant violence against priests and clergy. None of these was the exclusive domain of Jews, who were involved in various other subcategories of theft and burglary as well, but in these particular offences Jews were especially prominent. Many Jewish thieves specialized in urban theft from shops and warehouses, in theft at markets and fairs, and in picking pockets. They usually worked together in informal associations. In 1735–41 a loose network of Jewish thieves operated in the provinces of Holland, Zeeland, Utrecht, and Gelderland.[3] Among its members were Isaac Hajim, alias Rough Diamond (Ongesleepe Diamant), who was born in Germany in 1718, and the thirteen-year-old Abraham Moses, alias Cat's Paw (Kattenickel), born in Poland. Cat's Paw often worked with the much older David Abrahamsz Croo (born in Hessen in 1702), who had been a professional thief for more than twenty-five years. Men belonging to this network stole copper from artisans' workshops, silver from silversmiths, clothing, curtains, and linen from private houses, lace and textiles from shops, and coffee and tobacco from warehouses. They also stole purses from men and women in the market-place and in the crowded streets and squares of Dutch towns. Professional pickpockets – and this applies to Jews and Christians alike – usually operated in sets of three, four, or more: one stole the purse or watch and, for reasons of safety, would pass it on as quickly as possible to a respectable-looking accomplice. He or she passed it on again, or delivered it to the fence, who often played a central role in such associations.

Like picking pockets, the theft of textiles and of silver and gold was usually an urban affair – which gives us a first glimpse of the special bond between Jewish (urban as well as rural) thieves and towns. During the 1690s four men who had recently arrived in the Netherlands from eastern Europe specialized in the theft of gold, silverware, and watches. Two of them were born in Lublin, one in Prague, and one in Essen. They operated in various eastern towns in the Netherlands, before going on to The Hague. Between about 1690 and 1696 they broke into the shops of a number of silversmiths. Their earnings were not high enough to provide a living for all of them, so the leader, Abraham Jochumse, paid Philip Wolff (alias Phais), 'his accomplice, if their evil doings did not bring in enough money to pay for his upkeep . . . 30 *stuivers* a week, thus encouraging him to steal'.[4]

The third prominently Jewish category of offences was church robbery and the robbery of priests and clergy. Herry Moses may well have based his tale about the murder and robbery of the priest at Weesp on a robbery he had actually committed some years earlier in Friesland. With four accomplices he broke into the house of a Roman Catholic priest at Leeuwarden. The robbers trussed up the priest, maltreated him, and threatened to break his neck before making off with about 500 guilders in cash and some valuables. With respect to church robbery too Herry Moses's activities had already 'set' a pattern: after his detention at Weesp he stole the poor box, which contained about 80 guilders, from a Roman Catholic church in the eastern part of the Netherlands.

Some Jewish groups specialized in church robbery. A band of eight to twelve men operated in the north-eastern section of Brabant and the adjoining part of Gelderland during 1729–30.[5] Within a few months they broke into four Roman Catholic churches, stealing a large quantity of church silver, several priests' robes, and a small amount of cash. After each theft the silver was sold in Amsterdam. The much larger band of Michiel Feijtsburger, which was active in the 1760s, combined various kinds of urban theft and burglary with rural expeditions directed at farmhouses, churches, vicarages, and the houses of priests.[6] In September 1764 Feijtsburger and seven of his men broke into a church between Haarlem and Amsterdam. They forced their way into the house of the priest next door, beat him up, and stole clothes, linen, silverware, and some cash.

As noted before, violent robberies were by no means common in the Dutch countryside, especially in the province of Holland. By the mid eighteenth century the brutal violence of the gypsy robberies and murders near Haarlem and Kalslagen in the 1720s had not been forgotten. In 1742 the murder and robbery of a vicar in the area north of Amsterdam caused something near to panic among the district's rural inhabitants. There was a general outcry for special investigations, and suspicion fell on a group of Jews. Yet the local judicial authorities were not carried away by the call for a scapegoat. Again they proved capable of distinguishing between suspicion and fact. Only a few of the suspects were arrested and, although they confessed to another robbery and murder in the same area, their involvement in the priest's murder remained unclear. They were not convicted for it. Almost twenty years later some of the same men were involved in two burglaries, during which the houses of Roman Catholic priests living within about 20 kilometres of Amsterdam were robbed.[7]

From 1680 to 1795 the robbery of churches and priests and clergy was the nearly exclusive domain of Jews – for the whole of this period I have found only about a dozen such offences that were not committed by Jews (see also below). The good chance of finding church silver that was fairly easy to get at, the absence of guard dogs, and the minimal protection offered Roman Catholic churches by the Dutch authorities might explain why these churches formed attractive targets for burglars.[8] But why, in that case, did so few other groups take advantage of such opportunities? Besides, Jews robbed not only Roman Catholic priests and churches but Protestant ones too. It looks rather as if most Christian thieves stayed away from all churches, while Jewish thieves selected churches for more reasons than just convenience.

Religious awe may have been the single most important consideration keeping Christian thieves from what was, after all, seen as a desecrating enterprise. It cannot be a coincidence that the number of church robberies committed by Christians suddenly increased during the French Revolution: a large (Christian) band, for example, which was responsible for numerous armed robberies, burglaries, church robberies, and robberies in the houses of priests and parsons throughout the province of Brabant, concentrated its church robberies in 1793, when French armies were invading this part of the Dutch Republic.[9] More than the absence of religious restraints was needed, however, to induce thieves to turn to church robbery. Other motives appear when we consider the few groups besides Jews that took part in such activities. Gypsies carried out a small number of church robberies in the course of the eighteenth century. The aspect of desecration may well have been as important to them as the actual theft. In the rare cases of church robbery committed by Christian thieves before the revolutionary period it was stigmatized groups, such as skinners, who played a prominent role. Church robbery and attacks upon clergy and priests thus appear to have been acts of revenge and rebellion by groups of despised outsiders as much as 'easy' means of obtaining valuables and money. These crimes expressed resentment, anger, and protest against a dominant group, personified and symbolized by the men, buildings, and valuables most closely connected with Christianity.[10]

Exclusion and Identification

Jews were not treated in a different way from other inhabitants of the Netherlands as far as criminal law was concerned, as the case of Herry Moses indicated. But exclusion by means of civil law drastically affected the lives of all of them. Jewish communities formed separate *naties* (nations) within Dutch towns; charters demarcated their special position and privileges. Jewish communities were allowed and supposed to take care of all kinds of everyday business without recourse to the municipal authorities. Such privileges were offset by the restrictions imposed by the same Dutch authorities, who limited both the civil rights and the economic and sexual liberties of Jewish inhabitants. Local regulations varied considerably: in the worst cases towns – such as Utrecht – did not permit any Jews to settle within their city walls until the final years of the eighteenth century; the most lenient towns allowed them to settle and acquire *burger rechten* (civil rights, citizenship) in return for considerable payment. The few immigrant Ashkenazim who could afford such payments never attained the same position as Christian citizens, though. Jews were barred from public office: honourable functions, such as membership of the town militia (*schutterij*), remained closed to them, and they were not allowed to act as councillors or bailiffs. (Roman Catholics and Protestant dissenters were likewise barred from holding public office, but in practice this rule seems to have been applied less strictly in their case, particularly, as already mentioned, in the south.) Their sons did not inherit citizenship. Nor did Dutch tolerance extend to sexual relations and economic activities – a tell-tale combination. Sexual contact and marriage between Jews and Christians were forbidden. Jews were excluded from most branches of agriculture (by being barred from owning land) and from all activities controlled by the guilds, which included artisan occupations as well as some types of retail trade. Among the relatively small number of activities left open to them were cutting and polishing diamonds, drying and cutting tobacco, book-selling, engraving (seals, etc.), cattle-dealing, moneylending, cleaning and selling fish, and many types of unskilled labour and retail trade.[11]

These were no empty rules. Contravention of economic regulations generally resulted in the imposition of a fine, but might also entail the loss of civil rights or the withdrawal of a residence permit. Infringements of the sexual rules (which mainly involved contact between Jewish men and Christian women) were regarded as moral and physical outrages.[12] In 1752–3 several Jews accused of petty theft were convicted by the town court of Rotterdam, which severely reprimanded them on account of their involvement with Christian prostitutes. One year earlier a Jew had stood trial in the same town for marrying a Dutch Reformed woman while pretending to be a Christian. The court dissolved the marriage and condemned the man to a lifelong banishment from the province of Holland.[13] For any real or imagined violation of established norms, for any encroachment on Christian-Dutch economic and sexual prerogatives, the authorities could thus resort to a large number of restrictive regulations, which might be enforced at their discretion. There was no need to take recourse to criminal law as long as the simple withdrawal of a residence permit had the same effect. Dutch local authorities made an active – though not particularly consistent or strict

– use of these regulations in their efforts to control established Jewish communities and to get rid of individuals who threatened to become a nuisance.

In 1743 the Jewish butcher Ysaak Moses and his family were ordered to leave the town of Enkhuizen in North Holland on account of their frequent contacts with poor and itinerant Jews suspected of involvement in a 'confederacy'. Ysaak Moses came from Geldern in Germany and had been living at Enkhuizen for a number of years. He was 'six feet tall, fat and thickset, round of face, big eyes . . . forty-three or forty-four years old; wears a brown coat and a wig when in Enkhuizen, but has been seen in Amsterdam wearing the outfit of a gentleman [*heerschap*]'. Together with his nineteen-year-old son Moses Ysaak he frequently toured North Holland and visited farmers in order to buy sheep. After their move to Amsterdam the son tried to earn a living by selling goat's milk and poultry from door to door; he also worked on a fishing-boat or at the fish-market.[14]

Like gypsies, Jews were set apart by Dutch regulations that aimed at containing and confining their movements and activities – in short, their existence. Poor Ashkenazim in particular were seen as a lesser sort of people by Dutch established society, a point of view epitomized by the frequent use of the pejorative term *smous* (sheeny, or Jew), in the criminal records. Jews were not persecuted by the Dutch authorities, and nor were they treated in entirely the same stigmatizing manner as gypsies. It is not surprising, then, to find that Jews followed a different approach from the defensive strategies used by gypsies when confronted by the criminal courts.

Their identification as Jews seems to have posed no problems for the courts. Personal descriptions do not indicate special (for instance, east European) dress, hairstyles, or headgear but frequently mention dark hair and dark eyes. They include specifically Jewish names besides references to family connections with other Jews, and to typically Jewish occupations.[15] A list drawn up by the provincial Hof van Holland at The Hague in 1769 offers some good examples:

Nathan Focks, alias Nathan *Gannif*, born in Amsterdam, twenty-four years old, rather tall and good-looking, light skinned and round faced, wears a black wig, uses coarse language, has a cut across the palm of his hand, speaks Dutch; and has been in prison in Amsterdam for the last five years.

Joseph Hamburger, born in Hamburg, lives in Amsterdam, about thirty-four years old, tall and slender, round faced and white skinned, black eyes, a thin line of black beard round the chin, wears a wig.

Nathan Beellte, born in Amsterdam, fifty years old, tall and thin, dark skinned and gaunt of face, wears a little black goatee, an old wig and an old coat; his wife lives in Rotterdam; he lives in Amsterdam; has been in detention in Rotterdam.[16]

Names in particular were typical. Nathan, Hertog or Hertz, Salomon or Schlomme, Jacob, Meijer, Aaron, Juda, Levy, Abraham, Moses, David, and Isaac were among the most common first names. Many Jews had no fixed surname. Like Moses Ysaak, they used their father's first name (Jacob Isaacs, Moyse Daniels, Isaac Samson, and so on) or added their place of birth (Polak, Hamburger, Feijtsburger, Bamberger, from Kinsbag, Elsasser) or occupation (Hooijbinder: hay binder; Visschoonmaker: fish-cleaner) to their first name. Some of these additions eventually became established family names, and the same occasionally happened to the fixed nicknames and aliases characteristic of Jewish thieves. The brothers Moses and Joseph Lion were nicknamed the Wine Boys (de Wijnjongens) because their father, a vinegar-seller, had carried the same nickname. The variety was enormous. Names like Juda Galg (gallows) or Nathan Gannif (thief) speak for themselves. Some nicknames referred to physical characteristics, such as Black Mortje Derbach, or Crooked (Kromme) Borach. Others mentioned professional specializations, and many pointed both to occupations and personal qualities. In a few cases we may still guess at double meanings and allusions. Rough Diamond, the nickname of a very young thief, might have referred to his (still) unpolished technique as well as to his exceptional (though as yet hidden) qualities. Since diamond cutting was a typically Jewish occupation, it may also have hinted at his own (or his father's) training and professional knowledge of jewellery. The name of Lijp Goudvogel (golden bird) had similar connotations.

It is hard to distinguish between first names, surnames, nicknames, and aliases in these circles. Since a person's 'real' name usually consisted of only one first name, supplementary names or descriptive terms were needed for clarity's sake. How otherwise could they keep apart all those Abrahams, Nathans, and Moyses in the criminal business? Because of the extensive territorial range and the particular way Jewish bands were organized, identification was as important to the Jewish thieves themselves as it was to the Dutch authorities. The situation was entirely different from gypsy society, where everyone was familiar with each other's identity, whatever the names they were using.

Once chosen, Jewish nicknames and aliases remained remarkably fixed. In the course of a lifetime few Jewish thieves used more than one or two – whether among themselves or when interrogated by the courts. Nor did they continually change their statements about other aspects of identity (such as age or relatives), or about travels, associates, and activities. The absence of the strategic devices used by gypsies in their continued struggle with established society does not, of course, imply that Jewish defendants made no effort at all to prevent conviction: their methods were simply different. Just like all other defendants, the majority confessed soon after arrest, during the first or second interrogation, and without torture being applied or even announced. Jewish defendants who had begun denying, however, persisted in their denial longer than any other category of suspects, even under torture – much as Herry Moses had persisted in his (false) confession. Meijer Feijst, for example, also called Maijer Gasim or Marom Tijfels, toured the Dutch countryside, begged, and sold spectacles. Feijst had been in detention at 's Hertogenbosch in Brabant from 22 August 1783 until 21 March 1785 on suspicion of burglary, robbery, and violence and membership of a band of (Jewish) housebreakers. In the face of considerable evidence, which included the testimony of his associates, Feijst continued to deny the charges so vehemently that he collapsed and passed out before torture could actually be applied. No further torture was allowed and the court eventually released him. Half a year later (in the spring of 1786) he was detained again, this time at the village of Loosdrecht (in the border area of Holland and Utrecht), where he had been noticed by several inhabitants shortly before a local shop was robbed at night. Again he categorically denied not only his alleged involvement in the burglary but also his presence in the village, and even his detention at 's Hertogenbosch. (Two of his former warders travelled to Loosdrecht and talked to him for hours, but could not bring him to admit that he had been detained for more than a year at their prison.) Feijst was sentenced to fifty years' detention, and eventually released in 1800, when he was about fifty-eight years old.[17]

Most of them categorically denied their involvement in the offences of which they were accused. Hertogh Joseph and several others went further and altogether disclaimed being the persons they were said to be, thus dissociating themselves from any criminal involvement. Hertogh Joseph, or Herts Mepje, was born at Magdeburg in Germany.[18] By the time of his sentence at Dordrecht, in 1801, he was between seventy-four and seventy-six years old; his career in crime – which consisted mainly of picking pockets, petty theft at markets and fairs, and burglary – spanned more than fifty years. He had toured every part of the Dutch Republic and worked together with dozens of well-known Jewish thieves and burglars. Herts had been living in many different towns, including Amsterdam, Dordrecht, Groningen, Brussels, and 's Hertogenbosch. Arrested and interrogated by the town court of Dordrecht, Herts did not deny being called Hertogh Joseph but disowned the name of Herts Mepje: the name by which he (or, according to him, someone else) was known among thieves. The evidence of his involvement in several offences, the personal descriptions provided by former associates, and the face-to-face confrontations with some of his colleagues made no difference. His fellow thieves could provide as many details about their mutual exploits as they liked, but without effect. Abraham Gerson told the court in the presence of Hertogh that they had met in 1794 in Brussels. Together with Juda Galg they toured all over Brabant and Flanders, picking pockets and cutting purses at markets and fairs. As a final detail Gerson added that Herts, having 'earned' 20 ducats by picking pockets at 's Hertogenbosch, sent the money to his family at Groningen by regular post. The money somehow disappeared on its way to Groningen, but upon Herts's repeated complaints the post office finally covered the loss. By 1801 torture had been abolished for several years, and eventually both the court of Dordrecht and his fellow thieves gave up trying to 'convince' Hertogh that he was indeed Herts. He was condemned to six years' detention – not on account of theft, which the court considered not proven, but for infraction of a previously imposed banishment.[19]

Up to a point, then, such a way of dealing with the criminal courts could be successful: it might (but by no means always did) lead to the imposition of a lighter penalty or even to the release of the suspect. Unlike the gypsy tactics discussed previously, it was a highly individualistic and even divisive strategy, detaching and alienating the person concerned from his former colleagues, friends, relatives, and in the end even from part of his own identity and history. Instead of creating and adding new identities, it reduced and detracted from the existing one. It negated former bonds, and as such neither inspired nor expected mutual loyalty. As the testimony of Hertogh's companions indicates, allegiance did not extend very far among Jewish thieves. In the following paragraphs we will see that dispersion and a continuous reordering of associates were characteristic of Jewish organized crime.

The Infrastructure of Crime

Exclusion by social custom and containment by civil law marked Jewish life in the Netherlands – not least Jewish involvement in organized crime. This applies not only to their specialization in the theft of silver, gold, and textiles and their prominence in church robbery but also to two equally salient characteristics of Jewish organized crime: its near-monopoly in the buying and selling of stolen goods and the central importance of towns to all its activities.

As we have seen, Dutch economic regulations were strict. Even if

Jews had not been formally barred from numerous occupational categories, few occupations would have been accessible to first-generation Jewish immigrants from Germany, Poland, and the Baltic States. These Jews arrived in large numbers, penniless, often without training, and without knowing the language. As Endelman has pointed out, the trade in scrap, textiles, and old clothes required almost no capital and hardly any words (see Endelman 1979, pp. 178–90; cf. Bloom 1937, pp. 66–7). It was not a controlled business, and entailed many contacts within the growing and continually changing community of poor Jews. Those Jews who managed to settle in Dutch towns and to extend their contacts to non-Jewish salesmen, publicans, carters, local officials, and artisans acquired an enormous amount of local knowledge and information, besides the special asset of linking two worlds. Fences belonged to this category. They were brokers, middlemen, and organizers, and reliable information was their chief capital.[20]

One example is the German-born Salomon Sanders, who in 1712 was hanged in the town of Vianen for his complicity in the murder and robbery of an old widow. He had been convicted twice before; his uncle and former accomplice had been hanged some years earlier. Sanders was

> famous among the thieves of his nation because he had made it his profession to spy out the houses, to offer advice and suggestions, and to provide assistance for the purpose of theft and housebreaking; and for his [practice of] defrauding people by selling his wares, and for his selling and reselling of stolen goods, in all of which he always had his share and advantage . . . and, moreover, he was known to have paid his accomplices with counterfeit coins on various occasions.[21]

The near-monopoly of Jews in the fencing business indirectly contributed to the prominence of other Jews in organized crime. Few things are more valuable to a thief, burglar, or robber than good connections with and easy access to such 'nodal' figures in the criminal infrastructure. Many fences not only bought and sold stolen goods but also acted as informants and organizers. In rural areas it was mainly Jewish butchers and cattle-dealers – like Ysaak Moses and his son – who provided information to Jewish and, occasionally, non-Jewish bands. Most of them combined the two activities: buying cattle in areas that might cover almost half a province and selling meat to both Jewish and Christian customers. As with the urban fences, there was a clear connection between their occupation and their acting as informants and brokers. (Guild regulations generally did not apply to Jewish butchers, who were allowed to live and work in most rural parts of the country.) Butchers came into contact with Christians belonging to various social strata, and cattle-buying involved frequent tours throughout the region, paying visits to wealthy farmers, discussing prices, chatting about the weather, markets, the sale of animals and land, and recent bad luck or good fortune. It is hard to imagine a group better situated to assess wealth and take note of the location of valuables and money in farmhouses. Joseph Levy is a fine example. He was born near Mannheim in 1755, and in the 1790s lived in the village of Sprang in Brabant, working as a cattle-buyer and butcher. He provided information to members of the Great Dutch Band, who broke into several farmhouses in the same area (see Egmond 1986, pp. 164–73).

Jews involved in organized crime were based mainly in towns. This applied not only to pickpockets and thieves who specialized in theft in an urban setting but also to Jewish bands which operated mainly, or even exclusively, in the countryside. In this respect they differed from all other rural bands in the Dutch Republic – Christian as well as non-Christian. Members of Jewish rural bands might spend most of their time in the countryside, criss-crossing the Netherlands and selling their wares. Yet whatever the pattern of their travel, towns remained central to their existence, and their outlook was predominantly urban. Jewish band members do not describe their travels as tours in the countryside but as journeys from one town to another. Most of them lived in towns: they rarely stayed in one city for any length of time, however, but spent some months in Amsterdam, then travelled to, say, Groningen, and from there to Zwolle, Maastricht, 's Hertogenbosch, Rotterdam, The Hague, Delft, and back again to Amsterdam. Towns were the place they regarded as 'home', as well as the point of departure for their activities in the countryside. In 1711–12, for instance, a small Jewish band operated both in the rural areas and the towns of Holland. Five to eight men robbed farmhouses, country houses, and Roman Catholic churches throughout the countryside of South Holland and the border region of Holland and Utrecht. In towns they stole various goods from warehouses, shops, and the houses of wealthy citizens. All the men lived in the larger towns of Holland.[22]

Why did towns play such an important role in Jewish organized crime? First, a large number of Jews involved in criminal activities in the Netherlands had been born in towns, whether in Germany, eastern Europe, or the Dutch Republic. Secondly, as we have seen, Jews were not permitted to settle freely. In many parts of Europe rural areas were closed to them, and in several Dutch provinces official regulations either prevented Jews from settling in the countryside or severely restricted the number of permits. In 1726 the estates of Gelderland announced restrictive measures; the province of Overijssel issued placards 'against foreign German Jews' in 1724, 1739, and 1765. The fear of Jewish robber bands inspired some of these measures, but the problem of economic competition outside the guild-controlled towns was considered even more important.[23] With very few exceptions Jewish settled communities of any size and importance thus developed only within towns.

Jews involved in organized crime in the Dutch Republic rarely belonged to these settled urban communities. Most of them lived on the fringe of their own society, partly because they were poor and travelled often, partly because they were kept at a distance by other, established Jews. The latter had sound reasons for doing so. Settled Jewish communities were dependent on the continuing goodwill and tolerance of the urban authorities, who held Jewish leaders responsible for the good behaviour of their people. This was especially true in Germany, where relations between urban authorities and Jewish communities were often precarious. A similar situation obtained in the Dutch Republic. In the eighteenth century, when the number of poor Jews seeking assistance increased rapidly, a form of Jewish poor relief developed that can only be described as a 'push and shove' system. Poor Jews were not allowed to enter German towns but were given food and lodging in special Jewish inns, located on the outskirts of the towns; the local Jewish community paid for these forms of assistance. Itinerant Jews were permitted to stay no longer than one day and night, each receiving some money to continue his or her journey. Had they wished to do so, economic reasons and the simple matter of space would have made it impossible for most urban Jewish communities in Germany to accommodate the entire mass of poor, homeless Jews. But established Jews regarded itinerant Jews as a potential threat to their own respectability and moral integrity, and thus to their continued communal existence.[24]

To Jews who were refused entry towns were still the principal point of orientation. They provided a recognizable destination during their migrations through western Europe. For those who had a little money and some skills German towns too – despite their strict regulations of admittance – held the promise of joining a Jewish community and belonging. This was even more strongly the case with Dutch towns, in particular Amsterdam. From the mid seventeenth century the attraction of Amsterdam as a centre of economic opportunity and a developing focus of Jewish life in western Europe was enormous.[25] It is true that housing conditions were abominable, that the number of poor Ashkenazim dependent on some form of poor relief increased during the eighteenth century, and that Ashkenazim of uncertain reputation were kept at a considerable social distance by both non-Jewish citizens and the established Jewish community.[26] Still, for those who found employment, wages were slightly higher than in other parts of western

Europe, municipal regulations were not as strict as in many German towns, and the presence of what would become the largest Jewish community in western Europe was an attraction. Among the poor, homeless Jews who entered Amsterdam, found lodging, and tried to make a living were most of those who became involved in the Jewish bands active in the Dutch Republic.

Migrations

Almost without exception Jews involved in organized crime were Ashkenazim; most of them were poor, and a large majority were first-generation immigrants from eastern and central Europe, many having only recently arrived in the Dutch Republic. This was the case throughout the eighteenth century. Both in 1695 and in 1795 between one half and two thirds of all Ashkenazim convicted of burglaries, theft, or robberies had been born outside the Dutch Republic. Among the forty-eight men figuring on a list of names and personal descriptions which covered a large part of a network of Jewish pickpockets and urban thieves operating all over Holland between 1764 and 1770 thirty came from eastern and central Europe, while about ten were born in Amsterdam.[27] This does not imply that they were all newcomers to crime; on the contrary, some had already been operating in Germany and a few even travelled back and forth between Germany and the Netherlands. But the predominance of recently arrived immigrants among those sentenced implies that continuity in the 'criminal business' was heavily dependent on the influx of large numbers of poor Ashkenazim.[28]

It is by no means easy to pinpoint connections between patterns of migration and the long-term chronology of Jewish involvement in organized crime in the Netherlands. The latter looks as follows. Before the late 1650s almost no Ashkenazim are noted in the records, and from 1660 to about 1690 criminal cases against Jews are still scarce. The 1690s yield a few groups of Jewish thieves and burglars, while between 1705 and 1715 a 'wave' of Jewish criminal activities and groups is recorded. A short phase of relative 'quiet' follows between about 1715 and 1725, but the number of sentences against Jewish thieves rises again in the late 1720s and 1730s. The period between about 1740 and 1765 can be regarded as *the* phase of expansion of Jewish crime. After that Jewish involvement in organized crime continued at a consistently high level.

Waves of immigration correspond to certain phases of increased criminal activity. This is especially clear at the beginning of the period discussed here. The first notable involvement of Ashkenazim in organized crime (between about 1690 and 1715) followed closely upon the first wave of Jewish immigration. In the course of the second half of the seventeenth century Jews from the Ukraine, the Baltic States, and various other east-European regions joined Polish Jews in their migration to the west. According to Shulvass (1971), they were as much pushed away by the horrors of pogroms, warfare, and the economic misery caused both by the end of the Thirty Years War and the demise of the Polish state as attracted by prospects of economic growth, religious tolerance, civil liberties, and a safer existence. The anti-Jewish reaction in many German territories in the 1650s and 1660s and the more liberal admission policy of Dutch towns must also be taken into account. In any case, the 1690s saw large numbers of mainly German-born Jewish immigrants arriving in the Netherlands. The last decades of the eighteenth century present a similar pattern. From the mid eighteenth century onwards waves of westward migration from eastern Europe had begun to overlap with new migrations in Germany, caused largely by demographic growth and the exclusion of poor Jews from various German towns and principalities. As a result of both immigration and natural population growth the total number of Ashkenazim in Amsterdam almost doubled between 1748 and 1780 (from 10,000 to 19,000); it grew at about the same rate towards the end of the century (21,000 in 1795 to 24,000 in 1805). At the same time housing conditions in Amsterdam deteriorated, food prices rose, and opportunities for employment became more limited.[29]

The problem lies in the period 1730–60 – a 'quiet' phase for nearly every other group involved in organized crime but a phase of expansion and increasing activity for Jewish bands. Information about immigration and the general demography of Ashkenazim for this period is contradictory. According to Shulvass, the 1730s and 1740s – when the upsurge of Jewish band activities began – saw diminished immigration. Bloom's figures also indicate that the increase of the total number of Ashkenazim living in Amsterdam slowed down between 1720 and 1748, to pick up speed again from the mid eighteenth century.[30] On the other hand, the number of marriages of Ashkenazim living in Amsterdam began to grow quickly from the early 1720s, and at Leiden it is during the 1730s and 1740s that more and more complaints are heard about the rising number of poor Jewish immigrants.[31] The economic position of Jews living in the towns of Holland may also have taken a turn for the worse during these years. New restrictive regulations were proclaimed in Amsterdam in 1731, prohibiting Jews from selling new clothes, wine, beer, and fish (see, for example, Bloom 1937, p. 67).

Whatever the precise nature of the links between immigration and criminal activities, the biographies of Ashkenazim who joined bands of thieves, burglars, robbers, or pickpockets in the Dutch Republic were indistinguishable from the personal histories of those poor and recently immigrated Jews who did not enter the world of organized crime.[32] Again and again particular regions and towns noted for their high number of Jewish inhabitants are cited in the criminal records as their places of origin. Most frequently mentioned are East Friesland (the German area bordering on the Dutch province of Groningen), Frankfurt am Main and the surrounding area, the region of Mannheim, Nuremberg and its environs, the land of Mainz, the region around Neuwied on the Rhine, Hamburg, Paderborn, Osnabrück, Prague, various towns in Poland, rural Bohemia, and Alsace. Jews who joined bands in the Netherlands came not only from the same regions as most poor Jewish immigrants were from, they also followed the same routes of migration to the west, and had often travelled in Germany and eastern Europe for an extended period before arriving in the Netherlands (on routes of migration see Shulvass 1971 and Reijnders 1969).

We can follow some of these routes by tracing the geography of criminal activities, arrests, and convictions. The biography of Bohemian Meijer is a case in point. Salomon or Abraham Levy, alias Bohemian Meijer, was born in 1709 near Nuremberg. During the first part of his criminal career he journeyed extensively in Germany, and was detained and sentenced in Aurich (East Friesland), Hamburg, Düsseldorf, and Elbersfeld. On his second arrest in Hamburg he was tortured on account of his presumed involvement in an important robbery, but he persisted in his denial and was probably released. Having moved on to the Dutch Republic, Bohemian Meijer was twice arrested in the eastern provinces of Overijssel and Gelderland. In Holland he resumed his usual activities: urban theft and rural burglary. He spent most of his time at Amsterdam and became engaged to a Jewish girl. In Amsterdam too he soon had to appear in front of a criminal court: to answer the charge of nearly killing his future mother-in-law by throwing her into a canal. In March 1730 Meijer was again arrested and detained, this time for theft. The court eventually released him 'for special reasons' – probably because he had informed against his companions – and banished him from Holland and Zeeland. Meijer moved to the town of Hoorn in North Holland, but was soon caught again for stealing pearls, money, and diamonds. In July 1730 he was sentenced to whipping and twenty-five years' banishment. By then, he was just twenty-one years old.[33]

Parallels between the lives and backgrounds of Jewish immigrants who were involved in criminal activities and those who were not did not end with their regional origins and itineraries. The story of Isaac Heijman from Germany reads like a classic tale of social exclusion, poverty, migration to a free country, subsequent bad luck and lack of judgement, involvement in bad company, plain stupidity, and, finally, death on the scaffold. Even if Isaac Heijman invented some of it himself to enlist the sympathy of the local court in North Holland where he stood trial in 1760, it is still worth taking a closer look at his story.[34]

Heijman was born in 1720 near Nuremberg. He worked as a cattle-dealer but was forced to leave Germany 'because the farmers accused him of introducing the cattle plague into the region with his cattle, and also because he had stolen forty crowns from a farmer who had hidden them in his bedstead, because of his poverty, and because he had to leave anyhow'. Heijman arrived in Amsterdam around 1753. He moved in with a certain Lijp Koch, and it was at Koch's house that he met Salomon Reijsig, or Schlomme Reijsiger, a professional burglar and captain of a Jewish band. Heijman soon joined the group. His first trip was an expedition to the province of Groningen, where the band attacked, robbed, and murdered a parson. Reijsig was arrested not long afterwards. Some of the others fled, and Heijman spent some time with the camp of the Hanoverian army in Germany, where he sold coffee-grinders. Several members of the band eventually returned to Amsterdam, where Heijman again joined them. In 1755 they broke into the house of a woman living not far from Amsterdam; they threatened her with a knife and robbed the house. Heijman combined his criminal activities with part-time work as a barrow man in a vegetable market. When the band split up, he gave up crime for the time being and earned some money buying scrap and skins in the countryside. Once more he decided to try his hand at burglary: 'seeing so many foreign Jews arriving here, he thought that he might try again to steal alone, because he imagined that no one would suspect him' – a telling comment, by the way, on the bad reputation of newly arrived poor Jews.[35] He broke into a country house, where some men surprised him and tried to detain him. When he threatened them with an axe, Heijman was arrested and subsequently sentenced to death by hanging in March 1760.

One of the things Heijman's story reveals is that poor Jewish immigrants were immediately received into an urban Jewish subculture. It also presents us with a range of occupations that were traditionally Jewish, and bears witness to the astonishing mobility and occupational diversity that was typical of many Jewish pedlars and retail traders. Each of these elements was as much part of the ordinary existence of poor Jewish immigrants as a crucial ingredient in the organizational structure of Jewish crime.

Criminal Organization

Apart from a strongly urban orientation and a pivotal position in the criminal infrastructure, it was the loose framework, shifting coalitions, and territorial range of Jewish criminal networks that formed the main characteristics of Jewish organized crime.[36] The extensive operations of Jewish thieves, their mobility, and a specialization in certain trades went hand in hand. As we have seen, the combined effects of legislation prohibiting free settlement and of regulations restricting Jews from working in agriculture or as artisans helped push poor Jews into the few remaining 'free' occupational categories, several of which entailed at least part-time itinerancy. Jews involved in organized crime in the Netherlands were often active in the retail trade – selling haberdashery, spectacles, textiles, jewellery, lottery tickets, fish, kosher meat, old clothes, scrap, and various other types of used materials. Some made a living as itinerant musicians (mostly fiddlers); many were employed in a range of unskilled occupations (such as fish-cleaners, barrow men, porters); a small number worked as artisans in the handful of occupations that were not controlled by the guilds; and quite a few served at one time or another as sailors with the Dutch East India Company or temporarily joined one of the European armies.[37]

The mobile way of life of most of these trades was, as noted above, urban based. Professional contacts with customers and suppliers were varied and often short-lived; they were determined primarily by the context of buying and selling goods and services, which provided excellent opportunities to gain information and a perfect excuse to be almost anywhere at any time. Extensive travelling also meant numerous contacts with other Jewish pedlars. These men met at inns frequented by itinerant salesmen, made new friends when staying with relatives or colleagues in provincial towns, or simply struck up an acquaintance on the road. The typical far-flung and loosely arranged Jewish criminal networks thus developed out of the professional contacts of men who were selling, buying, performing, and, above all, travelling throughout the country during a large part of the year. In short, they originated in occupational activities characteristic of many poor Ashkenazim.

These networks were hardly visible to the local population and their judicial authorities. All they saw were men travelling alone or in groups of at most two or three. It was only during the large-scale armed robberies that more than four or five men could be seen together. The composition of the small itinerant groups varied. Sometimes they consisted of chance acquaintances, or of a mixture of new-found colleagues and old friends. At other times small sets of trusted friends, relatives, and colleagues went out to reconnoitre a village or an entire region. Jewish women (and children up to the age of fifteen) hardly ever accompanied the men on these tours, and nor were they present when the men conducted their legal or illegal business. Apart from occasional assistance in the sale of stolen goods, women did not participate in the criminal activities of the bands. Most of them stayed at home with their children, and home was usually one of the big towns of Holland, such as Amsterdam, Rotterdam, or The Hague.

The almost invisible role of Jewish women was an extension of the traditionally Jewish division of male and female domains: public, outside, and itinerant for the men; private, within the family and household, and static for the women.[38] Women's names – or rather the way in which Jewish men referred to them – reflect their subservient position as regards contacts with the outside world. Women were either designated by their first names alone (just Abigail, or Rebecca) or were defined in terms of their husbands and kinsmen: Sara 'housewife' of Baruch Meijer, or Gaije wife of Juda Marcus, or Rachel widow of Hersch.[39] In public matters women attained a definite identity only by reference to a male person.

Yet women were far from incidental to the criminal activities of their husbands, fathers, and other kinsmen. First, their absence from the criminal scene was an important asset. Women and children slowed down a mobile group considerably – as frequently happened with gypsy companies. Accordingly, within a fairly short period Jewish bands could cover a much larger territory than 'family bands'. Women and children were arrested more easily, and might be induced to confess and accuse their kinsmen, because they themselves were rarely involved in the most serious crimes. Jewish women thus formed less of a 'security risk'. A more indirect but crucially important contribution was their provision of a home base and the elementary links of kinship, so cementing shifting male coalitions that were founded largely on companionship and shared professional activities. While staying at home, the women formed invisible ties between the men who actively participated in thefts and robberies. They anchored the men to their urban bases by giving cohesion to far-flung networks and providing continuity. Kinship ties thus strengthened the bonds of belonging to a religious and ethnic minority and sharing a common language. In fact, the typical structure of Jewish networks and their urban leanings – both so unlike the clans and rural orientation of the gypsy bands – were predicated upon the 'absence' of women from business, the importance and strength of Jewish kinship ties, and the special character of Jewish gender relations.

Kinship ties were also generational, and underpinned continuity in a criminal business which depended heavily on the influx of new immigrants. Continuity was based on more than kinship ties, however, as is illustrated by the case of Nathan Moses, whose career in crime spanned roughly forty years. (He was hanged at Alkmaar in 1768 at the age of seventy-two.) At first glance there is no discernible pattern in the various networks to which he belonged over several decades. As might have been expected in a situation of incessantly shifting coalitions, the names of his companions changed from one year to another, from one region to another, and even from one journey to another. During the 1740s he had operated with Barend Worst, Ysaak Peskele, Levy Hertog (alias Swansburger), Ysaak Abrahams (alias Abraham Diersum), Handsome Little Barend, and Hertogh Joseph, alias Herts Mepje – to name only a few. As his accomplices of the 1750s to 1760s he designated Samuel Abraham (alias Fathead), Michiel Feijtsburger, Schimmetje Hensbach, Moses Topmeijer (alias Moses Marcus), Isaac Hajim (alias Rough Diamond), David Hertog, Salomon Reijsig, and Mozes Thickhead. And so on, and so forth.[40]

Yet from the moment we shift our perspective by focusing not on the individual but on connections among the men named as accomplices the consistency in this pattern of change becomes manifest. Rough Diamond belonged to the network of pickpockets (mentioned at the beginning of this chapter) which operated all over the western part of the Netherlands during the late 1730s. With his associate Abraham Moses, alias Cat's Paw, he was hanged at Dordrecht in 1752 on account of numerous thefts and burglaries. Michiel Feijtsburger was still in the early stages of his career when he worked with Nathan Moses. It is no coincidence that another colleague of Nathan Moses, Schimmetje Hensbach, was a member of Feijtsburger's later band, nor that Salomon Reijsig was the same man who invited the hapless Isaac Heijman to join his band. Samuel Abraham, who operated with Nathan Moses in the 1760s, appears again in the late 1760s in another network of pickpockets. The principal fence of that network, Jonas Maij, later played a crucial role in the Great Dutch Band of the 1790s, and Jonas Maij's son, Afrom Jonas Maij, acted as one of the commanders of a branch of the Great Dutch Band (see Chapter 7). Each of these men was thus linked to several other bands.

Individual names do not really matter here. The point is that the tangled mass of names and alliances provided by Nathan Moses should be taken as evidence of his contacts with Jewish bands and networks (active between about 1740 and the 1760s) which were interconnected, instead of as mere references to random and varying sets of acquaintances. It remains to be seen whether we may speak of a single Jewish underworld, but within the Jewish section of organized crime there was certainly continuity over time as well as a high degree of interaction (if not cooperation) between contemporaneous networks. Connections between Jewish bands can be traced from the early 1730s to the beginning of the nineteenth century.

None of these aspects changed much in the course of the eighteenth century. During the upsurge of Jewish organized crime in the course of the 1740s, 1750s, and 1760s the geographic range of the networks increased and those parts of the networks involved in more serious types of property crime began to coalesce. From the 1750s onwards slightly more closely-knit groups are noted in the records, and most of the references to leaders, captains, and hierarchically organized groups date from the second half of the eighteenth century. At the same time the role of violence, especially against church officials, progressively decreased. (Families such as the Feijtsburgers, who had become prominent in the Netherlands by the 1740s and 1750s, may have played a vital part in this development, mainly by providing expertise and connections to which newcomers could attach themselves.) The more closely-knit sections never developed into separate bands but remained part of the larger networks. Nor did the shifting coalitions turn into tightly bound family groups, extensive clans, or strictly demarcated and hierarchically structured bands. Up to the first decade of the nineteenth century they continued to form part of loosely arranged networks, held together by ties of kinship, occupation, and ethnicity.

Jewish prominence in organized crime thus cannot be reduced to poverty and social or economic exclusion, important though they were. Their particular criminal 'style' was rooted in their own culture – the culture of poor Ashkenazim who were respected neither by established Christians nor by established Jews. Occupational specialization, mobility, urban orientation, an extensive range of fluctuating contacts, a specifically Jewish definition of gender roles, and, most probably, shared beliefs and cultural practices all contributed. By the last decade of the eighteenth century many of these features had converged in the international, mixed Jewish and Christian Great Dutch Band. The next chapters trace how and when interconnections between the various criminal circuits in the Dutch Republic came into being.

Part IV

The Changing Structure of the Rural Underworld

7

Mixing Minorities, 1720–1800

Groups currently denoted as ethnic minorities played an important part in organized rural crime in the Dutch Republic. They did so during different periods, which only partly overlapped. Jews became especially prominent from the 1730s and 1740s onwards, when the heyday of gypsy band activity was already over and persecutions had resulted in the almost total disappearance of gypsies from the Dutch Republic. Gypsies stayed away from these parts until more than a hundred years later, when new groups reached the Netherlands in the course of the nineteenth century. That, at least, is the widely accepted version of gypsy history in the Dutch Republic (see van Kappen 1965 and especially L. Lucassen 1990).

Although accurate in most respects, this account needs some revision. Whereas gypsy bands operating out of large encampments located in inaccessible areas are indeed conspicuously absent during the period 1730–1800 – as are provincial placards against gypsies and references to *Heijdenjachten* (gypsy hunts) – an extensive and diffuse network of apparent gypsy origin materialized some three to four decades after the supposed disappearance of gypsies from the northern Netherlands. In the course of the 1760s this network, the Band of Rabonus, developed into one of the three major rural bands of the period. Only the Jewish Feijtsburger network and the Band of Calotte, which operated in Brabant, were of equal importance.

The arrival of the Rabonus Band cannot but raise serious doubts about the presumed absence of gypsies from these regions after the 1730s. Was it merely a lack of information which kept them out of sight until then, or did all gypsies stay away from the northern Netherlands until this sudden reappearance during the early 1760s? Did the Rabonus Band herald a new wave of gypsy migrations, and was it in fact a gypsy band? It closely resembled segments of the White Feather circuit of the 1720s and the preceding Garneson band, yet even a first reading of the extensive records indicated that the Rabonus Band did not fit the pattern of previous gypsy bands in a few important respects. In the long run it turned out to be impossible (as well as useless) to define the Rabonus Band as either gypsy or non-gypsy.

The uncertain and perplexing character of this band itself eventually provided a crucial clue. The Rabonus Band did not fit the pattern of the bands that had been operating during the first half of the eighteenth century because slightly different types of bands were beginning to appear in the Dutch Republic from the 1750s onwards. Instead of a rather unsatisfactory 'appendix' to the White Feather circuit, Rabonus's group – however idiosyncratic – proved to be a guide to some of the changes in the structure of rural organized crime during the second half of the eighteenth century.

Rabonus and His People

If Dutch historiography has almost completely neglected Rabonus and his band, it cannot have been for its commonplace character, the insignificance of its activities, or lack of evidence.[1] About thirty-five to fifty men and women were involved and, if we include some groups linked to the Rabonus Band by multiple ties of kinship and complicity, the whole network comprised about seventy to one hundred adults. They were active mainly between about 1755 and 1765, but the roots of this band reached back to the early decades of the eighteenth century. Their journeys and operations covered nearly every part of the Dutch Republic, besides the Flemish-speaking areas of the southern Netherlands and some German territory. The regional focus of their activities shifted slowly in the course of the years. During the period 1750–60 members of the band toured western Brabant and the environs of Antwerp and Brussels. Even then a few expeditions already extended far into the northern half of the Dutch Republic.[2] Between 1761 and 1765 members were active largely in the west and south-west of the Dutch Republic (Holland, Zeeland, Utrecht, western Brabant), with occasional excursions to the eastern and northern provinces. Other parts of the network concentrated their activities in the last area (Overijssel, Gelre, and occasionally Friesland).

The Rabonus Band has remained the most visible part of a very loosely structured network of interrelated families or clans. Even within its more closely-knit segments various small groups and families met only a few times a year. They generally knew where to find each other, however, and some of them spent months or sometimes years together touring the Netherlands. Both the judicial authorities and the members used the term *bende* (band) to describe these close-knit sections. Rabonus himself referred to '*his* band', and his grandson, the nine-year-old Jan Grijskeremoer, told his interrogators at Rotterdam that 'the band to which they belong consists of about thirty persons'.[3] Rabonus's band never became a strictly demarcated group, but it had a definite identity, partly because of a shared history. By 1765 Andries Melser and Jan Rijnhoud (or Arnoldus) and their wives had been members of the group for eight or nine years. Johanna Florusse had belonged to the same band since she was sixteen or seventeen years old, and she thought it likely that her mother had already participated in the band long before she herself was born.[4]

Like many other bands, Rabonus's group did not limit its activities to one type of offence. The women were involved mostly in petty fraud and theft, such as ringing the changes, shoplifting, and stealing poultry, cats, food, clothes, money, and jewellery from farmyards, barns, and farmhouses. The men likewise stole cats and clothes, besides pots and farm utensils; but they also broke into barns and stockyards, taking cheeses, big jars of butter, and occasionally sacks of flour. Among their more daring activities were burglaries in farmhouses – when they often broke through walls, risking a confrontation with the inhabitants – and assaults upon carters and travellers, as well as a considerable number of fully-fledged armed robberies. On these occasions they regularly attacked, trussed, injured, and even murdered farmers and rural shopkeepers. In 1755 two members accosted a sailor travelling on foot along the sea-dike to the port of Den Helder at the northern tip of Holland. They wanted his money, struck him with their knives when he refused, and robbed him of a few guilders; they finally left him severely injured on the side of the road.[5] Both Rabonus's section of the network and the eastern division commanded by Fat (Dikke) Piet committed such violent armed robberies. During the night of 18 March 1761 six to nine members of Piet's company used an axle-tree to ram the front door of a farmhouse in Gelderland. They tied up the occupants and beat the farmer's wife, until her son-in-law – who had been asleep in another part of the house – appeared with a loaded gun and shot and killed one of the band members.[6]

Women belonging to Rabonus's group – unlike female members of most other bands – occasionally attended these extremely violent episodes. If they had merely been passive spectators, we might have compared them to the female members of the French Bande d'Orgères, whose presence during robberies appears to have stimulated the use of violence as part of sexual rivalry among the men (see Cobb 1972a, p. 199). That aspect may have been a factor here as well, but in the

Rabonus Band some of the women took an active part in the violent activities. They never took the lead, however. During the autumn of 1757, for instance, Rabonus, his son Abraham Bastiaensz, and several other members decided to rob the house and inn of a man called Gampelaere who lived in a small village in the southern Netherlands. They planned to kill the inhabitants. Upon their arrival Rabonus's half-sister – who was known to Gampelaere's family – knocked on the door and asked for some gin. At the same time the men knocked on the back door and immediately attacked Gampelaere when he let them in. The murder of Gampelaere closely resembles some of the ruthless killings committed during the 1720s by gypsies of the Band of the White Feather. Rabonus used his pistol; another man stabbed the victim with his bayonet, while Abraham Bastiaens hit him with a coulter. Meanwhile the women got hold of Gampelaere's wife; she was likewise beaten up and stabbed by the men, while Rabonus's half-sister hit her with a heavy stick. The woman seems to have survived.[7]

A certain Johanna Hendriks, alias Henke, epitomizes the relatively prominent role of women in the Rabonus Band. She was one of the very few women to be broken on the wheel in these parts of the Dutch Republic during the whole of the eighteenth century. Henke was the widow of an important elderly band member called One-eyed (Eenoog) Jansse or Equerry (Stalmeester) or the Old Wolf (de Oude Wolf); her four children all belonged to the band. In 1767 she was convicted on account of numerous thefts, burglaries, and robberies committed during a period of about twenty-five years. If this had been all, Henke might have been hanged or perhaps garrotted. The court imposed an aggravated death penalty because of her active participation in church robbery and sacrilege, and because of her share in the murder of a hatter's assistant in Friesland: she had held his head while her husband cut his throat. By the time of her death sentence she was forty-eight years old.[8]

Henke's way of life closely resembled that of the gypsies of the 1720s. As one of her young companions told the court, their small group travelled all over the Dutch Republic: from South Holland to Groningen and Friesland, and from there back again through Overijssel, Gelderland, and Brabant to Utrecht and North Holland.[9] Like most members of the larger network, the men and women belonging to Rabonus's group earned some money by casual farm-work, and especially by selling herbs and medicines, grinding knives and scissors, peddling haberdashery, tinkering, mending chairs, selling songs, and playing the flute and violin. Of course, their illegal activities – which included the selling of stolen cats' skins – also brought in a certain amount of cash. A few of the men served in the armies for brief periods; some had enrolled in the

Dutch East India Company, only to disappear from the sight of their families as well as the judicial authorities.

Apparently fewer women were involved in fortune-telling and laying ghosts than during the 1720s, and the big encampments of those years no longer existed, though band members still built smaller, temporary encampments in the same regions as before: one woman said 'that 'a whole band stayed for some time near Winkel and Nierop [in North Holland] in a wood, and that she has seen the smoke from their fires rising above the trees'.[10] They also held annual meetings, which resembled the annual gatherings of the Garneson and White Feather years. It seems that some of the men formed a small court, and discussed matters of general interest and legal business. According to Henke, a woman called Rosine was punished at one of these meetings because she had stolen and killed a cock: three of her fingers were cut off and she was scorched with fire.[11]

Their vagrant way of life, the occupations, the location of the encampments, the annual meetings, and the *modus operandi* all point to a gypsy background. Some other, equally important characteristics support this view: self-definition and names, physical appearance and dress, language, religious affiliation and ritual, and finally the structure of the bands. In each of these respects the Rabonus Band resembled the gypsy bands of the 1710s and 1720s.

Rabonus's colleagues occasionally used the term *Heijdens* to denote their associates and relatives, and referred to themselves as *volk* (people, tribe). When confronted with his accomplice Jan Arents – probably in front of a military court at Delft – Rabonus declared that Arents 'is of the same people to which he himself belongs'. Jan disputed this statement and argued that he had proof in the form of a certificate of baptism issued at the Westerkerk in Amsterdam. Rabonus then asked in a positively cynical manner whether this certificate also listed Jan's offences.[12] Apparently Jan himself equated being a gypsy with not being a Christian – and this is not the only evidence pointing to antagonism between Christianity and gypsy identity. Like the Jewish bands discussed in the previous chapter, members of Rabonus's band committed church robberies, in several of which the violence used against the priest and members of his household was accompanied by the deliberate desecration of holy objects. Henke took part in at least two such robberies. During the early 1740s members of the Rabonus Band broke into a Roman Catholic church in the eastern part of the Netherlands. They tied up the priest, stole silver, gold, and vestments, and robbed the image of the Virgin Mary of its robes and smeared some of the holy oil on their shoes. Almost twenty years later another Roman

Catholic church in the same region was broken into by the same Henke, her daughter and two sons, and a small group of Jews. This time they smashed the image of the Virgin Mary and urinated in the aspersorium.[13]

Gypsy identity by no means precluded Christian baptism, however – either in the bands of the 1720s or in Rabonus's group. Many 'Christian' names commonly used in the latter (such as Maria, Johanna, Catherina, Theresia, Severinus, Vicentius, Anna, and Christina) had a distinctly Roman Catholic flavour, and several members mentioned being baptized and married by Roman Catholic priests.[14] Again we are confronted by cases of double (or even multiple) identity. Nearly everyone in the band with a 'Christian' name had a 'gypsy' name as well: Rabonus's daughter was Johanna Catherina Grijskeremoer or van Erp, called Rooseboom 'in their band'; Johanna Theresia Janssens or Gipte Wanne; Johanna Hendriks or Henke; Marietje van den Hove or Alemondus Sjouwele. As before, most of the gypsy names had a distinctly exotic character. During the 1720s we found Lucretia and Aquatina, Alewijn Aardappel and Marcus Allemonde, Sibora and Antichoon. Now we find Gipte Wanne, Mellesine, Gaudele, Arorus Florusse, Galathe, Teijtigue, Tittie Ranittie, and Josias Valentijns – names sounding as if they had been picked and adapted from current literature or popular tales, as perhaps they had. Rabonus himself offers the best example of a proliferation of identities which alternated between gypsy and Christian: his other names included Pieter van Erp, the Old Egyptian, Jacobus Grijskeremoer, the Old Jacob, and Father Abraham.

'Blackness' too turns up again, both as a descriptive and as a generic term. Personal statements suggest that several band members were indeed dark skinned. About three years before his arrest Jan Rijnhoud, according to his accomplice Joseph Bilouw, was 'a small fellow, black eyes, grey wig, brown skin, a big hook-nose, big mouth, large black teeth, with these he can bend more than one coin at the same time'.[15] The expression 'brown of countenance' was used by Christina Jans of her husband Arorus Florusse, and by his sister (Johanna Florusse) of the captain of the band, Frederik Jansse.[16] The distinction between dark and white skin, as used by the band themselves, seems to have coincided with that between members and outsiders. Johanna Florusse told the court at Rotterdam that a certain woman 'is white and does not belong to [our] troop'; when asked whether one Laurens was a member, she said, 'Yes, and . . . he is black and hardly speaks any Dutch.'[17] Rabonus used the term 'black' in a more general sense: 'Their troop, called the black troop . . . counted about thirty members when all were together.'[18] In this case 'blackness' may have related to a distinction dating back more than half a century: between the White, Black, and Red Feather companies.

Why not simply regard the Rabonus Band and related groups as gypsy bands? Because, whatever the category – religion, names, language, or appearance – ambiguities remain. This is particularly clear in the case of language. There is no doubt that band members spoke a 'foreign' language, which was described by the authorities as a 'thieves' language'. Johanna Florusse told the court that she had learned it as a child from her parents, adding that 'such people as they are, that is *Heijdens* and vagrants, all know it and particularly those who belong to the band of Frederik Jansse'.[19] Elisabeth Josephs described their language as 'the *Heijdense* language' and said she had learned it from her father when she was about ten years old, 'and that since then she had kept it up by talking to other *Heijdens*'. She also affirmed that band members knew each other by their language and that as far as she knew all those 'who spoke this language belonged to one band'.[20] Apparently, then, it was not her first language. Her statement implies that we are dealing here with a specialized professional vocabulary rather than with an 'ordinary' gypsy language. This would not contradict what other band members told the authorities, and it tallies with Arorus Florusse's remark 'that this is the language of the itinerant musicians [*speellieden*]'.[21]

Several band members, moreover, did not speak the thieves' language or had only learned it later on. They did not have gypsy names, but made do with just one or two 'ordinary' Dutch Christian ones. Some members were not dark skinned, and to quite a few Roman Catholicism was definitely more than just a convenient cover. In all these cases the term *Heijdens* is conspicuously absent from the personal descriptions compiled by the judicial authorities. This was not an oversight, as is most clearly attested by the profile of Jan Arorus in a list of band members drawn up by the court of Alkmaar: 'thirty-four years old, moderately tall, brown and smooth skinned, black curly hair, brown eyes; the little finger of his right hand is crooked; and is half *Heijden* and half Christian'.[22] Finally, the descriptions and biographies of several important members simply do not fit a 'gypsy pattern'. Andries Melser, for instance, spoke French and probably some Dutch, but no other languages as far as we know. He was born in 1728 near Maastricht and married Christina van Doorn – a white-skinned woman – in the Roman Catholic church at Breda. Melser earned his money in a variety of ways: he worked as a pedlar, selling haberdashery and spectacles, lace, and combs; he knitted gloves and small purses, and occasionally sold potatoes; during the summer he worked as a casual rural labourer. Melser had blond, curly hair; he usually dressed like a farmer. In other words, he was more like a member of the poor and itinerant sections of the Dutch working classes than like a gypsy. Several other members of Rabonus's band were just like Andries Melser.

A gypsy background and even belonging to one of the gypsy families involved in the band did not grant automatic admission. That, at least, is what Johanna Florusse told her interrogators, confirming that no one became a member unless the others approved of it. She had been very young at the time, and her mother had promised the captain on her behalf that she would steal as much as she could.[23] This promise may have attended the oath which every band member – gypsy or non-gypsy – had to swear. A young boy heard Andries Melser 'swear the Oath to Captain Frederick Jansse in the presence of Catrijn and a certain Syme'.[24] Rabonus's thirty-year-old daughter, Rooseboom, gave a detailed description of the ritual, saying that

> all of them together had sworn an Oath of Secrecy to Jakob Bull called the greatest, and currently living at Little Amsterdam [a hamlet in western Brabant], and after that another oath to Frederik Jansse called Captain. The oath includes the following: first saying (while holding up the first two fingers of the right hand) now we know there is a God in heaven, now we know we have to bow to our greatest, now we part from Our Lord and go alive to the Devil. And now we accept the Devil as our Lord. Then the greatest says to them: if we find ourselves in jail and one of you discloses anything, then your life is in my hands in the same manner as I wring a dog's neck.[25]

In itself swearing an oath was nothing new. We saw earlier that promises of mutual assistance and oaths of secrecy had also been sworn by members of gypsy bands during the 1690s and early 1700s. The character of the oath had changed to some extent, as had the sanctions. Previously there had been no mention of the devil or of renouncing God and, if it had ever been safe in the past to ignore the threat of punishment by death, it was definitely no longer so by the 1760s. Even in detention at Rotterdam Rabonus did not refrain from publicly uttering similar threats when informed by the authorities about the willingness of some of his associates to part with information: 'as soon as he learns that the other prisoners split on him, he will take care that all of them will mount the scaffold together with him'.[26] In such ways leading band members, like Rabonus, Henke's husband One-eyed Jansse, and a certain Prince Charles (Prins Carel), made themselves respected, and at the same time ensured the cohesion of the band. During his fourteenth interrogation Rabonus quoted One-eyed Jansse and Prince Charles as saying to another member: 'If you ever get caught, do not tell them anything at all or they will hang you; and if they let you go, we will cut your throat.'[27] Perhaps there was more need of oaths of allegiance to the devil – of rituals that united band members – when non-gypsies began to form a substantial part of the band.

One of the main grounds for cohesion, however, must still have been the pattern of organization that had been characteristic of gypsy groups for at least sixty or seventy years by this time. As we have seen, several bands, each with its own captain and leading members, operated within a large, loose-knit network. Fat Piet's group concentrated its activities in the eastern and northern Dutch provinces. In Rabonus's group Frederik Jansse acted as captain, while Arorus Florusse and Cornelis Jansse served as lieutenants.[28] No strict boundaries existed between these bands, and they were often linked by ties of kinship. Members of Fat Piet's group occasionally worked together with Rabonus and his people, and, as in the past, a captain's daughter might still marry one of the leaders of another band.[29]

In the second half of the eighteenth century this pattern proved flexible enough to accommodate members of other itinerant groups. In the Rabonus Band we find not only Christians, including Andries Melser and a small number of French-speaking Walloons from the region of Liège, but several Jews as well. Thus traditional gypsy patterns of organization provided a social, structural, and cultural framework to which itinerant non-gypsies could attach themselves. Of course, gypsy traditions did not remain unchanged.

Fisone and Her Kin

The history of a gypsy woman called Fisone and her connections with several members of the Rabonus Band epitomize this process of association and accommodation (see Table 3). Fisone's successive marriages, moreover, point to a transition from endogamy during the first part of the eighteenth century to a rather less exclusive marriage pattern after about 1740 or 1750. Fisone was born around 1700 in Alsteda (probably in Germany). Next to nothing is known about her early years, but it is likely she grew up in one of the extended gypsy families that we encounter again and again during this period. For most of her life she earned a living by begging, casual rural labour, selling herbs and other medicines, and by fortune-telling. Her first husband was a certain Jurriaan Jans or Lansprans, known among gypsies as Knolletje or Rossan Hoteij. He was probably the father of all her children except the youngest.

With Fisone and Knolletje we are suddenly right back among the 'hard core' of the White Feather circuit of the 1720s. Knolletje had been among the twelve band members who committed the brutal murders at

Kalslagen discussed in Chapter 5. The town court of Haarlem sentenced him to the severest death penalty: he was broken on the wheel in 1725.[30] Nearly forty years later his and Fisone's children and grandchildren in their turn belonged to the core of the Rabonus Band. After Knolletje's execution – and more specifically after the period of harsh gypsy persecutions – Fisone's choice of partners among gypsies must have been limited. Not surprisingly, she began to marry outside her own circle. Until her death on the scaffold in Haarlem in 1740 Fisone lived with a Christian, Focker Jongbloet, another gypsy, Engel Reijniersz, and a Jew, Lijp Diersum. It would seem as if from the 1730s onwards the small remnants of the gypsy population in the Dutch Republic began to look for outside support both in their criminal undertakings and as a more general survival strategy. Of course, this was not a one-sided development: it was not only gypsies who became interested in cooperation and (occasionally) intermarriage, but Jews and Christians as well.

At an individual level such marriages sometimes entailed fascinating forms of cultural and religious syncretism. Fisone's partner from the mid-1730s was a Jew at least fifteen years younger than she was, Levi Abrahams or Lijp Diersum. While Lijp was clearly a newcomer in a sizeable gypsy family, he continued to associate with his own network of Jewish thieves and other friends. To some extent Fisone adapted to Jewish customs. Lijp and Fisone were married according to Jewish ritual: they 'had made grave promises to each other'. Fisone, who for years had been going from one farm to another simply begging for food, began to beg in a different way: 'she had become a Jewess . . . and could not eat any meat [that is, pork] or bacon, and therefore did not beg her food but buys it'. Her youngest child, called Fockertje after his Christian father, Focker Jongbloet, was given a new, Jewish name by his stepfather.[31]

Fisone's relationship with Lijp was far from the only such case. Nathan Moses joined the Rabonus Band – or, if we may call it thus, the Fisone clan – in a similar way. In the previous chapter we saw how his career in crime had spanned about forty years by the time of his death sentence at Alkmaar in 1768. He was a circumcised Jew, born in Germany in the last decade of the seventeenth century. Nathan Moses was on familiar terms with members of nearly every Jewish network or band professionally involved in crime from about 1735 up to the time of his arrest.[32] His biography illustrates the slowly changing patterns of Jewish organized crime during the mid eighteenth century, as does his involvement with the Fisone–Rabonus circuit. It points to the growing interest in cooperation and intermarriage that existed among both gypsies and Jews.

Nathan Moses lived with gypsy as well as Christian women. Around

1732 he met the gypsy woman Koba, a sister of Fisone's third 'husband' Engel Reijniersz. Koba lived with him for at least twenty years, bore him eight children, and probably converted to the Jewish religion: we know that she took the name of Rachel. Eventually she was left by Nathan, who afterwards had affairs with at least five to ten Christian and gypsy women: the last one was Martijn Groen, who had been Rabonus's mistress a few years earlier. Although he 'married' into gypsy circles, Nathan Moses, like Lijp Diersum, kept up his connections with the extensive networks of Jewish thieves with whom he had undertaken hundreds of thefts and burglaries in the course of his long career. His involvement with Fisone and her extended family was in no way perfunctory. While Koba adopted a Jewish name, Nathan adopted obligations towards his new relatives and fulfilled them conscientiously. When Fisone was hanged in 1740, Moses took care of her children: Little (Kleine) Kees and Clarisse, then twelve and sixteen years old. They toured the countryside together; Nathan Moses taught them how to steal, and for a long time after continued to assist and advise Little Kees in all kinds of matters.[33] When asked by the court at Alkmaar 'what special affection he had for Little Kees and Clarisse, that he took them under his wings, and whether he is somehow a friend of Little Kees', Moses explained that their mother's (i.e. Fisone's) husband was a brother of his wife, Rachel. Both Clarisse and Little Kees were arrested in the course of the 1760s as members of the Rabonus Band: almost thirty years after his mother was hanged at Haarlem, and more than forty years after his father's execution in 1725, Little Kees died on the scaffold at the nearby town of Alkmaar – together with his guardian Nathan Moses.[34]

As Fisone's history shows, cooperation between gypsy and Jewish thieves slowly became a more regular practice from the mid eighteenth century onwards. In the first half of the century most bands active in the Dutch Republic had consisted of Jews, gypsies, or Christians, and cultural uniformity within bands was the rule before about 1740. Small numbers of gypsies joined Christian bands, but the reverse hardly ever happened,[35] and cooperation between gypsies and Jews was still exceptional. Personal ties of marriage heralded and symbolized new forms of association which were certainly not limited to the Rabonus Band. The more or less 'homogeneous' bands never disappeared completely in the period discussed here, but they gradually lost their prominent position to the composite bands that began to take shape around the middle of the century. Changing patterns of names epitomize this development. Before then a Jew or gypsy who joined a Christian band had a good chance of being nicknamed 'de Smous' (Sheeny) or 'de Heijden'. These names would have made very little sense if considerable numbers of Jews or gypsies had at the time participated in non-ethnic bands. The gradual disappearance of such nicknames in the course of the eighteenth century indicates increasing cooperation and mutual familiarity.

Association and Integration

Initiatives for cooperation came from more than one side, as Fisone's history shows. But what did increasing cooperation mean? Did it go any further than occasional professional collaboration and sporadic intermarriage? Can we find any evidence of cultural and social integration among the many vagrant groups in the course of the eighteenth century, and did they perhaps gradually merge into a more homogeneous *Gaunerschicht*?[36] Why, finally, did cooperation and intermarriage become attractive options at all? The histories of the Rabonus Band and of Fisone and her Jewish associates provide some tentative answers to the questions of when and why the different circuits became interested in joining forces.

Mutual though not identical concerns of gypsies, Jews, and Christians provided the main impetus for the growth of 'mixed' bands. As we have seen, it was mainly gypsy women who married Jews, and hardly ever Jewish women who married gypsies (or Christians, for that matter). Again, it was predominantly Jewish men who married Christian women, and not Christian men who married Jewish women. As Fisone's biography indicates, the new forms of cooperation came into being soon after the period of harsh gypsy persecutions, by which time very few gypsy men were left in the Netherlands; gypsy women had had less to fear. During the same years the share of unmarried young men among poor east-European immigrant Jews had begun to increase, and it would rise even faster in the second half of the century (see Shulvass 1971, p. 66). The number of available Jewish women must have been small at the time, and no respectable Christian woman would even have considered marrying a Jew. Since many Jews may have objected to marrying outside their circle unless their future wives (whether Christian or gypsy) were prepared to adopt Jewish customs and beliefs – as Fisone and Koba/Rachel did – the choice of marriage partners for poor Jewish men was extremely limited. Gypsy women had similar difficulties in finding partners within their own circle; their choice outside was slightly larger, and religious matters or customs do not appear to have kept them from marrying either Jews or Christians and still remaining part of their own families and culture.

In response to unusually difficult circumstances both gypsies (in particular women) and Jews (especially men) partly abandoned their usual endogamy, while at the same time looking towards each other and to various vagrant Christian groups for mutual assistance and an exchange of expertise in crime. Intermarriage itself must have led to more lasting forms of cooperation. Several 'external' developments characteristic of the second half of the eighteenth century, such as demographic growth, rising food prices, a contracting labour market, and the concomitant increase in the number of vagrant poor all over western Europe may also have contributed. More people than before took to the roads to find jobs, beg, sell their wares, or just to leave a place where they could no longer stay. Even if a marked increase in the numbers of people on the move did not automatically call forth new forms of interaction and criminal cooperation, it must at least have stimulated more frequent contacts between members of different cultures.

One more element may have been important: the evident success of the 'mixed' bands. Jews and gypsies had much to offer to Christian vagrant groups, such as extended and strong kinship networks, occupational and criminal expertise, flexible forms of organization, and possibly a positive self-image. Christian groups in their turn were just as important to members of either ethnic group – if only because they offered a large reservoir of potential recruits, a protective cover, and slightly smoother relations with rural inhabitants and local authorities.

Increasing intermarriage and the particular way in which gypsies associated with other itinerant groups to some extent clarify the 'problem of the disappearing gypsies' raised at the beginning of this chapter. Unquestionably, many gypsies had been executed or imprisoned during the first decades of the eighteenth century; many more must have left the Dutch Republic at the time of the persecutions. For those remaining in the area the safest way of vanishing from the sight of the authorities – and, incidentally, of historians – was to adopt the protective cover of a non-gypsy identity. Instead of a 'gap' in the history of gypsies in the Dutch Republic we have found a period of intermarriage and association, which entailed, step by step, both the 'absorption' of gypsies into the increasing mass of vagrant labouring poor and the disappearance of gypsy culture and perhaps identity.

Even by the late eighteenth century, however, gypsies had not completely vanished. We can still trace their presence in some of the networks active between about 1765 and the 1780s, when 'mixed' bands had definitely taken over from the strictly demarcated circuits of the early eighteenth century. In 1787 – nearly twenty years after the executions of Rabonus, Little Kees, Henke, and Nathan Moses – two gypsy women were whipped, branded, and sentenced to thirty years' detention by the town court of Haarlem. Maria Freduwa (aged fifty), alias Theresia de

Swol or Tittate, was born at Groningen and had spent most of her life touring the northern Netherlands. She sold haberdashery from door to door, begged, and specialized in shoplifting and ringing the changes. Her companion and colleague was the 25-year-old Maria de Laaij, born at Frankfurt am Main. She earned a living by selling scented waters and rubbers at markets and fairs. A third woman, Regina Christiaans (aged twenty), at first denied any connection with 'the band of vagrants and thieves to which her two companions had belonged for a number of years', but she soon admitted to being a member of this group of itinerant musicians and pedlars. She also told the court that a woman whose half-brother bore the familiar name of Jan Arendse (cf. Table 3) had taught her how to steal and ring the changes.[37]

This loose-knit conglomerate of vagrant families operated all over the northern Netherlands and in adjacent parts of Germany and the southern Netherlands. It comprised sixty to seventy men and women in all, who travelled in small family groups and used to meet each other at fairs and markets. Their customary criminal activities were petty theft and fraud. Gypsy and Christian families belonged to this circuit, but no Jews did. Some band members were conspicuous for their exotic names, such as Poeritang, Meilinde, and Giddia. Just like members of the Rabonus Band, they spoke a foreign language and used the term 'black' to describe themselves. Maria Freduwa told the court 'that she belonged to a certain Band or kind of people known as *Zwarten* [Blacks] or *Rommelscheelen* [related to Rom, Romany?] in Germany and elsewhere called *Heijdenen* and *Egyptenaren*, and that they speak an unknown language among themselves'.[38] Other band members had ordinary Christian names, came from Holland, Germany, or (more rarely) Brabant, and made no remarks about blackness.

Although strongly reminiscent of the Rabonus Band, cooperation had gone much further in the Freduwa group and had reached the point where a considerable part of the band could no longer be identified as either gypsy or Christian. Some members did indeed designate themselves as gypsies or 'blacks', but for the majority – many of whom spoke both a gypsy and a non-gypsy (Dutch or German) language – the distinction appears to have become irrelevant. All of them intermarried, if we may still use this term. Both Maria Freduwa's husbands were Christians, for instance. The first, Franciske Joseph, was an oboist and a member of a Prussian military band. The second, Cobus Henneberger, earned a living as a pedlar and organ-grinder. He came from a German family of thieves and change ringers whose roots lay in Prussian Geldern, just east of the Dutch border. Like Fisone's last husband, Cobus Henneberger was about fifteen years younger than his wife. During the 1780s he must have been in his thirties. His father had been hanged some time

Table 3 Fisone and Her Kin

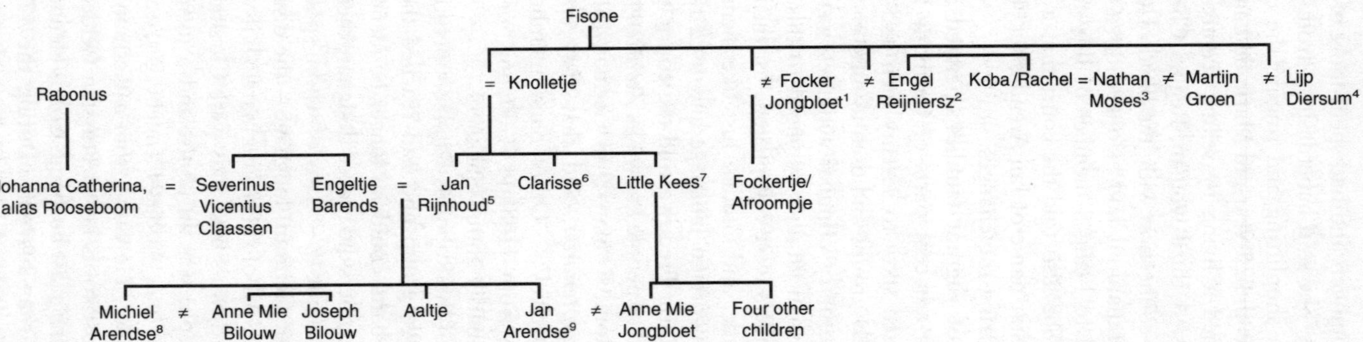

[1] Born in Amsterdam, 1708. Sailor and rope-maker. Banished at Wassenaar, 1730.
[2] Born between 1708 and 1718 in Princeland, Brabant. Chair-mender. Sentenced by the court of Schieland to fifteen years' detention, 1738.
[3] Born in Wartenscheid, Westphalia, around 1696. Pedlar, beggar. Hanged at Alkmaar, May 1768.
[4] Born in Hessen-Kassel around 1715. Pedlar. Hanged at Haarlem, April 1740.
[5] Born in 1719 and baptized in North Holland. Roman Catholic. Knife-grinder, tinker, chair-mender, dog seller, casual rural labourer. Sentenced by the court of Schieland to fifty years' detention and banishment, May 1765.
[6] Born in Amsterdam 1724. Beggar, fortune-teller, and herb seller. Sentenced at Haarlem to whipping and banishment, April 1740. Detained again at Amsterdam, 1768.
[7] Born around 1728, possibly near Copenhagen. Lived with many women, both gypsies and Christians. Knife-grinder, chair-mender, and casual rural labourer. Hanged at Alkmaar, May 1768.
[8] Born around 1742. Itinerant musician; served in the Prussian army. Lived with Anne Mie Bilouw; (earlier?) married to Lena, daughter of Fat Piet. No sentence known.
[9] Born in Amsterdam, 1745. Itinerant musician. Probably sentenced by a court martial at Delft to fifty years' detention, 1765.

earlier at hulst in flanders; his sister christiana was sentenced to whipping and fifteen years of detention at Rotterdam in 1784 at the age of twenty-eight.

By the late 1780s it was becoming more and more difficult (and pointless) to distinguish between gypsies and Christians living and working together in these vagrant networks. During the last two decades of the eighteenth century gypsies became completely 'invisible'. There are no references to either individual gypsies of gypsy bands in the criminal records of the years 1787–1807, by which time they must have merged completely with the other itinerant groups.

Jewish participation in non-Jewish networks followed a different pattern. From the 1740s onwards two by no means mutually exclusive forms of cooperation existed. Individual thieves, like Nathan Moses and Lijp Diersum, married into gypsy or Christian bands without loosing touch with their personal networks of Jewish friends, kinsmen, and colleagues. At the same time whole groups of Jews cooperated with non-Jewish bands. Both forms occurred in the Rabonus Band. An even larger Jewish contingent was attached on a more or less regular basis to the Calotte Band, one of the three major bands of the 1750s and 1760s.

Calotte was a Fleming with an impressive number of aliases (including Prince Carel, the Dissolute Student, and The Captain of a Hundred Thieves) and a just as impressive number of thefts, burglaries, and robberies to his name. By the time of his execution at 's Hertogenbosch in December 1766 he was thirty-two years old. For the preceding six or seven years he had acted as one of the captains of a huge network of vagrant men and women who committed petty thefts, extortion, burglaries (they regularly stole quantities of food from the cellars of farmhouses), and some armed robberies. Their activities covered a large area, ranging from the environs of Liège, Aachen, and Maastricht to central and eastern Dutch Brabant and neighbouring German territory.[39]

Lists compiled by the court of 's Hertogenbosch that aim to present a comprehensive view of the whole network mention 313 and 366 names respectively. As such they provide a rare view of a much broader set of predominantly poor and vagrant people.[40] They include active members and their closest companions as well as occasional assistants and relatives. With the exception of a few dozen men and women, all of them were Christians, born either in Brabant, Germany, or the southern Netherlands. Interestingly, the small number of gypsies was listed among the Christians and consisted exclusively of women, most of whom were living with non-gypsy men. All Jewish members, by contrast, were listed in one separate category. Most were men, and some of them had married (or were living with) Christian women. The lists thus point to the same marriage patterns that we have encountered before: gypsy women and Jewish men were marrying outside their own circle. The lists also graphically express the separateness of the Jewish contingent, in terms of both criminal organization and social matters. Jews did not take part in each of the band's robberies and, when they did, they did not mix much with the regular band members but arrived together and acted as a special company attached only for the duration of that specific expedition.

It will hardly come as a surprise to find the ubiquitous Michiel Feijtsburger and some of his kinsmen among the Jewish associates of the Calotte Band. Feijtsburger had incorporated a few Christians in his own Jewish network, among them the 34-year-old Pieter de Bast, alias Piet the Leper (de Lasarus), from Zeeland. He had served for a number of years in the French armies and, after returning to the Netherlands, found a temporary job as navvy; on his discovery that he had been infected with leprosy he soon managed to obtain a formal begging permit. Piet the Leper probably owed his connection with the Feijtsburger Band to another Christian, Joseph Rijckaart, who employed him from time to time to recruit soldiers and sailors. Rijckaart was the owner of an inn and lodging-house in the so-called Devil's Corner at Amsterdam. Like the Jordaan, this was an area of narrow alleys, lodging-houses, taverns, and small shops, mainly inhabited by beggars, pedlars, and a fluctuating population of people without fixed domicile. At Rijckaart's inn members of the Feijtsburger Band met and planned their robberies.[41]

Although these two Christians were important to the Feijtsburger Band for strategic reasons, both remained outsiders – and this was true of most Christians who joined Jewish bands, whether they acted as occasional assistants or as experienced members. This cultural and social 'segregation' of Jewish and Christian life can be closely observed in the Gossels Band, a relatively small group involved in armed robberies in Holland during the early 1770s.[42] Three Jewish brothers – Simon, Jacob, and Cosman Gossels – were among the leading members of this second instalment of the Feijtsburger Band, which also included two nephews of Michiel Feijtsburger. Three Christians participated in the band, all of them Germans and ex-soldiers. Jan Frederik Nijhuis from Osnabrück had served for at least five years in the French armies. He earned a living by selling textiles. Sebastiaan Wilter, who came from the county of Berg, had served for six years in the Prussian armies; he sold lace from door to door in Holland and northern Germany. Francis Schulz from Herzfeld had been in garrison at Amsterdam. He sold 'balms, elixirs, and herbs' and acted as surgeon and tooth-drawer.

These men differed from their Jewish associates not only in religious matters but also in occupational history, regional orientation, family connections, and language. Schulz became irritated when his companions continued to speak 'Jewish', which he could not understand. The Christian ex-soldiers made long tours in the Dutch provinces, selling new textiles, whereas the Jews were mainly active in Amsterdam and its environs, buying and selling second-hand clothes, hats, spectacles, mirrors, fish, or meat. They even inhabited different parts of Amsterdam. Jewish band members lived in the Jewish quarter; most of them were related to members of the large Jewish community. Levi Moses for instance, lived at Vlooienburg with his wife, Saartje, and his mother-in-law, Rachel. For a long time Cosman Gossels had been living in the house of his brother-in-law in the Jewish quarter. The three Germans, on the other hand, had lodgings in the Jordaan – a mainly non-Jewish working-class quarter. Their connection with the Jews was a strictly professional one. Differences between Jewish and Christian ways of life were considerable, and unless they adapted to Jewish customs, Christian band members stayed on the fringe.[43]

During the second half of the eighteenth century gypsies and Jews thus increasingly associated with Christian bands; to some extent Christians participated in Jewish and gypsy bands. The forms of association varied, however. Gypsies merged with Christian groups to the point of disappearing from sight by the late eighteenth century and, in all likelihood, of losing their identity as gypsies. Their language, meeting places, and occupational specializations may have influenced the Christian bands they joined, but their 'integration' seems to have been a largely one-sided process. They were absorbed by the diffuse and vagrant mass of Christian poor. Between Jews and Christians, by contrast, there was no question of social or cultural integration beyond the point of professional cooperation. Jews did not change their way of life and they did not relinquish their religious or sociocultural identity; nor did they change their names. When they married non-Jewish women, their wives usually adopted Jewish customs, and whenever Jewish and Christian robbers cooperated in large bands, Jewish patterns of organization were dominant.

The *Gaunerschicht* of the Late Eighteenth Century

Turning from cooperation within the framework of individual bands to interconnections and communication between the various circuits involved in organized rural crime, we may now ask again whether the formation of composite bands from the mid eighteenth century was part of the growth of a more homogeneous *Gaunerschicht*. Were there any far-flung composite criminal networks which united several criminal traditions? To what extent did individual bands or networks by this time know about each other's existence and perhaps coordinate their activities? And can we speak of an integrated rural underworld by the end of the eighteenth century?

Men like Nathan Moses and Lijp Diersum, who linked gypsy and Jewish circuits, must have provided information to both groups about each other's illegal activities, criminal specializations, and so on. There is no reason to assume that they acted as 'liaison officers', let alone as coordinators. A more than incidental exchange of information between bands of diverse ethnic or regional background also seems to have been unusual. None of the evidence points to concerted efforts of the various circuits, to territorial agreements between captains, or to coordination of their activities. Interestingly, suspects were hardly ever questioned about such matters, and we may safely assume that the judicial authorities would have been the first to suspect such interconnections. (Even during the revolutionary period at the end of the century the courts apparently did not fear the 'criminally dangerous' lower classes.) It seems likely, then, that links between the various circuits were rare; furthermore, some bands may not have been aware of each other's existence.

The few instances of communication between criminal circuits point in the same direction. Mozes Wijl, a German Jew who earned a living as a pedlar, was an elderly man by the time of his trial in 1765. He had been a member of the Feijtsburger Band (1763–5) and the court was convinced of his long involvement in organized crime. He was certainly known to Nathan Moses – a good indication of his professional standing. In the course of his interrogations Wijl provided the court with unasked-for and extremely interesting information about, among other things, the existence of a contemporaneous band: he said

> that they [he and his Jewish associates] live nowhere, but roam all over the countryside ... some will be in town after Easter and others ... at the time of the Amsterdam Fair, not knowing where their lodgings are ... There is another band consisting of Christians, all of them Brabanders, decked with gold and silver, and the women dressed like important ladies; they pass themselves off as merchants and usually go out on large and difficult exploits, and will also be in Amsterdam during the fair, and he knows a few of this company . . . A certain captain Veldmann is Captain of the Band of Brabanders . . . Hannes Manus [a member of the Feijtsburger Band] wanted to take him to this band of Brabanders, but he did not want to go, not trusting him.[44]

Wijl's account sounds rather like romanticized fiction, reminiscent of eighteenth-century picaresque novels. Which robbers at the time would have been wearing gold and silver or other costly finery? Even the captains of the Calotte Band – the only large group active in Brabant during these years and the only one to fit most (but not all) of Wijl's description – did not dress in this manner. His remarks thus convey a striking lack of familiarity between northern (and in this case Jewish) bands and the southern circuit of Christian Brabanders. Since it can hardly have been mere distance that kept the extremely mobile Wijl from contacting his Christian colleagues in the south, we must assume that these circuits remained separate for other reasons.

A story told by Nathan Moses likewise illustrates the casual and to some extent haphazard character of connections between the various criminal circuits. Moses

> was staying at the place of a Brabander called Van Rossum at Leiden in the beginning of 1765. Hendrikus Stoffe, alias Heijntje van Gog, and Hermondus Rijnhold, alias De Schot, were also in lodging there. Heijntje van Gog spoke to his mistress Marian . . . in *bourgouns* [cant, thieves' slang]; he [Moses] heard this whereupon they recognized each other as thieves, and he made a deal with Van Gog to sell a few pounds of stolen old silver which Van Gog would bring to Leiden.[45]

(Stoffe and Rijnhold were among the leading members of the Calotte Band; together with Calotte they were executed at 's Hertogenbosch on 13 December 1766.) It is notable that tentative contacts between criminal circuits occurred only when various forms of cooperation had already been explored at the level of individual bands and band members: that is, in the bands of Rabonus, Calotte, and Feijtsburger. Until the growth of the internationally operating composite network known as the Great Dutch Band such links continued to depend on a small number of individual thieves and robbers. Accordingly, they remained both tenuous and incidental.

During the decade of the Great Dutch Band's existence (1790–9) Jewish–Christian cooperation in organized rural crime assumed a more permanent character. It formed a framework flexible enough to accommodate the diverse criminal circuits that participated. To a large extent it was the creation of an elderly Jewish pedlar called Moyse Jacob, who played a central role in bringing together the various criminal circuits of the Dutch Republic within a more permanent organizational structure. Typically, this structure may have sprung from Moyse Jacob's own family arrangements. At the same time it epitomized the main developments in criminal organization of the past half-century.[46]

Moyse Jacob himself took an active part only in its first 'branch', the Brabant Band, which operated in the environs of Brussels, Antwerp, and Ghent during the years 1789–91 and 1794–6. Two thirds of the sixty men belonging to this branch were Jews. Individually they committed a variety of petty thefts; as a group both this branch and its successors specialized in large-scale armed robbery. They attacked isolated farms and village shops, rammed or broke open doors, gagged and trussed up the inhabitants, maltreated them occasionally, and robbed them of large amounts of money, gold, silver, textiles, and other valuables. In 1796 French reforms in the by then annexed southern Netherlands caused the disintegration of the Brabant branch. Three more branches followed. The Meerssen Band (comprising about sixty members, forty of whom were Jews) operated in the region of Aachen, Cologne, and Maastricht during 1796–8. The Dutch-Brabant Band (1797–8) was active in the area near 's Hertogenbosch and consisted of about twenty-five men (including sixteen Jews). The Holland Band (1797–9) alone had a Christian majority: only five of its twenty-one members were Jews. Membership of these branches partly overlapped. Taken together the whole network included at least one hundred and twenty members, not counting assistants such as informants, innkeepers, and fences.

The first, Brabant branch set the pattern with respect to criminal specialization, leadership, and forms of organization. All the principal commanders had been instructed (and probably selected) by Moyse Jacob himself. Each one of them, moreover, belonged to his extended family. His son Abraham Jacob was a captain of the first branch. The French Jew Abraham Picard – a commander of both the Brabant and the Meerssen bands – had married Jacob's daughter Dinah. Her sister Rebecca was living with the Christian Frans Bosbeeck from Antwerp, who acted as captain in the Brabant, Meerssen, and Dutch-Brabant bands. A third daughter may have been involved with either Marcus David or Mozes Ocker, both of whom were Jews and leading members of two or three successive branches. If we add the names of Afrom Maij – son of a well-known Jewish fence at Amsterdam – and of Frans Bosbeeck's twin brother, Jan Bosbeeck, we have an overview of all chief commanders of the Great Dutch Band.

In territorial range and flexibility this network surpassed any previous band active during the seventeenth and eighteenth centuries in these parts of the Netherlands. Patterns of organization characteristic of Jewish bands were dominant in every one of its branches, whatever their composition. Most band members had an itinerant way of life. Wives and children (whether Jewish or not) did not accompany the men on their tours – never mind during their criminal exploits – but stayed at home in the big towns of the southern Netherlands and Holland, as was customary in Jewish bands. The urban orientation was strong: whereas nearly all the robberies took place in the countryside, Jewish as well as Christian band members generally lived in towns. Towns also served as the basis for their expeditions – as had been the case in the early eighteenth-century Jaco Band and in all Jewish bands – and towns provided the crucially important services of Jewish fences and reliable innkeepers.

As a composite group the Great Dutch Band drew upon nearly the whole range of criminal traditions and cultures in the Netherlands. Even a glance at these 'roots' illustrates their variety and shows how far integration had proceeded in this section of society by the end of the eighteenth century. As we have seen, no gypsy bands were left by then, and no gypsies participated in the Great Dutch Band. Yet at least one person formed a link between this network and gypsy traditions in crime, as epitomized by Rabonus, Henke, Fisone, and the early eighteenth-century Captain Garneson: Cobus Henneberger, organ-grinder, member of a Christian German family with a long-standing involvement in crime, and second husband of Maria Freduwa. (At the time of his involvement with Freduwa's part Christian and part gypsy band in about 1787 Henneberger had already been on friendly terms with Jews like Abraham Levi Singer, Mozes Gaas, Afrom Maij, and Mozes Ocker. All these men became leading members of the Great Dutch Band. Between 1792 and 1797 Henneberger participated in numerous burglaries and robberies committed by three of its branches. He was arrested in 1797; in a daring venture Frans Bosbeeck and some other band members liberated him from his German prison.) The dominant Jewish 'root' of the Great Dutch Band in itself formed an aggregate of diverse criminal specializations and traditions, ranging from picking pockets and shoplifting to certain forms of burglary and armed robbery. Most Jews in the band had a long history of professional involvement in crime, interspersed with months and even years of imprisonment. During the late 1770s Mozes Ocker, for instance, had belonged to a medium-sized group of highly mobile urban thieves and burglars who specialized in picking pockets, shoplifting, and petty theft at markets and fairs.[47] At the time one of their fences had been Jonas Maij from Amsterdam, father of Afrom Maij. Perhaps it is no longer surprising that there were even some links between the Great Dutch Band and the by now famous Feijtsburger family: during the early 1780s Salomon Isaak, alias Salme Gast, belonged to the Jewish band of Joseph Michael Feijtsburger which was based at 's Hertogenbosch and committed burglaries all over Dutch Brabant. By the mid-1790s Gast had joined the Meerssen branch of the Great Dutch Band, while also committing robberies in the province of Utrecht together with yet another Jewish band.[48] Finally, numerous

Christian groups contributed to the Great Dutch Band. Among them were professional urban burglars from Amsterdam as well as German vagrants, rural Brabanders from both Dutch and Austrian Brabant, and inhabitants of the Dutch ports, such as Rotterdam and Dordrecht. It is to these groups – and to the theme of cooperation and integration within the non-ethnic, Christian segment of rural organized crime – that we will turn in the next chapter.

By drawing upon a huge range of criminal traditions the Great Dutch Band advanced and broadened cooperation between the various criminal circuits. Communication had definitely improved by the 1790s, and contacts between Christian and Jewish band members were no longer strictly limited to matters of business. To some extent the Great Dutch Band may even have served as a social and cultural 'melting-pot'. Neither Jews nor Christians now operated as separate contingents 'added' to the main body of the band; both acted as leaders, sometimes together. There was still a considerable cultural gap, none the less, between these two main segments. They differed in language, occupations, kinship obligations, patterns of recruitment, the position of women, housing, and so on. Intermarriage remained exceptional, and we hear very little about Jews and Christians drinking together in taverns, visiting fairs, dancing, or joining in other forms of leisure. Integration did not extend this far, even though Christian members (as a minority) had adopted characteristic aspects of Jewish criminal tradition.

For criminal purposes there was no need of further integration. Moyse Jacob and his associates had, after all, brought together various criminal circuits precisely because they differed. Each criminal tradition contributed special qualities, skills, contacts, and forms of knowledge. Association and the coordination of these criminal traditions, rather than integration, were the main basis for the flexibility of the whole network. Flexibility in its turn formed the principal reason for its success and survival during a decade of revolution, warfare, economic upheaval, and later, harsh persecution by the newly organized judicial authorities. The history of the Great Dutch Band shows how the diverse traditions came together at the end of the eighteenth century: it also shows that there was never any question of an integrated rural underworld in the Dutch Republic.

8

The Brabant Connection, 1730–1810

Within the Christian segment of organized rural crime in the Dutch Republic a similar process of increasing cooperation and association can be traced. The main dividing lines in their world were based on geography: whereas nearly all the gypsy bands, Jewish networks, and mixed bands discussed in the preceding chapters operated throughout the Dutch Republic, even the largest non-ethnic bands tended to confine themselves to either the northern or the southern half of the country. The natural barrier formed by the so-called big rivers separated criminal domains, as it did so many others. (The best known, of course – even in the modern Netherlands – being the division between a largely protestant north and a predominantly Roman Catholic south). At least until the mid eighteenth century connections between the northern circuits and those active in the south remained minimal.

The mixed composition of the northern bands reflected the international background of the general population in this area. As we saw in Chapter 3, these bands included men and women born in Holland, Germany, Flanders, Scandinavia, England, Scotland, Ireland, and Wales. Composite though they were, these groups comprised only very few members of ethnic groups or 'southerners' from Dutch Brabant. Similarly, the large military bands active in Brabant, such as the Zwartmakers and Moskovieters, counted no outsiders at all among their members: that is, no people from outside Dutch or Spanish-Austrian Brabant. In many respects Dutch Brabant was oriented towards the south rather than towards the northern Dutch provinces. The recruitment of additional band members from the whole of Brabant rather than from Utrecht or Holland simply followed a pattern set by family connections and economic ties. Recruitment of Brabanders by the northern bands – rather than the reverse – would have been logical, since seasonal migration from the predominantly poor and politically dependent southern regions to the urbanized and affluent northern ones had always been greater than vice versa.[1]

From the mid eighteenth century onwards, however, the Brabant bands gradually began to associate with Jews and French-speaking Walloons, and to establish connections with northern non-ethnic bands. Here, the slow process of cooperation and association between the various Christian circuits will be looked at from the south, from the perspective of the Brabant bands. In order to understand why particular forms of cooperation developed (and others did not), and why they took shape only in the late eighteenth century, we will have to go back to the early eighteenth century to come to grips with patterns of organized rural crime in Brabant.

Roots

The activities of the big military bands of the years 1690–1715 were, as we have seen, predicated upon their links with local rural society. They relied on local assistants; local knowledge enabled them to select their victims, and most band members had grown up in the area of their operations. Yet most of them no longer belonged to the respected part of village society. They were either on the brink of becoming social outcasts or had already crossed the borderline between a fixed residence and a life of nearly permanent vagrancy. This pattern was characteristic of almost all large and small, military and non-military Christian bands active in Brabant during the first half of the eighteenth century and of a good many more operating in the 1750s, 1760s, and 1770s.

A few 'non-military' examples serve to illustrate this strongly local and regional orientation. Between 1709 and 1713 a group of ten to fifteen men and women committed numerous thefts and burglaries in and near Zundert, a village on the Dutch-Spanish border between Breda and Antwerp. They confessed 'to having formed a company [*compagnie*] for the purpose of robbing and despoiling the houses and goods of honourable country folk'. The band was formed in 1709, 'when grain was extremely expensive', and in the course of the next five years regularly stole quantities of rye, wheat, grain, peas, apples, meat, butter, sheep, and so on. Unlike the small family groups involved in the theft of bread, fruits, and vegetables in and around the towns of Holland during years of food crisis (such as 1740–1), the Zundert Band was stealing mainly for commercial purposes. Members did not take one loaf of bread or just a piece of meat, but stole barrels of butter and large quantities of grain. At least part of their booty was sold.[2]

In some respects members of the Zundert Band followed a pattern set by the military Zwartmakers, whose activities had ended only a decade earlier. They carried arms during robberies, posted sentries, and sometimes threatened to kill the houses' inhabitants. On such occasions they blackened their faces, while some used chalk to draw white circles around the brims of their hats. The main purpose of this masquerade was probably to confuse and terrify their victims, for the Zundert Band was exclusively local: an extended family enterprise of kinsmen born and living in or near this village. It consisted of an elderly couple, Adriaan Willem Coppens and Jenneke Marijnis van Zittert (both in their sixties), and their numerous sons, nephews, daughters, and sons-in-law, all of whom were in their twenties or early thirties by the time of their arrests in 1713–14.[3] Their greatest fear must have been recognition by victims, who were their own neighbours and fellow countrymen.

A second and much larger company, the Band of Engele Jantje, operated all over Dutch Brabant during the 1720s and comprised forty to sixty men and women, all of them without fixed residence.[4] It was a loose-knit association, mainly held together by ties of kinship. Along with Engele (Angel) Jantje we find his wife and child, his parents (or parents-in-law), a niece, and his mother's half-sister among the members. They travelled in pairs or small groups from one market or fair to another, occasionally working as day labourers, selling and singing songs, begging for food, and stealing fruit, vegetables, meat, and bread. They often spent the night in barns and haystacks, at cheap inns, or even outside in the woods. Some members were second-generation vagrants. Anne Griet Hendrikse, for example, was arrested at least three times on account of vagrancy and petty thefts at fairs. Her mother had been a vagrant and beggar; her father was hanged at Cleves.

Besides petty theft, the people in this group were involved in burglaries, occasional church robbery, and frequent extortion under threat of murder and arson. Such threats could not be ignored. Like many other bands active in Brabant, this one did not hesitate to use violence. In 1726 the occupants of an isolated farmhouse – the Nonnenbosse Hoeve not far from 's Hertogenbosch – apparently refused to give bread and butter to about fifteen band members who camped in a nearby wood. Upon a second refusal Engele Jantje said to the farmer, 'Tomorrow you may be as rich as we are'. A few hours later the group of vagrants met and decided that the man or woman among them who drew the ace of diamonds would set fire to the farmhouse. Griet, who drew the card, made all her companions assist her in lighting the roof, saying, 'all of you will have to join in, for if they arrest me I will betray everyone'. The whole farm was burnt down, and a child died. In the course of the next few weeks several members were arrested in different parts of

Brabant and eventually sentenced to death; their penalties often involved scorching and were meant to mirror their crimes.[5]

Relations between members of the Zundert and Engele Jantje bands and the local inhabitants of their respective districts varied considerably, ranging from closeness and belonging – though not necessarily respect – with regard to the former to social distance and fear with regard to the latter. There is no doubt, however, about the regional character of both. Each consisted of men and women born and bred in Brabant, as their surnames or the references to places of birth that were used as such indicate. In the company of Engele Jantje we find names like Elisabeth van Oirschot, Peter Thijsse van Uden, Pietje van Middelrooij, Anne Catrien van 's Hertogenbosch. Their first names likewise point to 'southern' origins in the abundance of those with a distinctly Roman Catholic flavour and of abbreviations that were and still are peculiar to Brabant: Domien (Dominicus), Arike (Adriaan), Jen or Jenneke (Johanna; cf. Janneke in Holland), Giel (Machiel; cf. Michiel in Holland), Trieneke (Catherina), Trui (Gertrudis), Peerke (Peter), Jennemie (Johanna Maria), and numerous variations of Maria, including Mie and Maaij.

Whatever their relations with the local population of the hamlets and villages where they had grown up, these band members still shared many important cultural characteristics with 'non-itinerant' rural society in Brabant. As we saw earlier, patterns of Jewish organized crime highlighted Jewish gender roles and reflected particular types of mobility and occupational specializations. In a similar way the structure of bands deeply rooted in local Brabant society illuminates and reflects the wider setting of the local social strata in this predominantly rural part of the Netherlands. The three familiar themes of urban/rural orientation, occupations and mobility, and names, kinship, and the role of women may again serve as guidelines.

The urban experience of members of the Brabant bands was limited and only rarely extended further than the main towns of Dutch and Spanish Brabant: 's Hertogenbosch, Breda, and Antwerp. They were not at home in towns, and, unlike Jewish pedlars, for instance, they regarded towns as places to go to for specific purposes, such as buying, selling, or entertainment, rather than as places to return to and live in. During the 1730s Black (Swarte) Cas was an important figure in a loose-knit conglomerate of about forty to sixty vagrants and beggars involved in various kinds of theft, extortion, and violence. Besides illustrating the violent tenor of existence in rural Brabant, the activities of Black Cas and his accomplice and friend Hein de Ruijter evoke a way of life centred on the countryside. In 1735 Hein de Ruijter, then aged twenty-seven, escaped from the house of correction at Breda where he had spent some five years and re-joined Cas; seven years earlier he had been convicted by the court of Breda to whipping and thirty years' imprisonment on account of vagrancy, theft, and burglary. Cas too had escaped, after a conviction for extortion, stabbing, and threatening passers-by on the public road. Both men thereupon joined a large company, or *troup*, of

> tramps, beggars, vagrants, and vagabonds . . . which was at least forty strong, among whom there were men who carried pistols and sticks with pointed metal pins. This *troup* . . . spoke a so-called Bourgounse language to prevent local people from understanding what they said. These people, usually travelling in pairs, beg all over the Meijerij, though strong and healthy, and occupy themselves in this way, but now and then up to six, eight, ten or even more men may be found together.[6]

Black Cas, Hein de Ruijter, and their companions spent most of the summer of 1736 begging and tramping the countryside of western Brabant; sometimes they found jobs as casual rural labourers. In June they stole and skinned a sheep, cooking it in a big kettle on a fire they had made behind a hedgerow. Two weeks later they entered the stable yard of a farmhouse not far from Roosendaal and stole clothes, money, and some small utensils. Soon afterwards they broke into another farmhouse, taking clothes, linen, and sheets. Part of the booty was sold in the town of Bergen op Zoom. Finally, in August 1736, Black Cas, Hein de Ruijter, and a third member of this company encountered a local constable in the middle of the heathlands of central Brabant. They attacked him, robbed him of his flintlock, stabbed him several times, and beat him up with a wooden club. The three men then joined their wives and girlfriends who were staying at a nearby village. Black Cas was eventually hanged at 's Hertogenbosch in 1736; a few months later his friend Hein met the same fate at the village of Loon op Zand.[7]

Towns hardly figure at all in the stories of these two men and, if they do, it is either as places they visit to sell the booty or as the location of the judicial authorities, as places of justice. Towns were irrelevant in precisely the same way to most other vagrant groups operating in Brabant, whether they were involved in violent crime and armed robbery or 'only' in petty theft and begging. A vagrant existence in Brabant meant sleeping at cheap rural inns, in haystacks, barns, and stables, or outside in the open; eating food bought from the rural population or obtained by begging and stealing; and travelling on foot along dusty roads which crossed the wooded areas and heathlands of eastern and central Brabant, the eastern moors, and the rich and often waterlogged clay soils of the west.

Patterns of mobility too differed from both the long-distance travel in small, exclusively male groups and the brief tours circling a particular city which were characteristic of Jewish pedlars. Members of Brabant bands spent the larger part of the year tramping, begging, and working in the countryside. Their tours had a more or less random character; as a rule they did not start and end in towns, and there is not much sense of direction in their itineraries. Travelling together, these men and women criss-crossed the countryside of Brabant, went from one farm to another, and then again spent a day in town to visit a fair. Obviously they only rarely toured the countryside totally without purpose – though much of it seems to have consisted of meeting each other at specific locations after having first split up because of judicial persecution, personal enmity, or the hope of obtaining more money and food when travelling in pairs instead of a larger group. This type of 'random' mobility was linked not only to their illegal business but to other professional activities as well. For part of the year many band members still belonged to the mass of casual day labourers looking for jobs on the big farms of western Brabant and Zeeland. Quite a number of them spent the summers in the fields and nearby heathlands and woods (on migrant labour see J. Lucassen 1984). In late autumn some returned to their home regions, the poorer eastern section of Brabant, Limburg, and Wallonia. Others stayed in western and central Brabant, and took up begging, mending chairs, peddling, sweeping chimneys, buying and selling scrap, knitting, and repairing items such as nets, baskets, and broomsticks. The combination of rural labour during the summers and artisans' work, retail trade, or begging during the winters was typical.

For many vagrant people involved in the Brabant bands, though, no former or current occupations – apart from begging, theft, and so on – can be traced at all. More often than in Holland, sentences pronounced in Brabant simply describe convicts as 'earning their livelihood by tramping, able bodied, along the roads and begging for things'. Begging and vagrancy had become their principal trade, a main source of income and a way of life all in one. This was particularly true of the members of several well-known vagrant families who turn up again and again in the criminal records of this region. Especially during the second half of the eighteenth century no bailiff in Brabant can have felt any surprise when a vagrant man, woman, or child of the names of Stap, Trap, Sestig, Trieste, Stulp, or Trompet was brought in. The ubiquity of these families can hardly be overestimated and their number increased during the final decades of the century. Their presence in nearly every band of any importance during the period 1760–1805 points to a certain measure of interconnectedness in these circles.

These same vagrant families also exemplify the value of kinship as one of the main bonds keeping this mobile and fragmented part of society together. They demonstrate which particular kinship relations and family structures were important in lower-class rural society in Brabant, and how they were expressed. The position of women in the Brabant bands formed a striking contrast with the role of Jewish women as discussed in Chapter 6. Even in predominantly male bands – such as the military bands of the 1690s to 1710s – women like Barbel de Clercq and the innkeeper Kee Vuijlhemd had been key figures. Besides supporting and assisting, they organized, planned, and inspired. In non-military bands their role was even more crucial. The men usually monopolized the more spectacular illegal activities, but begging and petty theft (which were central to the everyday existence and livelihood of these groups) belonged largely to the women's domain. As long as their children were still very young, the women were less mobile than the men. They spent nearly as much time on the road as the men, however, and did so for much the same reasons: to earn a living by begging, peddling, washing, cleaning, hoeing, and any other type of unskilled rural labour. During these tours they did not necessarily accompany their menfolk.

It was not only in economic terms that women formed the backbone of many vagrant groups in Brabant. In addition to a few nuclear or slightly extended families, such bands regularly included a number of women related by kinship ties – mothers, daughters, sisters, aunts and nieces, sisters-in-law, cousins, and even grandmothers and granddaughters – as well as several male and female children and youngsters aged between ten and about eighteen. The women might be joined by current husbands or lovers, sons-in-law, cousins, and occasionally brothers and nephews. Even then it was still the women who provided a measure of coherence and permanence; they were the mainstays of these groups – and they were recognized as such. Names and nicknames commonly used in the Brabant bands reflected their special position. Children were often known by their mother's surnames.

The case of Catherina (Kaat) Hendriks de Bruijn and her relatives illustrates most of the current naming patterns in the Brabant bands. Kaat, the daughter of Hendrik Hendriks de Bruijn, was born in Brabant around 1730. Her father had served in the Prussian army; later he earned a living by casual rural labour and begging. During the late 1750s and early 1760s Kaat belonged to the band of Dirk Verhoeven, which operated in Gelderland, Utrecht, the northern section of Brabant, and the area between the big rivers. She evidently regarded Catherina Hendriks de Bruijn as her 'real' name, that is, as a formally recognized name sanctioned by baptism. Nobody knew her by this name, however. Her companions usually referred to her as Harelipped (Hazemondse) Kaat, but she might as well have been called Kaat Trap, after her mother (Mie Trap), who belonged to the well-known vagrant Trap family. Kaat's brother was known by their mother's surname – as Cornelis Trap, and never as Cornelis Hendriks de Bruijn – and he transferred this surname to his young son, who was called Jantje Trap. Tracing this family name back in time we discover a certain Thomas Trap (a former soldier) who spent some time in the Amsterdam house of correction during the 1710s and who died about 1722. He had married Catharina Bernards, who earned a living by selling shoelaces, pins, and needles; their son Hendrik Trap was a professional soldier. Their daughter Anna Maria Trap (Trappe Mie) married a ballad singer and was among the members of the band which set fire to the Nonnenbosse Hoeve in 1726. This Trappe Mie may have been Kaat's grandmother: definite proof of a connection between Kaat and this earlier section of the Trap family is lacking, but it can hardly be a coincidence that Kaat's mother was called Mie Trap.[8]

The surname of Trap was thus first transferred from a father to his male and female children, and then from a mother to her sons, daughters, and some of her grandchildren. Other names might also derive from the mother's side of the family. Several men and even more women belonging to the Brabant bands were known by a combination of their own and their mother's first names: Hendrien's Beth, Anna Marie daughter of Agnes, Anna Catrien's Hein and Anna Catrien's Jan (all of whom belonged to the Calotte Band). Now and then a mother's nickname stuck to all her descendants, as in the case of Maria Mombers, alias Stumpfoot-fat (Stompvoets-Dikke) Mie, who belonged to the Calotte Band of the 1760s. Her daughter Anna Catrien van Boekelt was always called Stumpfoot's or Fat Mie's Trien; her son or nephew was called Fat Piet or Stumpfoot's Piet and her second daughter was referred to as Stump Mie's daughter.[9]

Names like these underscore the pivotal role of mothers in the vagrant groups touring Brabant as opposed to the more peripheral position of fathers. It was not only mother's names, moreover, but also the first names, nicknames, and surnames of wives, mistresses, and possibly sisters too that served to identify men in Brabant. Jan Mareau, who was sentenced to death in 1741 at 's Hertogenbosch on the charges of theft, burglary, and violence, was usually called Maaij Wellens's Jan after his wife Marij Wellens.[10] Even more elaborate names can be found in a company of semi-vagrant beggars and rural labourers which toured western Brabant during the 1750s and 1760s. Jenna Pieterse Luijckx and her brother Anthonie Pieterse Luijckx were called respectively Maaij Lieven Jennen Jaan and Maaij Lieven Jennen Teun – after their mother Jenne and grandmother Marij Lieven.[11]

Names which defined men in terms of their mothers or wives were much more rare in the Christian bands operating north of the big rivers, and the position of women in these northern bands differed from their southern counterparts. Individual women might be as influential in 'the north' as in 'the south'. In the Thorn-bush Band (Doorne Boske Band) of the 1770s, which operated along the big rivers in the border area of Holland, Gelderland, Brabant, and Utrecht, two middle-aged women dominated a company that consisted largely of their children, sons and daughters-in-law, grandchildren, nieces, nephews, and other relatives.[12] But on the whole women were less prominent in the northern bands – a result of the different structures of northern and southern bands, it would seem, rather than a reflection of any more subservient position of 'northern' women in general.

Names also reflect and symbolize other structural differences between north and south. In the northern bands nearly all nicknames referred to individual characteristics – such as physical qualities and defects, habits, exceptional feats, occupational activities, and so on. In the south names and nicknames that defined people in terms of kinship were much more prominent. As we have seen, the northern bands generally formed composite, loose-knit networks, which consisted of indigenous urban and rural Hollanders as well as Germans, Englishmen, Frenchmen, and Irishmen of varied occupational backgrounds. Most of these men had joined the vagrant groups as individuals or in pairs. In Brabant whole families (or even extended networks of kinsfolk) at the margins of local society joined in organized criminal activities: women, men, and children.[13] It is only in such a context that the use of nicknames referring to kinship and in particular to female relatives makes sense. And it is only in groups where family ties of this type provided coherence and some measure of continuity that women could reach prominent positions.

The First Strand of the Brabant Connection

Both the ubiquity of certain vagrant families and the importance of kinship relations in the vagrant circuits of Brabant during the second half of the eighteenth century indicate a measure of interconnectedness between non-ethnic bands operating in this region. The histories of two families with a long-standing criminal reputation may serve to demonstrate how such links between bands in Brabant slowly multiplied during the last decades of the century, and how, eventually, a tenuous Brabant connection came into being with professional bands operating north of the rivers.

When Marijn Jansse Jaspers acted as a fence for the Zundert Band (1709–13), the Jaspers family already resided at the small village of Rucphen in western Brabant which continued to be their principal base for the rest of the century. Nearly twenty years later, in 1729, the same Marijn and his brother Cornelis Jansse Jaspers were sentenced to whipping and twelve years' detention for similar activities: they had been lodging thieves in their house at Rucphen and lent them their ox cart for the transport of stolen goods. Cornelis had also stolen beehives – an offence punishable by death – in the wide surroundings of their native village.[14]

If we move on from the 1710s and 1720s to the second half of the century, the number of Jaspersens prosecuted on account of a large range of illegal activities increases. It is nearly impossible, in fact, to go through the criminal records of the 1770s, 1780s, and 1790s for any jurisdiction in western Brabant without encountering members of this family, or their regular associates, the families Rommens, de Bruijn, Heeren, Luijckx, and Catoen.[15] Between 1756 and 1763, for instance, Machiel Antonisse Jaspers, alias Bare-toed (Lugte Tonen) Giel, was arrested and convicted several times by different courts in western Brabant on account of cattle thefts, violent disturbances on the public road, theft of beehives, burglary (stealing clothes, silver, and 150 kilos of pork), and alleged manslaughter. Among his accomplices were two members of the Luijckx family whose names may sound familiar: Anthonie or Maaij Lieven Jennen Teun, and his sister Jenna, alias Maaij Lieven Jennen Jaan. Having escaped from prison, Machiel continued to tour the region of Breda with a friend and their respective mistresses. They combined their occasional jobs with burglaries and extortion from passers-by. In 1763 – at the age of twenty-eight – Machiel Jaspers was sentenced to an especially severe form of death penalty by the town court of Breda: he was garrotted, his face was scorched, and his body was afterwards exposed on the wheel.[16]

After about 1770 it was no longer a matter of individual members of the above-mentioned families being involved in a variety of criminal offences: the families as a whole joined forces (together with a number of others) and began to engage in organized theft, burglary, and robbery. From a small family enterprise, in which the innkeeper Marie de Klerck was a central figure, this association gradually expanded during the 1770s to include twenty-five to thirty-five men and women by 1778.[17] Although some of these families might best be described as semi-vagrant, the village of Rucphen and in particular the nearby hamlet of 't Heike (Little heath) provided a home base for all of them. By the late eighteenth century this hamlet, which was nicknamed Schooiersheike (Tramp's heath) or Kleijn Amsterdam (Little Amsterdam), had about 175 inhabitants. Many of them belonged to six to ten intermarrying families, among whom the Jaspersens are considered one of the oldest.

'T Heike was a poor village, for much of the infertile soil was covered with brushwood and heather. The people lived in huts and cottages, and quite a few could provide for themselves and their families only by leaving the region during part of the year to find work as casual rural labourers, soldiers, or pedlars. Some literally made a living from their own soil (which consisted of fine sand), selling it either by cartloads or by baskets; others manufactured brooms and brushes and sold them all over the province; several earned a living by weaving baskets and collecting refuse (on 't Heike and its inhabitants see Schreurs 1947 and Slootmans 1956). Clearly the lack of economic resources had something to do with the frequent involvement of the villagers in illegal activities. Besides poverty and concomitant forced mobility, however, the location of the hamlet itself and its marginality in terms of the administration of justice were important. As Schreurs has pointed out, 't Heike served as an informal sanctuary because it was right on the borders of the two largest administrative districts of western Brabant: the barony of Breda and the marquisate of Bergen op Zoom (1947, pp. 11–21). Administrative as well as judicial control over the territory of Rucphen and 't Heike was contested for a long time, thus creating a no man's land where the bailiffs of nearby jurisdictions feared to intervene. In 1756 the bailiff of the neighbouring Zegge certainly felt he needed every single one of his constables to arrest Machiel Jansse Jaspers and his two associates. To that purpose he organized a nightly expedition to 't Heike reminiscent of a raid rather than an orderly arrest.[18] Naturally this policy – which took collective resistance for granted and simply assumed that an arrest would be followed by concerted efforts to liberate the detained person (as indeed happened occasionally) – only solicited further action by the local population and helped to perpetuate their fearsome reputation.

The hamlet of 't Heike formed a special community, characterized by strong family ties and kin-based solidarity, poverty, low social status, particular occupations entailing mobility and other tactical qualities, a suspicious (not to say hostile) attitude towards the authorities, and a lack of state control which enabled the inhabitants to use their village as a relatively safe home base. ('T Heike may have been special only to the extent that so many of these characteristics were combined in this one community; other hamlets in Brabant which formed a base for local bands probably showed some resemblance. Oss east of 's Hertogenbosch is another village in Brabant known for similar, long-standing criminal traditions, which continued far into the twentieth century.) Most of these aspects contributed to the formation of both the band of the 1770s and its more impressive successor, the Catoen Band, which likewise originated as a family enterprise. In 1787–8 Marijn de Bruijn, his sons Willibrord and Marijn Junior, and a few others committed a number of thefts in the environs of Roosendaal. By 1789 some more members of the de Bruijn and Rommens families had joined the group, besides four of the Catoen brothers, three Jaspersens, and several other inhabitants of 't Heike. By the early 1790s the band had grown to include about thirty-five people, and between 1789 and 1791 it committed numerous thefts, burglaries, and large-scale armed robberies. Band members showed a marked preference for the large and isolated farms of the Roosendaal and Bergen op Zoom area.[19]

The target of one of their expeditions was Matthijs Rampaard's farm near Steenbergen in western Brabant. All the band members carried flintlocks and knives. At midnight on 7 December 1791 they knocked on the front door, demanding money and shouting that they were going to cut the throats of the cows and set fire to the house. They also vowed to surrender body and soul to the devil if they did not kill every one of the farm's inhabitants, including the baby in its cot. The robbers smashed most of the windows, fired a shot into the house, and continued to beat upon the doors with the butt-ends of their rifles until the farmer finally had to admit them. Some remained on guard outside while three robbers ransacked the house. They stole not only the farmer's money, gold buttons, and other jewellery but also the savings of the two farm-hands and a servant-girl.[20]

Their reliance on 'local roots' constituted both the strength and the weakness of the bands of 't Heike – and, in fact, of all locally based bands. Unlike mobile ethnic groups of the composite network of the Great Dutch Band, these local bands could not shift their activities to any other region. They were finished as soon as regional bailiffs joined forces and thereby increased the risks of continued operations in their 'home region', as the history of the Catoen Band, which fell apart because of a number of arrests in 1793–4, shows. Jan Catoen escaped from prison, however, and attempted to organize a new band in Zeeland during the late 1790s. Among the men he invited were Francis (Cis) Mertens from Tongerlo or Antwerp and several former fellow inhabitants of 't Heike: the brothers Jan and Andries Jaspers, and Kees de Bruijn, who had been living for some time with Thona (Anthonia) Jaspers, a sister of Hendrik Jaspers. The 'new' Catoen Band was not a success. It remained small and lacked both cohesion and continuity. Jan Catoen and Cis Mertens were finally hanged at Middelburg in 1802.[21]

This short detour along the sundry illegal activities of 't Heike's inhabitants has brought us back to the Jaspers family and thus to the issue of the connections between late eighteenth-century bands. It was to the villagers of 't Heike – in particular to Jan and Andries Jaspers, their kinsman Kees de Bruijn, and Cis Mertens – that the captains of the Holland branch of the Great Dutch Band turned when their band extended its operations from Holland to the south and south-west in 1797–8. They needed experienced band members who were familiar with western Brabant as well as the islands of South Holland and Zeeland. By hiring these four men they gained access, in a manner of speaking, to the accumulated criminal expertise of the whole community of 't Heike. This is how the first strand of the Brabant connection came into being.

The link between northern and southern bands remained tenuous. As we saw in the previous chapter, the Great Dutch Band formed a large, loose-knit, and internationally operating network, in which men from diverse regional and cultural backgrounds worked together. Apart from a few Jews, its Holland branch included Germans, Hollanders, and men from the southern Netherlands as well as the small division formed by the Jaspersens, Mertens, and De Bruijn. Like the rest of the band, these Brabanders spent much of their time in Amsterdam and Rotterdam; some of them married or lived with women from Holland, and in many respects they seem to have felt at home there. Yet, other than the Jews, the Brabanders were the only ones who remained a distinct contingent in the band. They stayed together, visiting taverns, going to markets and fairs, working, and stealing. They even bought a small barge, ostensibly for the transport and sale of potatoes, but actually (according to their fellow band members) to enable them to go out stealing by themselves. It is no coincidence that they were regularly referred to as 'the Brabanders' by their colleagues (see Egmond 1986, pp. 54–5).

The partial integration of the Brabanders in the Great Dutch Band epitomizes the tentative character of this first strand of the Brabant connection and the still strongly regional orientation of 'the southerners'. The initiative for cooperation had not come from them, after all, but from the chief commanders of the Great Dutch Band. While there were certainly more contacts between the criminal circuits of Holland and western Brabant, they had as yet failed to attain any degree of permanence.

The Second Strand of the Brabant Connection

The history of the Jaspers family has shown how by the end of the eighteenth century increasing mobility and the growth of interconnectedness among groups operating within Brabant had resulted in a tentative link between the criminal circuits of western Brabant and Holland: the first strand of the Brabant connection. The following history of the Albert family reveals how connections between the bands operating in central and eastern Brabant multiplied, just like those in the western half, and eventually led to the second strand of the Brabant connection. The Alberts' activities also illustrate how the Dutch authorities managed to increase their control over the countryside just when a more structural integration of the Dutch rural underworld seemed imminent.

For a first reference to the Albert family in the criminal records we have to go back to the late 1770s and move to the border area of Brabant, Utrecht, Holland, and Gelderland. Between about 1776 and 1783 a vagrant band of about fifty people in all operated in this region: the Thorn-bush Band, named after an eighteen-year-old boy called Hermanus Caspar le Dove, alias the Water Rat, Manus the Fiddler, or the Little Thorn-bush. Most members came from the villages of Loon op Zand or Oss in the northern part of Dutch Brabant bordering on the river Maas; the reputation of the latter has already been mentioned. The extensive Rustevelt–van Gaalen clan formed the backbone of the band, but the oldest and most redoubtable band member was Christ the Skinner (de Vilder) from Oss, who was born about 1723 and described as follows:

> average height, relatively thickset, with black curly hair, full face, walks in a slightly lopsided manner, with a cut on the right cheek; on his left hand he has a little bit more than the thumb and first finger, having shot off the rest. He is married to Fair [Schoone] Kaat, alias Skinner's Kate, and has Willemijn Rustevelt for a mistress.[22]

Members of this band spent a large part of the year on the road. Some earned a living as pedlars and fiddlers, others begged, sold medicines, and served intermittently as soldiers. Men as well as women and children toured the countryside and slept in barns and haystacks. Their illegal activities consisted largely of petty theft (stealing from walled gardens, barns, stables, cellars, and occasionally shops) and, more rarely, of burglary and robbery.[23]

Several members of the Albert family belonged to this band: Joseph Albert, alias the Frenchman (de Fransman), his son Jacobus, his daughter Marie Elisabeth, alias Mie the Frenchman (de Fransman) or Frenchman's Mie, and her husband, Frederik van Yzendoorn (see Table 4). Joseph Albert was indeed a Frenchman, born in 1728 at La Croisette in the Languedoc. He must have migrated to the Netherlands when still relatively young, for both his first and second wives were Dutch. There were five children from his first marriage and two small children from the second. According to one of his sons, the family used to spend part

Table 4 The Albert Family and Their Involvement in Bands

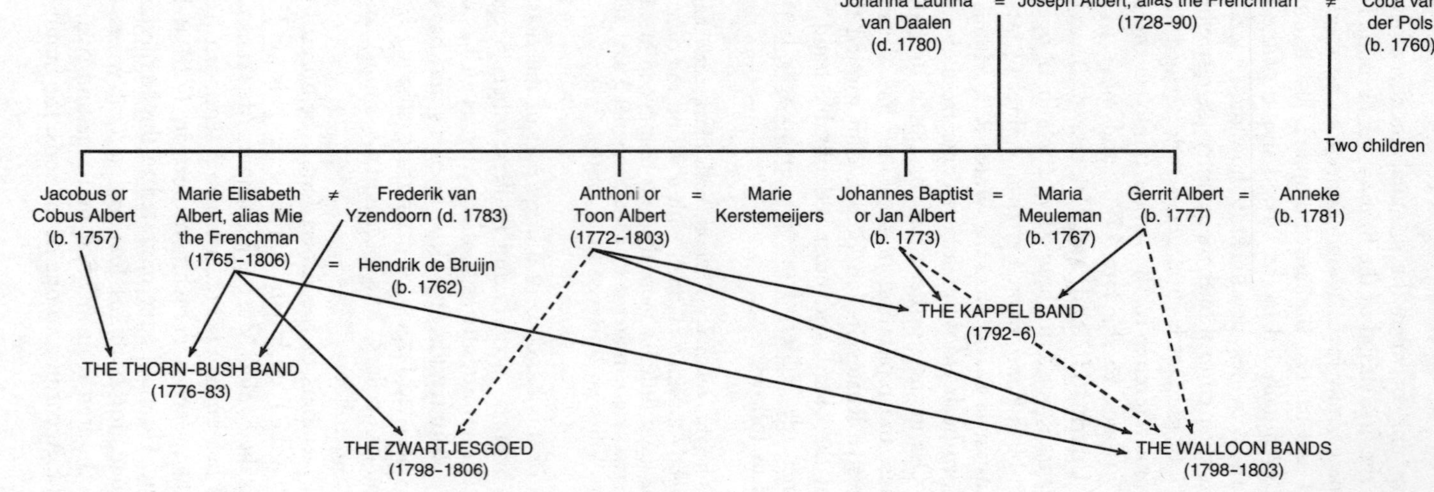

of the winter at 's Hertogenbosch. During the rest of the year they toured the countryside of Brabant while begging, mending chairs, and hawking. Joseph himself occasionally crossed the rivers into Holland in order to find casual jobs as a rural labourer, and two or three of his sons briefly served as soldiers. The women generally begged, collected and sold rags, hawked, took care of the children, and intermittently worked as seamstresses and cleaning women.

Albert senior was well known as a thief, but the second generation of the Albert family is of more interest here. They participated in four major bands between about 1778 and 1806, most of which were in their turn linked to other criminal groups and networks. The range of the family as a whole may be compared with that of Nathan Moses, whose personal network covered parts of nearly every Jewish (and a few non-Jewish) bands operating in the Dutch Republic during a period of nearly forty years. In a similar way the ramifications of the Alberts' personal networks highlight the interconnectedness of the Brabant bands of the late eighteenth century.

By the early 1790s the younger siblings of Mie the Frenchman and her brother Jacobus had begun to make a criminal reputation for themselves. Jan, Gerrit, and Toon Albert – collectively nicknamed the Frenchman's Boys – were becoming important figures in the Kappel Band, which specialized in armed attacks on farms, shops, Roman Catholic churches, and the houses of priests in the region of Eindhoven and the northern part of Brabant along the river Maas.[24] During the robberies most members carried arms; some had blackened their faces, rather like the Zwartmakers of the 1690s. Operating in groups of about six to ten, the men rammed open doors, tied up and occasionally beat the inhabitants, and plundered their houses. The booty usually consisted of money, silver, gold, jewellery, church valuables, linen, and textiles. During its first phase (1792–4) the home base of this Kappel Band was Eindhoven, or rather a tavern at Eindhoven called de Reijsende Man (The journeyman). The innkeeper, Sebastiaan Kappel, acted as the central figure of the band. Several smaller taverns further to the north were likewise used by the band, but the Kappel inn remained their principal base until a series of arrests cut short their exploits in 1794.[25] The Albert brothers and the rest of the band were soon back into business, however. They moved their base to a hamlet near Oss and directed their expeditions of the years 1795 and 1796 at the north-eastern part of Brabant.

Among the most interesting features of the Kappel Band is the prominence of ex-soldiers during its first phase and of former constables in the second. The presence of former soldiers among the members of any band operating in the Brabant during the early 1790s was only to be expected – French, Dutch, Austrian, and German armies were contesting precisely this area at the time. (In 1792–3 the French advance through the southern Netherlands and Dutch Brabant had stopped just short of the river Maas. The defeat at Neerwinden forced the French armies to retreat for the time being, but during 1794 they reoccupied most of the Dutch Brabant and in the winter of 1794–5 they marched on into the northern provinces.) Just like the Zwartmakers and Moskovieters of a hundred years before, these soldiers did not participate in band activities because of lack of military employment. Most of them were professionals with an extensive knowledge of the military trade. Georg Herlein's case is typical. Born in Germany around 1764, he fought with the Hessian troops in North America and on his return to Hessen served for another two years. After working for two years as a tailor, he again joined a German company, but deserted five years later. He travelled to the Netherlands and worked as a rural labourer near Oss; having fetched his wife and two children from Germany, he went back to Brabant, where he became involved with the Kappel Band.[26] A similar story was told by Johannes Scheffers Deckers.[27] He was born at Oss in 1756 and served for about sixteen years in a German company. Twice during this period he deserted – once to enlist with the Austrian troops, with whom he stayed for six years – but each time he eventually returned to his old regiment. When he joined the Kappel Band he had once again deserted and was trying to earn a living in his native region by selling and buying rags and scrap. By this time he was not a newcomer to the illegal business. Fourteen years earlier (about 1780) he had committed a few burglaries and thefts with two close friends and associates. Their names will sound familiar: both Christ the Skinner and Cees van Gaalen (Rustevelt) were important members of the Thorn-bush Band at that time.

The Kappel Band resembled the military bands of the late seventeenth century in more than one respect. It operated during (and not after) a period of warfare; its main expeditions affected areas just outside the battle zone; it included deserters and men still in active service rather than disbanded soldiers; and, like its predecessors, it was made up almost completely of local people. Innkeepers and village constables epitomize the importance of these local 'roots'. Among a total of thirty-five to forty band members we find at least three innkeepers (besides Sebastiaan Kappel himself) and five constables. They must have been extremely useful to the band for more or less the same reasons. Both occupied strategic positions in the local community, gathering, distributing, and controlling information.[28]

The Kappel Band was a traditional Brabant band in most ways, yet its outlook was less confined and its boundary less strictly defined than had been the case in former times. Several members of the Kappel circuit were at the same time involved in other bands – just like the Alberts – and intricate family ties linked the Kappel Band to at least four other groups active in Brabant during the 1790s. One example serves to illustrate the labyrinthine character of these connections. Five members of the Kappel Band also participated in the band of Jacobus Geerts, alias Luije Maan, which concentrated its activities in western Brabant (1790–3).[29] One of these five men – Pieter Paans – had previously been connected with the Catoen Band of 't Heike, just like Stinus de Groot, alias Stien Pape, who was the stepson of Jan Baptist van Veen, a member of both the Kappel Band and Jacobus Geerts's group. Two of Pieter Paans's brothers subsequently joined the small band of the basket weavers Jacob and Hendrik Blok (1795–6).[30] The connections between the Kappel Band and several other bands active in Brabant during the late 1790s and early 1800s followed much the same pattern.

The general impression, then, of late eighteenth-century rural bands active in Brabant is one of a multitude of small to medium-sized local and vagrant bands, and a small number of large and loose-knit networks, almost all of which were connected by intricate ties of kinship, locality, occupation, and, of course, complicity. Most of these groups closely resembled their predecessors: nearly all shared a predominantly rural orientation, strong local ties, and a relatively homogeneous composition. They consisted mainly of indigenous 'professional' vagrants and semi-itinerant local people with a low income, low social status, and (often) military experience.

In some respects, however, the bands of the 1790s were clearly different. Mobility had increased; communication between the various districts of Brabant was becoming more frequent, and connections between the numerous local and vagrant groups were multiplying. No doubt this was partly a consequence of revolutionary and wartime conditions. But the proliferation of bands in rural Brabant during the 1780s and 1790s should also be seen in the context of mass impoverishment in the whole of western Europe during the second half of the century. It cannot be a coincidence that from the 1760s onwards we hear of more and more second- or even third-generation vagrancy, begging, and serious crime. More often than before, whole families seem to have become involved in illegal activities.

It may have been the demise of the Kappel Band which inspired the Alberts to join a new and in many respects foreign association. During the 1780s and early 1790s the five Albert siblings had usually belonged to different bands, but by 1800 all of them except the eldest, Jacob, had joined a large and predominantly Walloon network, the Band of

Dossain and Prudhomme (1798–1803).[31] A list drawn up in 1802 and used by the authorities to trace members of this network describes Toon Albert and his sister Mie the Frenchman as follows:

> *Toon Albert,* otherwise called Frenchman's Toon, thirty-eight years old; is short and fat . . . pock-marked, but pale and narrow faced; black, slightly curly hair, the nose a bit broad and swollen; with fat legs, but small feet, and graceful of gait. Speaks *Hollands* [Dutch] well; dressed probably in a blue serge coat with a broad collar; wearing a fine three-cornered hat . . . he has served in the army of Holland, and may have been whipped at 's Hertogenbosch. He is a knife-grinder; his barrow is painted blue with red trimmings. His wife or mistress is of average size; she has red hair and is called Mie Kerstemeijer or Tonia, who is slightly hunchbacked or has one shoulder higher than the other. He is also accompanied by a boy called Piet who is a fiddler, and by a girl of about ten to eleven years old; and also by a big black and white dog (more black than white), sleek haired and with small ears. This man spends much time in the region of Cleves, also in the area between the rivers Maas and Waal . . . and at Easter he can usually be found at an inn between Megen and Macharen [northern border of Brabant]; also on the Veluwe . . . and along the river Linge. He is the brother-in-law of Hendrik de Bruijn, and is at the moment in North Holland.
>
> *Mie Albert*, aged about thirty, neither fat nor thin, and fairly short; with beautiful long black hair, black eyes and ditto large eyebrows, pock-marked, and dark skinned; a short pointed nose, narrow thin lips, cultivated speech, with a proud air and gait, fat legs, and generally poorly dressed.[32]

The Band of Dossain and Prudhomme committed illegal activities ranging from petty theft, vagrancy, and begging, to burglary, armed robbery, and finally murder and robbery. The band eventually included seventy to a hundred people in all, but it started as a rather smaller conglomerate of immigrant Walloons from the region of Liège and Luxembourg. Most of them had left the southern Netherlands to find work as rural labourers in Dutch Brabant. Some had already committed thefts and burglaries in their native region.[33] In Brabant this band soon attracted new members: among them were the Alberts as well as several other former members of the Kappel Band and related groups. The influx of Brabanders did not turn the Dossain and Prudhomme network into a typical 'Brabant' band. Instead, the reverse happened. It remained a network of itinerant (often French-speaking) men and a few women, most of whom lacked close ties to any particular Dutch area, while Brabanders who had joined the band found themselves moving out of their own territory when the Dossain and Prudhomme network gradually extended and eventually shifted its operations to the north and north-east. From the central and eastern parts of Brabant it slowly moved to the area between the big rivers, to Gelderland, the Veluwe and Overijssel, and to adjacent German territory. Toon, Gerrit, Jan, and Mie Albert moved along. Gerrit and Jan remained peripheral members and seem to have been able to avoid detention. After, that is, a brief spell in 1797 at 's Hertogenbosch and Nijmegen on account of their activities with the Kappel Band; both escaped from prison in Nijmegen. Gerrit and Jan earned a living as casual rural labourers and chair-menders. Toon reached a prominent position in the band, and was punished accordingly: he and two of his colleagues were the only band members to be sentenced to aggravated death penalties by the Hof van Gelre (1803). They were partly strangled and then broken on the wheel. Several others were hanged or sentenced to combinations of whipping, branding, and banishment.[34]

For their sister, Mie Albert, the same transfer to the north opened up new sections of the Walloon network as well as yet another criminal circuit: the Zwartjesgoed (1798–1806).[35] Together the Dossain and Prudhomme Band and the Zwartjesgoed may be regarded as the second strand of the Brabant connection, linking southern and northern criminal circuits. The two bands were quite different, however. Whereas the Walloons had shifted their activities from Brabant to the north, the Zwartjesgoed originated as an interregional band which from the start operated all over the Dutch Republic and 'absorbed' new band members from diverse cultural and regional backgrounds. Its name – het Zwartjesgoed (Black fry) or de Zwarten (Blacks) – like so many other names of robber bands suggests dark skins, perhaps even gypsies, and at least hints at obscure and dangerous nightly exploits.

Many band members were dark skinned, and the link with gypsies is less far-fetched than it may seem. In a letter to one of his colleagues, bailiff Meuleman of Woerden, the principal prosecutor of the band, bailiff F. Blok of the court of Rijnland describes the wife of a senior band member, Harmen Hendriks Wijnands, as follows: 'She is fifty-two years old . . . rather small of stature, has a face like a *heijden*, black, grubby, peculiar eyes with the eyelids drawn down; wears a pelerine; is very brown of hands.'[36] Some of the members themselves referred to a gypsy background. It was Mie Albert, in fact, who stated that the Wijnands family was known as 'the Blacks because they are *heijdens*'.[37] Not only appearance but language as well pointed to gypsy influence. Several band members spoke a 'peculiar language, called *rommisceers*', a name that cannot but refer to some type of Romany language.[38]

It would be a mistake, though, to infer that gypsies had suddenly returned to the Netherlands. Characteristic gypsy names and occupations (such as fortune-telling) were lacking in the Zwartjesgoed, and band members did not build huts or live in tents. The case of the Zwartjesgoed rather shows to what extent gypsies had become integrated into the larger mass of vagrant and itinerant poor in the Dutch republic. By the early 1800s some noticeably dark skins, occasional references to a *heijdense* background, and some knowledge of a Romany language appear to be all that was left of gypsy identity.

Even a brief inspection of the backgrounds of a dozen or so men and women arrested and sentenced in Holland in the course of 1805–6 reveals that the Zwartjesgoed drew upon a range of different cultural and criminal traditions. Among those denoted as 'blacks' we find a very senior band member, Harmen Hendriks Wijnands, a fifty-year-old knife-grinder from Groningen; his wife, Elisabeth Walters (described above), who sang songs and sold them from door to door; and their son Harmen Hendriks Wijnands Junior, born in Friesland, also a knife-grinder. Hanna Broens from Hamburg and Hannes Baptist, a 32-year-old knife-grinder and ex-soldier born in Amsterdam, belonged to the same category. Mie the Frenchman and her husband Hendrik de Bruijn need no introduction. Among the 'non-blacks' were Walloons from the environs of Liège as well as immigrant German rural labourers, Dutch girls who had run away from an orphanage, former seamen from the coastal towns of northern Germany and Holland, a Dutch puppeteer and fiddler from The Hague, a Hungarian ex-hussar, beggar, and former stocking weaver, an itinerant German quack, and several more knife-grinders, chair-menders, tinkers, fiddlers, and vagrant actors of uncertain regional provenance.[39]

In many respects the Zwartjesgoed was quite unlike its counterpart, the Great Dutch Band, which formed the first strand of the Brabant connection. Its size and territorial range were smaller; it had neither a hierarchy nor different segments; and band members with a strongly urban orientation (such as the Jews and Hollanders whose presence marked the Great Dutch Band) played a minor role. Yet in its own way the Zwartjesgoed was as much an extensive, loose-knit network as the Great Dutch Band. Both combined a composite structure, mobility, and a large interregional and occasionally international field of operations. Both drew upon a wide range of criminal traditions, and both strands of the Brabant connection only came into being during (and perhaps thanks to) a period of extraordinary political and administrative change. The itinerary of the French armies – who crossed the frozen rivers during the winter of 1794–5 and marched to the north, from Brabant into Utrecht and Holland – as well as the French plans for the political integration and unification of the Dutch Republic almost literally pointed the way to all kinds of interprovincial communication. Boundaries that had served as barriers were slowly breaking down.

The consequences of this affected the Zwartjesgoed and Great Dutch Band alike. The activities of the two alarmed both the rural population and the local authorities to an uncommon degree. Confronted by these mobile offenders, bailiffs recognized the necessity of mutual assistance. They could avoid cooperation no longer; some even appealed to higher judicial and administrative echelons for assistance and protection. The robberies of the Great Dutch Band had been noted mainly for the huge amounts of money and valuables stolen, and for their efficient execution and predominantly non-violent character. (Victims were often trussed up, though, and locked in cellars or attics.) The Zwartjesgoed, by contrast, became known for its excessive and ostensibly random violence. This band interspersed its 'everyday' illegal activities – such as begging, vagrancy, shoplifting, and petty theft at fairs and markets – with several extremely brutal murders and robberies.

The first one in particular caused general shock and outrage among the rural population of South Holland. Reactions included requests for police protection and for an increase in the number of nightwatchmen and the frequency of nightly patrols by local civil guards. What exactly had happened? In October 1798 approximately ten members of the Zwartjesgoed – including Harmen Hendriks Wijnands, his son Harmen Junior and Mie the Frenchman – waited until the last customer had left a small tavern called the Halfway House or the Last Penny, which lay halfway between The Hague and the coastal village of Loosduinen. At about 10.30 they broke into the house through a back door and immediately attacked the owners (an elderly couple), who were half asleep. The robbers had brought pistols, knives, a sabre, and several wooden clubs. Both victims were brutally battered and stabbed to death: the autopsy showed that their heads had been bashed in and each had received about ten wounds. Most of the men then sat down beside the bodies and drank some gin before proceeding to ransack the house, taking cash and valuables worth about 1,200 or 1,300 guilders. Similar violence accompanied the robberies of a postilion (October 1799, near Leiden), a travelling salesman (around October 1799, not far from Groningen), a travelling saleswoman (summer 1804, between Utrecht and Amersfoort), and a skipper from Groningen (February or March 1805, near Zaltbommel). All of them were brutally murdered. On two occasions, moreover, constables who threatened the band's safety lost their lives: in 1801 or 1802 the members killed a constable or bailiff's assistant on the road between Putten and Nijkerk shortly after having robbed a shop near Putten, and around 1803 they murdered a constable (using a knife and a pistol) between Dordrecht and Gorinchem the morning after they had robbed a house near Gorinchem.[40]

As noted before, such violence was rare in the province of Holland, and it may have been the infrequency of such acts as much as their brutality and ruthlessness that caused vehement reactions. Feelings of shock and outrage reverberate in the sentences of most band members: 'they had not been harmed or insulted by any of their victims, but had murdered them for foul profits alone, and to get hold of their money and goods'. A female band member who tried to find excuses by pointing 'to misguidance by others, to a bad education and poverty, and finally that God has deprived her of her reason' was reproached by the court for 'imputing as it were, even indirectly, her own vices to the Supreme Being, and locating them outside her own person'.[41] Mie Albert's sentence was no different from any of the men's – she appears to have been one of the very few women in the band who participated actively in at least some of the armed robberies. After being questioned eighteen times between February 1805 and the beginning of 1806 Mie the Frenchman was finally hanged at Rotterdam on 5 March 1806.[42]

The arrest of Mie Albert was part of a more general 'round-up' of members of the Zwartjesgoed. In the course of 1805 and 1806 courts at Leiden, Rotterdam, Oudewater, The Hague, Woerden, Naarden, and Schagen pronounced sentences against twenty-six band members: thirteen were condemned to death and several others were sentenced to periods of detention ranging from ten to fifty years. The demise of the Zwartjesgoed – like the downfall of the Great Dutch Band during 1799–1800 (see Egmond 1986) – was the outcome of increased cooperation among the numerous local courts of Holland (see especially the correspondence between bailiff Blok and his colleagues, which also refers to the state of alarm among the local population).[43] Bailiffs began to inform their colleagues about the results of interrogations and even met once or twice to discuss further measures. They sometimes allowed each other the use of their prisons to prevent the numerous suspects from passing on information from one cell to another in their 'secret' language. Some of the most active local bailiffs frequently contacted the prosecutor general (Procureur Generaal) of the provincial Hof van Holland at The Hague.[44]

Such forms of cooperation should not be regarded as structural judicial reorganizations, however (cf. van Weel 1989 and Zwaardemaker 1939). As yet they were largely *ad hoc* measures, initiated and activated in the case of the Great Dutch Band by this same prosecutor general, C.F. van Maanen, and in the case of the Zwartjesgoed by both van Maanen and bailiff Blok of Rijnland. Cooperation depended to a large extent on their personal contacts. As soon as the two criminal networks had been eliminated, each local court again concentrated on its own business. Even in the midst of the prosecutions against members of the Zwartjesgoed, rivalry among local bailiffs had by no means disappeared. Considerable friction arose for example, between bailiff Blok of Rijnland and the town court of Leiden over the transfer of an important band member from one jurisdiction to the other. Each wanted the public acclaim of sentencing and executing such a key criminal.

Still, the initiatives of van Maanen and Blok, the slowly increasing willingness of the local courts to cooperate, and the concerted efforts of the judicial authorities formed part of the gradual judicial centralization and unification of the northern Netherlands. Privileges and boundaries that had protected local and regional 'autonomy' in the past were slowly being broken down. With regard to the organization of criminal prosecution, this process can be traced back to the first treaties concerning interprovincial judicial cooperation against the gypsy bands of the 1720s. It gained momentum during the French 'occupation' of the Netherlands and culminated in the legal, political, and administrative measures of 1798, 1806, and finally 1810, when the Netherlands became part of France.[45]

During the French revolutionary period the same political and administrative developments that stimulated interregional mobility and the concomitant cooperation of criminal circuits thus contributed to similar developments on the side of their opponents. As we have seen, these were initial stages of integration on both sides. Intermittent forms of cooperation and association which depended to a large extent on personal contacts were characteristic of both criminal networks and judicial authorities. Whereas political, administrative, and judicial integration eventually proved to have lasting effects, the western and the eastern branches of the Brabant connection were cut short when contacts between the various circuits had just begun to develop and multiply.[46] Neither branch constituted a permanent link between northern and southern bands. The Brabant connection did not prefigure a general integration of the criminal networks operating in the Dutch Republic – but it might have done so.

Part V

Conclusion

9

Contrasting Designs

During the seventeenth and eighteenth centuries, as we saw in the first chapter, continuities prevailed in the terminology and concepts used by the Dutch judiciary to describe, define, and condemn people involved in rural organized crime. The few changes that occurred seemed to point to an increasing sense of distance between respectable citizens (as represented by local judicial authorities) and the 'infamous' part of the nation. Regional differences in terminology, though, were noticeable. If we take the case-studies into account, the parallels between linguistic continuity and regional differences in terminology on the one hand and the actual chronology and geography of organized crime on the other are difficult to ignore.

Chronology

The most striking characteristic of the chronology of Dutch rural organized crime is its lack of unity. The chronology of indigenous (non-ethnic) bands did not correspond with that of either Jewish or gypsy groups, and the Brabant bands were often – though not always – most active at times when bands in Holland kept fairly quiet. Each type of band followed a different chronological course. If we put all of them together for a moment, their activities form an intricate and nearly continuous pattern.

Whereas the 1650s, 1660s, and 1670s saw the growth of loose-knit 'post-war networks' in Holland and Zeeland, the 1680s to 1710s were dominated by an apparent explosion of urban organized crime in these parts, matched by the upsurge of wartime banditry in southern rural districts. At the same time – in particular between 1690 and 1725–30 – gypsy bands became increasingly active, only to be wiped out almost completely during the 1720s and early 1730s, when a number of smaller, loose-knit vagrant groups took over in Holland, Utrecht, Zeeland, Brabant, and Gelderland. Jewish bands became prominent only from the late 1720s onwards; they formed particularly extensive networks during the 1740s and 1750s, and continued to grow and branch out into numerous types of property crime until the end of the eighteenth century, when they dominated the international network of the Great Dutch Band.

The elimination of gypsy bands around the late 1720s, the temporary decline of urban organized crime after about 1720 (it revived spectacularly during the final decades of the century), the disappearance of the major wartime bands which had been active in Brabant between 1690 and 1718, and the relatively unspectacular activities of the rural bands which continued to be active in the countryside of Holland, Utrecht, and Brabant all contributed to the comparative calm of the 1740s and early 1750s. Jewish bands were nearly the only ones to bridge this 'gap' of the mid eighteenth century.[1] From the early 1750s onwards the reverse process can be observed. In Brabant big, loose-knit networks reappeared, drawing on family traditions and connections which might date back to the 1720s and 1730s. Descendants of formerly well-known gypsy families joined non-gypsy travellers; Jewish networks were expanding and formed tentative connections with non-Jewish bands. By the early 1760s the Rabonus Band, whose composition was mixed – part gypsy, part Christian, part Jewish – was operating all over the Netherlands. In Brabant regional bands were gradually broadening their territory and increasing their mutual connections during the last quarter of the eighteenth century. The 1790s in particular saw the rise of the composite interregional networks, but these never completely supplanted the more 'old-fashioned' regional Christian bands and mobile Jewish networks. By this time gypsy bands had disappeared completely – most probably because gypsies had been absorbed by the growing mass of vagrant poor.

It makes far more sense, however, not to force all these different bands into one 'neat' chronology, since there was no corresponding general development of rural organized crime in the Netherlands. On the whole bands did not become larger – or smaller – in the course of the seventeenth and eighteenth centuries; there was no question of increasing specialization, a growing division of labour, drastically new techniques, or of centralization in the rural 'criminal circuit' as a whole. To put it briefly: organized rural crime did not become more (or less) professional in the period 1650–1800. If we consider the size of networks, their structure and hierarchy, leadership, access to the criminal infrastructure as well as planning and technical expertise, specialization, and mobility, some bands were obviously more professional than others. But the most professional groups can be found both at the beginning and at the end of the eighteenth century, or for that matter during the 1650s, the 1760s, or the 1780s. Was the Jaco Band of the 1710s any less professional than the Great Dutch Band of the 1790s? And how about the large segmented network of the Brabant Zwartmakers (1690s) versus the Jewish Feijtsburger Band (1760s)? Small, un-hierarchical vagrant bands which regularly committed property crimes but did not specialize can likewise be found at any time during the period 1650–1810.

The slow increase of cooperation and association between the diverse ethnic and Christian bands and the concomitant 'disappearance' of gypsy bands during the second half of the eighteenth century were the most drastic changes to take place during the whole period. As we have seen, cooperation and various forms of association did not result in mergers, except in the special case of the gypsies. The interconnections between the northern and southern criminal circuits – that is, the two branches of the Brabant connection in the shape of the Great Dutch Band and the Walloon and Zwartjesgoed networks – only came into being in (and probably depended on) the special circumstances of the revolutionary years 1789–1806. Even these new north–south connections did not result in an integrated criminal circuit, let alone in a centrally organized rural underworld. There was never such a thing as one criminal circuit or one underworld in the Netherlands; not even, it seems, in the minds of the authorities, who never managed to think of one term covering all the groups involved in rural organized crime.

There existed no dangerous or subversive criminal counter-society or counter-culture, then, in the Dutch Republic. (In so far as organized rural crime represented social protest – as may well have been the case in the ethnic bands and in some of the military bands active in Brabant – this protest remained verbally inarticulate, and was certainly not recognized as such by the rural population.) Nor did the world of crime form a homogeneous, infamous domain, even though it was separated and excluded – in terms of the social hierarchy – from 'respectable', established Dutch society by legal and social rules. If we look at its organization, it was internally divided in two (by no means totally separate) large segments: the urban underworld with its overlapping networks of thieves and burglars; and the rural domain of mobile and often vagrant bands, which comprised many underworlds. Culturally, it consisted of many different circuits, based on ethnicity, regional background, occupational specialization, and so on. Contacts between these segments were infrequent, especially during the period 1650–1750, and increasing cooperation during the second half of the eighteenth century did not result, as we saw, in cultural integration. In none of these segments did 'crime' form a constitutive element of group culture: band members generally continued to observe the religious customs, follow the naming patterns, speak the language, and hold on to the occupational specializations and gender roles of the larger 'subculture' to which they belonged. That there was never one thieves' language in the Dutch Republic is worthy of note.

The absence of any general long-term development should make us question the value of several ideas and opinions which surface again and again in discussions about historical crime patterns. One of these persistent notions regards the eighteenth century as *the* age of banditry (as compared with the seventeenth century), and either explicitly or implicitly links the supposed increase of band activity to the demographic growth, rising food prices, and increasing numbers of poor and vagrant people of the decades after 1740. A second one, which can still be found in many surveys of modern crime, lumps together all kinds of property crime – ranging from petty theft and shoplifting to armed robbery and professional urban burglary – for no other reason, it seems, than that they are all covered by the (modern) term property crime. Again, the main purpose is usually to relate rising crime rates to economic depression and increasing poverty.

Information about eighteenth-century bands is certainly much more abundant than about their seventeenth- or sixteenth-century colleagues (except for a few towns in Holland, Dutch sixteenth-century criminal records are scarce and fragmentary).[2] But the available evidence does not point to important qualitative differences. The activities of, for instance, the Band of Hees (1650s) and Stoffel van Reenen's group (1660s) in Holland, and the exploits of the big military bands of the 1690s in Brabant definitely matched those of their eighteenth-century colleagues. Should we therefore infer a smaller amount of seventeenth-century band activity simply from the more fragmentary character of surviving seventeenth-century records? The image of the eighteenth century as the age of banditry may, in other words, rest completely on the more exhaustive information we have about this period. (This might also apply to other west-European countries, in particular Germany, for there too seventeenth-century political and administrative conditions did little to contribute to continuous registration or undamaged survival of local court records.)

Dutch evidence confirmed the the conclusion reached by Hay and Beattie for England: organized crime followed different patterns from petty theft, and links between crime and poverty were anything but simple and direct. Certain types of theft did indeed coincide with periods of scarcity and high food prices. During the early 1740s numerous poor families living in the towns of Holland started stealing fruit, bread, cabbages, and peat at the height of scarcity. Organized crime, however, kept remarkably quiet during this period. All over Holland, Zeeland, and Brabant the 1740s were among the most 'peaceful' years of the period 1650–1800, whereas the first few decades of the eighteenth century – a phase of relative prosperity – were notable for the proliferation of many different types of bands.

Yet it is nearly impossible not to search for links between the growing interconnectedness of organized rural crime during the last three or four decades of the eighteenth century and the swelling numbers of poor and vagrant men and women looking for work and assistance all over Europe.[3] The increasing sense of distance between the judicial authorities and the vagrant part of the population – as conveyed by the terminology used in criminal sentences – perfectly matches the growing distance between the well-to-do and the poor. Whatever their regional, ethnic, or non-ethnic background, or their area of operations, rural bands consisted exclusively of poor men and women, most of whom tried to earn a living by a combination of various seasonal activities which required little capital investment. They mended chairs, grinded knives and scissors, performed at fairs as jugglers, actors, and musicians, sang songs from door to door, and sold anything from glasses and mirrors to lace and haberdashery, pills and ointments, large quantities of textiles, or pots and pans. During the winters they begged or prepared their stocks for the summer season. Quite a few of the men had served as soldiers. Some had worked as artisans and combined spinning, weaving, making lace, knitting, carding wool, making clay pipes, cutting tobacco, or repairing shoes with summertime casual rural labour. Most of them begged – occasionally, seasonally, or full time.

Links between poverty and organized crime were indirect, however; other factors also contributed to the growth of a reserve of potential recruits for band membership and thus influenced the chronology of organized crime. In England the combination of economic factors and warfare proved to be especially relevant to fluctuations in serious property crime. The absence of many lower-class young men during periods of warfare considerably lowered the amount of property crime. In the Netherlands too fluctations in certain types of rural property crime were linked to periods of warfare – at least from the 1620s to the first decades of the eighteenth century. Thereafter the Dutch Republic largely withdrew from European warfare until the 1790s. Dutch criminal chronology differed drastically from one area to another, though, and it was only the non-ethnic bands which presented a war-related sequence. In Holland, as in England, such bands became particularly active just after periods of war; in Brabant, by contrast, military bands operated during these phases, while other non-ethnic groups could be found both during periods of warfare and in between. On the activities of ethnic groups – gypsies and east-European Jews – warfare had hardly any influence at all, except in so far as peace was conducive to long-distance travel in Europe.

For the Netherlands migration should be added to economic conditions and warfare as a major influence on the long-term chronology of organized crime. Even a short list of examples shows as much: the numerous groups of English vagrants of the 1620s; the fairly large proportion of Flemings in the post-war bands of the 1650s and 1660s; the Jewish and gypsy bands that date back no further than the 1690s; the Walloon bands of the 1780s and 1790s, and so on. The advent of each major new wave of poor immigrants – whether Flemish, English, Walloon, Jewish, or gypsy – was reflected in the composition of rural bands. Of course, immigration patterns do not explain the prominence of 'outsiders' in rural bands, but they make clear why the involvement of certain groups was linked to certain periods.

Poverty was often closely intertwined with social exclusion. One would have to be blind to ignore the desperate economic condition of the east-European Jews who had recently immigrated, many of whom joined the large criminal networks of the 1750s, 1770s, and 1790s. They had left eastern Europe because of political and religious persecution, social stigmatization, lack of economic opportunities, or a combination of these factors. On their arrival in the Netherlands they met with religious tolerance and could often rely on members of the large community of Ashkenazim in Amsterdam for temporary assistance. As in Germany, however, Jews were barred from many professions by civil law. Most of them eventually ended up in retail trade, which required little training or capital; it also provided a perfect cover for various illegal activities. It was the generally suspected combination of legal and illegal dealings that gave many poor Ashkenazim their bad reputation. As a consequence they were excluded twice over: by Dutch citizens and by established Ashkenazim and Sephardim, who took care not to let their own reputations suffer by contact with their 'infamous' fellow Jews.

The social exclusion of gypsies went even further: unlike that of any other group in Dutch society, their way of life itself had been declared punishable by criminal law. Yet in some respects their position was extremely ambiguous. (It is even difficult to decide whether gypsies were actually poor. Most probably were, but the way in which large sums of stolen money were apparently collected by band leaders – perhaps to be redistributed – at least raises questions about relative poverty and wealth. Nor can the theft of poultry, bread, peat, and farm utensils by itinerant gypsy families be understood in terms of destitution alone.) Gypsies provided important services by repairing pots, pans, and buckets, selling ointments and pills, telling fortunes, playing the fiddle, showing off their animals, and generally offering entertainment to the rural population. In spite of the considerable social distance and their formally illegal way of life, in spite of their reputation as dangerous but fascinating strangers, the women in particular were admitted to the houses of many rural families to look at a child who had fallen ill, to read palms, or to tell stories. Contacts with the local population were close and distant at the same time; the arrival of gypsies brought enjoyment as well as apprehension.

This uneasy combination of economic interdependence and alternating intimacy and social stigmatization decisively changed for the worse during the 1680s and 1690s. By then gypsies were apparently beginning to arrive in the northern Netherlands in larger numbers than before. The rural population soon felt threatened by their companies; the Dutch authorities issued harsh placards and punished more severely. Gypsies closed ranks; some became involved in organized and armed robbery. Both sides used more and more violence. This escalation had ended in the nearly total disappearance of gypsies from the Netherlands by the late 1720s. Many had been sentenced to death or to long terms of imprisonment, and many had fled the Dutch Republic. After about 1730 those who still remained were either in prison or had begun to ally themselves with other vagrant groups. During the rest of the eighteenth century gypsies were slowly absorbed by these groups: what had started as a protective cover had become a new, non-gypsy identity by the end of the century.

In varying combinations poverty, warfare, immigration, and social exclusion all strongly contributed to the formation of groups, bands, and networks involved in organized rural crime. The case-studies have shown that the men and women who participated in these bands were invariably poor; most of them did not have a permanent home; they either belonged to the fringe of local rural society or were – as recent immigrants or members of ethnic groups – outsiders. All were relatively powerless in political and social terms. Yet it is totally unconvincing and definitely unsatisfying to interpret organized crime with regard only to what was lacking: income, jobs, social status, a position in local society, power, a fixed residence, and so on. The participation of specific social categories in rural bands cannot be understood just in terms of what they did not have: as if the absence of means and skills reveals how someone becomes a professional in any occupation. The case-studies have shown that they had talents and qualities which many other lacked, such as mobility, family traditions and expertise in crime, familiarity with weapons, and access to local resources and assistants combined with a certain independence from local social control, leadership, discipline, and a measure of solidarity. The fact that some of these characteristics were not particularly appreciated by established citizens – we will shortly come back to this point – should not obscure that these were indeed qualities and skills, not failings.

The Geography of Organized Crime

The continuity which prevailed in the terminology used by the courts thus reflected the absence of any general development in organized rural crime in the Dutch Republic. In a similar way terminological variation from one part of the Netherlands to another indicated regional contrasts. The baroque vocabulary of the Brabant courts, their comprehensive terminology for the description of acts of violence, and their frequent use of the term 'band' in the sense of a close-knit and hierarchically organized group, as opposed to the regular use of 'company' in Holland, reflected differences – not only in the background, structure, and organization of bands but in their criminal activities as well.

The main exception should be mentioned first, however. Regional differences did not affect all bands to an equal extent, and were least important to the most mobile groups. Jewish networks, gypsy bands, and the composite vagrant networks of the late eighteenth century were familiar with many diverse regions: a continuous (though not erratic) change of territory was, after all, one of their main characteristics. Their criminal 'methods' and their way of life accorded with this pattern of mobility, and consequently did not change much from one area to another.

Although similar in this respect, Jewish and gypsy bands differed on nearly every other count. Jews generally operated in small groups of varying composition which formed part of loosely structured and far-flung networks. They were active all over the Dutch Republic. Gypsy bands too toured the whole country, but they consisted of larger family groups which tended to stay together or at least meet frequently. Jewish band members toured the countryside as pedlars, rag sellers and buyers, cattle-dealers, or itinerant musicians. They either covered large distances – travelling from one city to another and selling and buying from door to door in the countryside in between – or used one town as a base for short trips in the nearby countryside. Whatever the length of their tours, towns remained their point of departure and return. The orientation of gypsies was mainly rural: they went from door to door and earned a living by repairing pots and pans, selling pills and ointments, and telling fortunes. During these tours they spent the night in tents or slept in barns and disused farmhouses. Larger and more permanent gypsy encampments consisted of tents and straw huts. Most important of all, Jewish bands consisted not of families but of men alone: women and children stayed behind in the towns. They provided a permanent 'base' to return to and formed links between the men, thus encouraging solidarity and prompting some degree of coherence in wide networks which lacked a formal hierarchy. Gypsy bands, on the other hand, grew out of an extended family enterprise in which men and women shared in both legal and illegal activities. Leadership rested with a few men, and hierarchies usually followed military lines.

At the opposite end of the scale of mobility we find the 'local' bands which confined their activities to one district or even to one or two villages. To these bands particular regional circumstances were vital. Not surprisingly, they existed almost exclusively in Brabant, where all non-ethnic bands were predicated to a considerable extent on local ties. Such 'immobile' bands consisted mainly of indigenous families, and depended completely on local knowledge, local connections, and other local resources. As soon as circumstances in their particular district changed for the worse, they tended to fall apart and disappear.

It is in the broad middle range of mobile non-ethnic bands that regional contrasts within the Netherlands are most clearly revealed. As we have seen, local connections were crucially important to all Brabant bands – whether military, such as the Zwartmakers of the 1690s, or 'civil' like the late eighteenth-century Catoen Band. In Holland such ties were certainly not absent, but the diverse composition of the Holland bands – which included a high proportion of recent immigrants besides a number of indigenous urban and rural Hollanders – made reliance on any particular local community less likely. Not only the immigrants but the indigenous Hollanders too appear to have already lost or discarded close local ties before they became involved with the rural bands. (Such ties seem to have been more fragile in Holland than in Brabant, perhaps because Hollanders were much more used to a permanent influx of foreigners as well as continuous interurban mobility and the prolonged absence of seafaring men.)

Geography also affected the position of women in the bands and the relevance of kinship ties in general. In Brabant whole families or sets of relatives joined bands, whose coherence came to depend to a large extent on ties of kinship. Some groups might well be described as enterprises of several interconnected families. In such bands women – and in particular mothers – occupied a position similar to the central one they had in ordinary family matters, as may be seen from the nicknames and family names current in Brabant. Even when women did not actively participate in the robberies or join in the tours, they still formed crucial links, both between the band members themselves and between band members and established local people. Some of them came close to the position of backstage organizers.

In Holland no complete urban or rural families joined bands. Individual men and women – whether of a foreign or indigenous background – fell in with a small group, which slowly turned into a band or company. Relationships between male and female band members only rarely seem to have dated from the period before the beginning of their vagrant existence or their involvement in the bands: many immigrants married or lived with women born in Holland. Some of these women reached a prominent position in the bands, but their prestige was usually based on expertise and other strictly personal qualities. It did not entail power within the bands and it was almost never underpinned by family ties.

Another major difference between the Brabant and the Holland bands concerns their orientation. The proximity of numerous large and small towns in the western part of the Dutch Republic – and their near-absence in Brabant – profoundly influenced the bands' manner of operating and way of life. Brabant 'produced' only bands with a singular lack of interest in urban amenities. Unlike their counterparts in Holland, few members of Brabant bands spent the winters in town, and there were no southern parallels to the Amsterdam-based Jaco Band (1710s). In Holland, on the other hand, even the most rurally oriented groups rarely kept away from towns altogether, visiting them regularly for business as well as pleasure. Some band members lived in towns, and rural burglars were often known to members of the urban underworld: all of them met at certain lodging-houses and taverns. Urban thieves hardly ever turned into rural burglars, however; nor, as a rule, did members of rural bands become urban thieves.

Regional differences affected the offences as well. Certain illegal activities – such as picking pockets, street robbery, nightly mugging, and the theft of large stocks from warehouses – were typical of urban settings, while others occurred mainly in rural areas: the theft of poultry and livestock, the extortion of food and money under threat of arms, highway robbery, and, of course, vagrancy. So far, contrasts between the urbanized province of Holland and rural Brabant (including the larger part of Zeeland) are self-evident, but these were not the only and not even the most important differences between the two regions. Whereas burglary, plain theft, and armed robbery were carried out in both provinces, large-scale robbery and violence, especially with guns or other weapons, the posting of sentries, and a big group of offenders, were rare in Holland. The brutal murders by the gypsy bands at Kalslagen

(1720s) and by the Zwartjesgoed at Loosduinen (1798) and the extensive armed robberies of the Great Dutch Band (late 1790s) did not cause such a stir for nothing. (For the Kalslagen case see Chapter 5; for the Zwartjesgoed murders see Chapter 8.)

In Holland rural burglars generally preferred to make their way into a house by digging a small tunnel underneath the front door, by using a ladder and climbing into the attic through a hole in the thatched or tiled roof, or by sneaking in through an unlocked stable door. The number of people taking part in a burglary was generally small. They tended to make as little noise as possible so as not to wake the inhabitants, and sometimes even waited until the whole family had gone out. Naturally only thieves who were relatively well informed about the layout of the house and the habits of the occupants could proceed in this manner.

The situation in Brabant was different. There violence was almost a standard ingredient of any type of property crime committed by indigenous bands as well as some of the interregional networks. Members of Brabant bands frequently carried weapons – ranging from swords or sabres and bayonets to guns (such as flintlocks and pistols). Even band members who did not know how to handle a gun were often issued with one by their commanders, at the risk of shooting themselves or their companions. Vagrants commonly uttered threats of arson and murder while begging; knives and guns were regularly employed during highway robberies and extortion; and the larger expeditions of the Brabant bands frequently involved the battering down of front doors, the maltreatment, torture, and even murder of the victims, and the ransacking of whole houses. These expeditions entailed far more commotion than in Holland: the number of people involved was larger and, instead of taking care to go unnoticed, robbers often made a good deal of noise. Shouting at each other and the inhabitants, ramming open doors and windows, breaking into cupboards and chests, shooting their pistols, and leaving in an anything but quiet manner, the robbers' purpose was as much to frighten their victims and keep them from either helping each other or calling on the judiciary as to obtain booty. To intimidate and inspire terror: that was the point of these tactics. In Brabant violence was as much part of an individual lifestyle as of group activities, as is revealed by the violent personal histories of some of the Zwartmakers (see Chapter 4). Rather than a simple means to an end, to these people violence was part of their regular way of life, to be used both among themselves and against others, and was only to be expected from the authorities when caught.

The contrast between a 'quiet' burglary and a spectacular, noisy, and violent armed robbery epitomizes the main differences in criminal styles and modes of behaviour between Holland and Brabant. This contrast was not limited, however, to just two Dutch provinces: Holland should be read as the whole of the western, urbanized part of the Netherlands, while Brabant represents the predominantly rural inland provinces. This distinction already existed among the bands of the mid seventeenth century and did not change in the course of the next 150 years. It affected large as well as small bands; even the mobile interregional networks did not remain untouched. Clearly this contrast cannot be explained in terms of the people involved (though the prominence of men born outside Holland among those actively engaged in violence in the Holland bands is striking). Brabanders and people born in Gelderland, Utrecht, Flanders, or Germany may have been more familiar with warfare, weapons, and personal violence than many Hollanders, yet they generally refrained from using excessive violence as soon as they joined bands active in Holland or when their own bands moved to Holland because it impeded rather than contributed to their success and safety. (The best example is the van Exaerde Band, discussed in Chapter 4; cf. the Stoffel van Reenen Band in Chapter 3.) Even a brief look at the salient characteristics of the countryside in Holland should make the reasons plain. Then, as now, Holland was heavily populated in comparison with neighbouring areas. Distances between towns and villages were small, and a fairly dense network of canals and roads facilitated communications. No woods or hills limited visibility. Would it make sense for a band to ram open doors, make a loud noise, take their time to torture people and ransack a house, knowing that neighbours lived within shouting distance, the landscape offered little protective cover,[4] and a hasty retreat – where to, unless to the comparative safety of the towns? – might be observed by so many eyes? The few bands that committed such large-scale violent robberies in Holland had good reason not to rely on that particular region alone. The Jaco Band (1710s), the gypsy bands (1720s), the Great Dutch Band (1790s), and the Zwartjesgoed (around 1800) alternated robberies in the urbanized, western part of the Netherlands with periods of inactivity and expeditions to other provinces.

In Brabant conditions were more favourable for large-scale armed robbery. Extensive heathlands, woods, and moors provided shelter; roads were scarce and, apart from the western and northern fringes, access by water was limited. Population density was comparatively low: in the countryside neighbours only rarely lived within shouting distance. Moreover, the large and isolated farms on the rich clay soils of western Brabant and the northern section along the river Maas formed extremely attractive targets – all the more so since they were near the heathlands and woods of the poor, sandy soils.

Landscape, ecology, population density, and infrastructure thus did more than constitute a setting for illegal activities. They set limits to the specific ways in which burglaries and robberies were executed, and were a major influence on both criminal styles and the geography of organized rural crime. The same was true of the much discussed aspect of political and administrative borders. As Hobsbawm, Weisser, McIntosh, and many others have demonstrated, rural bands like border areas;[5] Dutch bands were no exception. Hobsbawm remarked that 'the ideal situation for robbery is one in which the local authorities are local men, operating in complex situations, and where a few miles may put the robber beyond the reach or even the knowledge of one set of authorities and into the territory of another, which does not worry about what happens "abroad"' (1981, p. 21; cf. McIntosh 1975, p. 31). This adequately describes the situation in the Netherlands. The large military bands of the south, for instance, operated across the border between Dutch and Spanish Brabant; the Catoen Band committed robberies in the border area of Brabant and Holland; the Thorn-bush Band of the 1770s toured the border area of Gelderland, Utrecht, and Brabant; and Stoffel van Reenen's band was frequently active in the border region of Utrecht and Holland, an area characterized by the extreme fragmentation of judicial territories. All of them fully appreciated safe escape routes to 'foreign' territory, whether it belonged to a neighbouring jurisdiction, another province, or another state. Gypsy bands more than any others made a skilful use of border areas. In order to profit from the best escape possibilities as well as the protective cover of dunes, moors, and woods and the amenities (food, work, and occasionally shelter) of nearby villages and farmhouses, they invariably put up their tents and straw huts near the intersection of provincial, communal, jurisdictional, and ecological borders.

Yet the 'border-region model' far too easily equates a proximity to political and administrative borders with a peripheral and even marginal character of such areas in terms of state control, accessibility, and economic importance, as happens in Hobsbawm's statement that 'brigands flourish in remote and inaccessible areas such as mountains, trackless plains, fenland, forest or estuaries . . . administrative inefficiency and complication favour it . . . Frontier regions – better still, regions of multiple frontiers like central Germany or the parts of India divided between the British and numerous princely states – were in perpetual difficulties' (1981, p. 21). In other words, the model continues to put bands in the place where they belong according to the tales: in mountainous regions, forests, and other out-of-the-way locations. Again – as when organized crime was explained in terms of lack – an example of the place being made to suit the social status of those concerned?

Although celebrated for its regional and local particularism, and abundantly provided with many kinds of borders and frontiers, the Dutch Republic as a whole cannot, after all, be regarded as a marginal or peripheral area in any terms. Nor was it inaccessible. A case might perhaps be made for the 'marginality' of Brabant – though even that seems unwarranted – but organized rural crime did not, as we have seen, confine its activities to Brabant. Moreover, in the Netherlands political fragmentation was strongest in the most urbanized and 'advanced' part of the Dutch Republic, where communication was easier and the opportunities for efficient state control may well have been better than in almost any other part of western Europe at the time.

The relevant point about organized rural crime in the Netherlands is, of course, that bands do not seem to have been much more active in one area than in another, but they were differently organized and went about their business in different ways according to the region concerned. This brings us back once more to the geography of crime and the subject of criminal styles. The 'border-region model' mainly distinguishes between regions in terms of more or less band activity, and lumps together bands of smugglers, groups of outlaws, gypsy bands, local associations of coin clippers, (presumed) cases of social banditry, mafia-type organizations, some forms of Mediterranean feuding, and so on. It might be helpful to introduce an additional, qualitative distinction in terms of criminal style, which includes aspects of organization and background as well as offences and ways of committing them. The major differences in criminal style between Holland and Brabant were not limited to just these two provinces: they indicated a more general contrast between the western half of the Netherlands and the rural inland provinces. Perhaps the Holland/Brabant contrast epitomizes a similar, more general distinction between the urbanized coastal zones of north-western Europe and the continental inland regions: a coast/continent contrast in crime.[6]

Marks of Marginality

Naturally bailiffs and courts did not completely ignore differences in criminal style. They distinguished between a pickpocket and an extortionist, between armed robbers and urban burglars, between a gypsy woman selling ointments and a boy belonging to a vagrant band, between members of a Jewish network of burglars and a military band operating in Brabant. These distinctions were primarily related to the practical business of catching and convicting criminals, however. For the rest, most bailiffs and courts could not have cared less about their defendants' background, traditions, or customs – not even if information about these aspects would have facilitated their investigations. (A few notable exceptions were C. F. van Maanen, prosecutor general for the Hof van Holland at The Hague during the 1790s and principal prosecutor of the Great Dutch Band; bailiff Blok, central figure in the prosecution of the Zwartjesgoed around 1805–6; and possibly the bailiff of Schieland who prosecuted and extensively interrogated members of the Rabonus Band during the 1760s.) To the authorities all defendants were first and foremost suspects – criminals – and always, if only for that reason, a lesser kind of people: marginal and dangerous figures who should be removed from society.

This attitude presupposes more than just a lack of interest in cultural (and other) differences; and the uniformity imposed on the suspects by the judicial authorities went much further than is suggested by the common denominator of 'crime' or 'criminal'. Instead of regarding them as a variety of groups involved in an assortment of activities defined as illegal, the judicial authorities tried to fit them into a homogeneous category of marginal and dangerous people. The terminology used to describe defendants – especially gypsies – indicates as much. By portraying, for example, a member of the Rabonus Band as 'in short a monster', members of the Jaco Band as 'some utterly godless thieves and rascals', or the military Moskovieters in Brabant as 'the scum of robbers and assaulters',[7] the courts relegated defendants to the realm of outsiders who no longer belonged to the moral community of decent people. This outlook could hardly be stated more succinctly than in the description of the Zwartjesgoed Band (1798–1806) as 'so many dregs of society who regarded the most appalling atrocities as a game'.[8]

By limiting the legal rights of people without a fixed domicile criminal law itself defined them as second-rate citizens at best and at worst as a lesser sort of people. The judiciary went further than that: it repudiated their cultural diversity by overemphasizing certain characteristics and selectively leaving out others. This process may be designated as the construction of marginality, as forcing suspects to fit a stereotype (while at the same time reinforcing that stereotype), or by any other phrase that underscores the fact that it entailed the (not necessarily conscious) construction of a largely negative image. The established authorities not only adhered to this negative stereotype – even in the teeth of the evidence – but actively and indiscriminately imposed it on a far from homogeneous collection of groups and individuals.

What exactly happened? It looks as if the authorities – and how many others besides? – could not believe that 'criminals' might at the same time be 'normal' people. Because the defendants had committed certain illegal acts, they must be violating other vital rules as well. The basic norms of established society – according to these respected and generally well-to-do bailiffs and local court members – pertained to three domains: to be established in the most literal sense of the word (having a fixed or at least known domicile); not to be poor, that is, being able to maintain oneself and one's family; and to belong to a family (having kinsmen and a name, a respected identity). These three aspects more than anything else formed the cornerstones of a good reputation: a man or woman without family, without a home and without possessions was almost nobody. It was to these that the courts returned again and again during interrogations, irrespective of whether the answers would contribute towards solving practical matters such as establishing identity or gathering evidence. In the concluding paragraph of criminal sentences, after the summing up of a series of illegal acts, bailiffs used to recapitulate some of these same points to emphasize once more that the person concerned was of ill repute – as if it lent credibility to the preceding accusations, as if to say, 'anything can be expected from such a person'.

Whether the defendants had or had not committed the acts they were accused of is, of course, completely irrelevant here. The important point is that in the outlook of the authorities particular forms of illegal and immoral behaviour belonged together. Interrogations most frequently focused on the twin themes of residence–mobility and of name–family–marriage that were at the core both of marginality as construed by the courts and of cultural differences as discussed in the preceding case-studies.

Any form of itinerancy was immediately translated as vagrancy. In the courts' opinion mobility could only mean not having a home, a fixed address, or even a roof to sleep under. A local court in North Holland described a small group of vagrant beggars touring the area during the 1760s as 'marching in troops through the villages and spending the night now here and then there at farmhouses, having no fixed domicile anywhere and thus being a burden on the rural population'.[9] Another court portrayed the Rabonus Band of the same period as 'most famous thieves, housebreakers, extortioners – touring the countryside as a troop or conspiracy . . . and loitering in woods, huts and tents'.[10]

In a similar way criminal records accentuated the absence of regular family ties and especially of marriage. Formal marriage and baptism were considered rare, and any instance of an unmarried man and woman living together or of children born out of wedlock served to confirm and underscore the wide gap between 'respectable' people and these 'infamous' persons. Suspects were commonly reckoned to be licentious, promiscuous, lacking a sense of responsibility for their children, and in general careless and unrestrained. Comparisons with animals appear especially in this sexual context. It was no slip of the pen when criminal sentences referred to gypsies as a 'brood' of 'so-called *Heijdenen* or *Egyptenaren*'. Female members of vagrant groups were immediately regarded as whores 'leading a dissolute and abominable life' and 'squandering their time with beggars in taverns until they had spent everything on booze'.[11] Once more a sentence pronounced against a member of the Rabonus Band offers a good example of the courts' viewpoint. Summing up, the town court of Rotterdam stated that Elisabeth Josephs had 'never been married but came to lead a repulsive and unrestrained life of collective licentiousness and profligate living like hares and foxes'.[12] Poverty – or rather the lack of visible possessions apart from the clothes worn by a defendant – was mentioned less frequently, as were speaking a foreign language, exotic dress, and unusual general appearance. These were details which only served to underline the principal marks of marginality.

Again, the point is not whether the men and women concerned actually spent the night out in the open, led a dissolute life, boozed away their money, dressed abominably, or spoke strange-sounding languages. Even if all of them had done so perpetually, it was still the courts who chose to highlight these real or imaginary aspects of their lives, to suppress other 'positive' aspects, and thereby portray the defendants as socially irrelevant, marginal, and yet at the same time dangerous people. In constructing this stereotypical image of marginal people and making the defendants fit this image the courts were simultaneously establishing a reverse (or negative) self-image and thus defining themselves by means of contrast and opposition:[13] a criminal was taken to do and be everything a respectable citizen did and was not, acting as 'a worthless, dangerous and harmful subject in civil society'.[14]

Such negative self-definitions were not created, however, by a 'plain' inversion of established values: by a search for opposite but equal characteristics facing a series of qualities connected with the self-image of the respectable citizen. The fabrication of marginality called for more creativity on the part of the judicial authorities. It required a finely balanced combination of downplay and overemphasis. We have seen how elements that did not fit the courts' concept of marginality were disregarded, sometimes to the point of disappearing from sight. (It is no coincidence that historians have long regarded members of the military bands operating in Brabant as foreign riff-raff. It would be difficult not to get that impression when reading the sentences and in particular their final paragraphs. It is precisely what the courts wanted [others?] to see. To recognize that instead of foreign rabble these men and women were local people – Brabanders born and bred in the villages they plundered – was inconvenient and perhaps even dangerous.) At the same time interrogations stressed and repeated every aspect of the defendants' appearance, conduct, and way of life that departed from the civic norm, especially anything connected with vagrancy, mobility, licentiousness, drunkenness, and unrestrained behaviour.

So, instead of equal features on the sides of 'citizens' and 'criminals', instead of an inversion, we find only the lack of positive qualities on the side of the latter. 'Vagrant' was definitely not a neutral term: it did not refer to a different way of life but in this context always implied the lack of a home. For the relations of men and women who lived together without being married, and for kinship patterns that did not precisely fit the civic model – such as extended gypsy families – there was not even a separate term. These people could only be described as not being married, as lacking 'family' in the sense of 'name' and 'status'. Taken together, the features on the side of 'the criminals' added up to nothing or even less than nothing: all these negative characteristics in the end signified the lack of the most important asset in seventeenth- and eighteenth-century society: social status. Here we have come full circle, for a lack of status, a lack of a specific identity and culture, had, of course, been central to the authorities' image of 'criminals' to start with.

In so far as the criminal records depicted defendants as a negative self-representation, their image must have served as a reminder of civic norms and duties. Indirectly it thus helped to emphasize the importance of public order and general adherence to established norms and rules. At the same time, and much more directly, it served as a practical means of control. All defendants were made to fit the stereotype of 'dangerous others', step by step, beginning with their first interrogation or even before. The process culminated in the ritual of public punishment. The display on the scaffold, the marks left by physical punishment (branding in particular), and the public reading of the sentence effectively excluded convicts from the category of 'normal' persons. (It was for good rhetorical reasons that the final paragraph of a criminal sentence not only summarized the defendants' illegal acts but also reiterated other aspects of his or her marginality.) By a symbolic declaration of alterity – expressed both in words and by means of the body of the convict – this ritual redefined the boundaries of the moral community. It made very clear who belonged and who did not, and it legitimized any further exclusion and persecution of the latter.[15]

By defining criminals according to what they lacked and thus stripping them of distinctive cultural and social characteristics the authorities ultimately created a blurred social category. How could anyone establish the position of a person whose identity remained vague and was mainly designated in terms of deficiency, of not having a home, a name, a family, relatives, possessions, status? The public proclamation of criminals as 'people without a clear identity' effectively reinforced their marginalization – and was, as we have seen, compelling enough to be adopted by many later historians. By explaining crime by means of poverty, lack of jobs, lack of status and power, deprivation, or social exclusion they followed in the footsteps of the judicial authorities of the past. And by following them historians have too often neglected the construction of marginality as well as the cultural and social diversity that is partly hidden behind this representation.

One of the main purposes of the preceding case-studies has been to show that no reader of the criminal records is totally and irrevocably bound to the idiom and outlook of the courts: not even the court members themselves. The records disclose, after all, how a particular stereotypical representation took shape in practice and thereby allow the discovery that we are dealing with one.[16] Court records, unlike fairy tales and other literary stories, proclaim to be about real crimes, real people, and real evidence. They cannot completely mask aspects that do not (or only partly) fit the stereotype. (As pointed out in Chapter 1, this was not a situation where cynical and arbitrary judges made up completely fictive cases against suspects.) Besides, criminal records – and especially the detailed accounts of interrogations – reflect a dialogue between judicial authorities and suspects. However unequal their position, defendants still had a say. Or rather, they had to speak about themselves and their activities in a way that would at the same time make sense to the authorities and serve their own purposes.

Captain Garneson, for instance, who commanded a small gypsy band at the beginning of the eighteenth century (see Chapter 5), was one of the few gypsy leaders to talk about gypsy customs and other 'inside' affairs. This fact alone should make us suspicious, not so much about the value of his statements but about why and how he was discussing these matters at all. We might speculate that he did so because he had been the loser in a conflict between gypsy clans; he may have desired revenge as well as remission of his punishment. So, even if the court was using Garneson to come to grips with gypsy bands, Garneson was using the court for his own purposes; and perhaps he had only been arrested because the rival clans in their turn had been using the courts to get rid of a leader who was causing trouble and standing in someone's way.

Such strategies may well have formed only a minor element in the usual dialogue between authorities and defendants, but in order to avoid or lessen punishment nearly every suspect made some effort to play down the importance of his or her illegal activities and also the value of the available evidence. (As we saw in Chapter 1, most defendants were well aware of the relevant aspects of legal procedure.) Gypsies were most proficient at this verbal contest, in which lives might be at stake on one side while all the rules had been set by the other. Unlike any other category of suspects, they – or at least some of them – refused to follow the rules. Instead of making a simple confession or plain denial some gypsies fabricated a multitude of continually changing identities, relatives, places of birth, journeys, and legal as well as illegal activities – until it had become both impossible and useless to try to establish what was true or false about their stories. They tormented the authorities by defying a form of control which depended on establishing a person's identity but at the same time aimed to obliterate every mark of cultural distinctiveness.

In the end, of course, the refusal to be pinned down to a specific identity did not help these defendants much, and they were convicted anyhow. Whatever their individual characteristics, they were still forced into the blurred category of marginal people – by an overemphasis on their lawless behaviour, promiscuity, erratic travels, and so on. Yet their way of answering questions and the maddening effect it had on the authorities clearly demonstrate how far the power of suspects reached. For a brief period they could succeed in subverting the authorities' way of thinking by overturning the negative self-image of the respectable citizen once more: instead of a lack they displayed an exotic surplus, an abundance of names, identities, places of birth, occupations, and so on . . . Thus they refused not only to fit the stereotype of the reverse self-image but also to comply with the current idiom of control. It is interesting to note that this strategy was deployed by the same people whose everyday self-representation as exotic persons was based on a similar, though rather more positive play upon these same categories.

Multiple identities, diversity, cultural differences – uncertainties, in short – were precisely what the judicial authorities did not particularly want displayed in their sentences, but this is exactly what may be uncovered by a close reading of the criminal records. In spite of the courts' attempts to gloss over the local origins of members of the Brabant bands, they can still be traced. In spite of their efforts to depict gypsies as lawless people who belong outside in the woods, like animals, and who live in huts and tents, we can still trace a few of their own customs as well as the infrequent urban sojourns of some gypsy groups. Most aspects that shine through are not completely opposed to the marks of marginality, but they point to individuality, to different styles, and to cultural diversity. It is in this way that the records themselves enable us to shatter the homogeneous image of 'criminals'.

Instead of revealing indiscriminate marginal people with a violent and dissolute predisposition the records allow glimpses of an enormous variety of groups with different customs, languages, occupations, kinship patterns, and criminal styles. Instead of lack we have uncovered many specific qualities and skills. Instead of a homogeneous collection of 'criminals' we have found cultural diversity. The single feature that connected all these people was that they had broken the law.

Appendix The Organization of Dutch Criminal Justice

One of the most striking characteristics of the structure of Dutch criminal justice is the absence of a national high court. Most provinces had central courts, but some of these dealt only with a small section of all criminal cases, while others controlled proceedings in nearly every criminal case that occurred within their region. In Friesland, for example, criminal justice had been centralized. But the Hof van Holland en Zeeland at The Hague, the provincial court of Holland, concerned itself with few criminal proceedings and functioned mainly as a court of appeal in civil cases. The Raad van Brabant (Council of Brabant) had a similar position. Because of the subordinate political and administrative status of Brabant and Limburg (the *Generaliteitslanden*), this council likewise resided at The Hague. In spite of the limited powers of some of these provincial courts, their influence should not be underestimated. The Hof van Holland was known for its attempts to encroach upon the privileges of the local courts of the first instance. Both it and the Raad van Brabant played an important role in outlining a policy of criminal justice, and their verdicts were probably used as models by some local courts. Their actual involvement in the day-to-day management of criminal justice was limited, however. Even as courts of appeal in criminal matters they dealt with only a small number of cases. Generally speaking, no appeal was possible against a criminal sentence pronounced by one of the regular courts of first instance if the usual 'extraordinary' procedure had been followed and if the defendant had confessed (see Huussen 1976, 1978, Faber 1983, and van de Vrugt 1978).

It was the regular local courts of first instance that dealt with by far the larger part of all criminal cases in Holland, Zeeland, and Brabant. Each of these courts had full competence in all criminal cases and each had its own territory: the jurisdiction.[1] Neither the size of these territories nor the number of their inhabitants made any difference with respect to the autonomy of such local courts. A death sentence pronounced by the court of Oegstgeest – a jurisdiction covering a few villages and polders to the west of Leiden – was no more susceptible to appeal than a sentence pronounced by the town court of Amsterdam.

In the province of Holland alone there were more than two hundred courts of first instance with full competence in criminal cases. The size of their territories was often small, but one – the jurisdiction of Rijnland, which convened at Leiden – covered nearly a fifth of the province. Some of these larger jurisdictions consisted of several fragments which might lie far apart. The 'judicial geography' of Holland thus displays a fine-meshed web of jurisdictions spread all over the province. In Brabant the size of jurisdictions was generally larger and their number consequently smaller. Whereas in Holland urban courts covered only the town itself and a one-mile zone around its walls, the most important town courts of Brabant – those of 's Hertogenbosch and Breda – also covered large parts of the surrounding countryside. The position of Zeeland lay in between: the judicial geography of its northern islands more or less followed the pattern of Holland; the southern islands and Dutch Flanders resembled Brabant (see Egmond 1987a and van Ham & Vriens 1980).

Information about the daily activities of these local courts is scanty. Even in small jurisdictions they seem to have convened at least once every month: partly to discuss civil cases, partly to deal with matters of police and public order, and occasionally to try criminal cases. Meetings took place at the town hall or, in the case of small rural courts, at a local inn. The courts, or *schepenbanken*, were called after their members, the *schepenen* (aldermen; cf. German *Schöffen*). Depending on local custom, size, and the importance of the jurisdiction, the courts might also be called *hof* (court) or *hoge vierschaar*. They ranged in size from about five people in small jurisdictions to eight or nine in larger ones. The town court of Amsterdam consisted of nine members (see Faber 1983).

Schepenen were always appointed for a period of one year, but a former *schepen* might again occupy this position after a certain interval. Normally the posts appear to have circulated among those inhabitants of a jurisdiction who qualified. Formally speaking, candidates had to be respectable, Protestant, male inhabitants of the jurisdiction; in fact, Roman Catholics were frequently appointed in the southern half of the Dutch Republic and in other predominantly Catholic areas. In large rural districts and in the towns this category often included jurists and other notables cognizant with the law. There families belonging to the local upper and upper-middle classes often successfully attempted to monopolize such positions. In smaller rural districts very few jurists were available, and the position of *schepen* circulated among well-to-do farmers, a few local notables, and some wealthy and respectable artisans (see Egmond 1987a; cf. Rijpperda Wierdsma 1937).

Schepenen had to make decisions at three crucial stages in a criminal procedure: they determined whether a suspect might be taken into custody by the bailiff; they brought in a written verdict granting (or withholding) permission for torture; and they pronounced the final sentence. In itself the presence of laymen in courts was nothing unusual in *ancien régime* Europe, but autonomous 'lay courts' with full competence in criminal cases were rare. The influence of trained jurists on actual criminal proceedings in the Dutch Republic was none the less considerable. Because so many *schepenen* were laymen, the legal advice of two or three impartial jurists (*onpartijdige rechtsgeleerden*) had to be asked for by any first-instance court before it could pronounce a sentence involving torture or corporal punishment. The records indicate that this rule was generally obeyed by the smaller rural courts; because of differences in registration less is known about this aspect in the large rural courts and town courts (cf. Faber 1983).

Thus, backed by the opinion of trained jurists, *schepenen* were able to provide formidable opposition, if so inclined, to the plans of high-handed bailiffs. Contrary to received opinion, *schepenen* did occasionally refuse to authorize warrants for arrest; they sometimes declined permission for torture; and they regularly imposed milder punishments than those demanded by the bailiffs.[2] The bailiff (called *baljuw*, *ruwaard*, or *drossaard* in rural districts, and *schout* or *hoofdofficier* in towns) remained the real linchpin of criminal justice in the Dutch Republic, however. He was the protagonist in court and the main counterpart (or even the opponent) of the *schepenen* as well as their principal ally. While the *schepenen* were charged with the double task of local administration and first-instance justice, bailiffs too were involved in activities that have now become separate responsibilities. They combined the functions of public prosecutor and chief superintendent of police.

There was no division between a bailiff's duties as keeper of the peace, criminal investigator, and public prosecutor. Together with a few assistants (called *schoutsdienaren* or *justitiedienaren*) he inspected the scene of the crime, interrogated witnesses, took down depositions, gathered material evidence, and tracked down suspects. As soon as they had been taken into custody, the bailiff (or his deputy) supervised interrogations and confrontations of suspects; if a confession was not forthcoming, he might ask the court to permit questioning under torture; and he finally summarized the case for the prosecution in his *Eisch en Conclusie Crimineel*, which usually included or referred to the defendant's confession. Unlike the *schepenen*, bailiffs were appointed for a long period of time – often for life, occasionally for five to ten years. Like the *schepenen*, many of them were laymen. (Only among the bailiffs of the big towns and the largest rural districts do we find a number of trained jurists. Many of these 'high' bailiffs delegated their duties to deputies, who might again be laymen.) All bailiffs should be regarded as professionals, if only because they could devote much of their time to judicial and police matters for a number of years on end. Many of them gained an enormous amount of practical experience during careers that sometimes spanned thirty years or more.

Abbreviations

ARA	Algemeen Rijksarchief at The Hague
ARB	Archives du Royaume de Belgique at Brussels
CR	Criminal Records
DA	District Archive
fragm.	fragmentary
frags	fragments
HvG	Hof van Gelre (the provincial court of Gelderland at Arnhem)
HvH	Hof van Holland en Zeeland (the provincial court of Holland and Zeeland at The Hague)
HvU	Hof van Utrecht (the provincial court of Utrecht at Utrecht)
MA	Municipal Archive
MAA	Municipal Archive at Amsterdam
MAB	Municipal Archive at Breda
MADe	Municipal Archive at Delft
MAH	Municipal Archive at 's Hertogenbosch
MAL	Municipal Archive at Leiden
MAR	Municipal Archive at Rotterdam
MATH	Municipal Archive at The Hague
RvB	Raad van Brabant (Council of Brabant; council for Dutch Brabant, Dutch Flanders, and the Landen van Overmaze)
SA	State Archive
SAG	State Archive for Gelderland
SANB	State Archive for North Brabant
SANH	State Archive for North Holland
SAU	State Archive for Utrecht
SAZ	State Archive for Zeeland

Notes

Chapter 1 In Bad Company

1 For Germany see Küther 1976, 1983, and Danker 1988; for France see Cobb 1970, 1972a, 1972b, 1975a, 1975b, 1975c, Hufton 1974, Farge 1986, 1993, Muchembled 1989, and Agulhon 1990; for England see Beier 1985, Beattie 1986, Hay 1982, Hay et al. 1988, and Brewer & Styles 1980, to name only a few of the best known authors.

2 See her innovating study *The Organisation of Crime* (1975). Cf. McIntosh 1971, McMullan 1982, Einstadter 1969, and Fijnaut 1985, 1989.

3 For a list of the courts see Archival Sources, and for a discussion of the organization of Dutch criminal justice see Appendix. The period covered extends from 1650 (sometimes 1612 or 1625, if the records were especially good) to 1795–1810 (likewise depending on the quality of the records).

4 MAA, CR 608 (1714).

5 See Chartier 1974, 1979, and Burke 1987 on early modern French and Italian concepts of a dangerous counter-society. On picaresque tales see Lüsebrink 1983, Müller-Fraureuth 1894, A. A. Parker 1967, and Babcock 1978; cf. Faller 1987.

6 For a discussion of picaresque tales and other literature related to crime in the Netherlands see van Gorp 1978, Buijnsters 1980, and *Feit en fictie* 1985.

7 This is both because of differing opinions about methods of computation and because of the inherent problems which *ancien régime* styles of record-keeping pose to any attempt at quantification. Among the most interesting and sophisticated examples (to name only some British contributions) – which often combine quantitative and other approaches – are Beattie 1974, 1986, Gatrell 1980, and Hay 1982. For a contribution to and succinct discussion of the violence/theft debate see Stone 1983.

8 For clear and helpful discussions of micro-history, its strong points and its limitations, and for some excellent examples see the essays collected in Muir & Ruggiero 1991; see also Ginzburg 1990b.

9 See, for instance, Ginzburg 1980, 1983, 1990b, Davis 1983, 1988, Beattie 1986, Hay 1982, Burke 1987, Gatrell, Lenman & Parker 1980; cf. Brewer & Styles 1980.

Chapter 2 Confronting the Authorities

1 See, for instance, van de Vrugt 1978, Gerbenzon & Algra 1987, and Egmond 1989a; cf. Langbein 1977.
2 On the by no means simple distinction between ordinary and extraordinary criminal procedure see, for example, Faber 1983.
3 See SAG, CR Buren 15/5 (1718).
4 See DA at Schoonhoven, CR Heeraartsberg 2 (1722); cf. ARA, CR Zuid-Holland 114 (1722), and MA Gorinchem, CR 35 (1722–3).
5 See MAL, CR 16 1668. That he felt the need to confess at all – and he was by no means the only one – gives us a glimpse of his religious sentiments.
6 See SAZ, CR Zierikzee 3850 (1723).
7 A case could be made, though, for the construction or invention of the crime of sodomy by the Dutch authorities of the 1720s to 1730s. Cf. van der Meer 1984 and Rousseau 1987.
8 See Langbein 1977 on differences between theory and practice in this respect in several European countries. Cf. Faber's critical comments on Langbein's thesis (1983, pp. 13 and esp. 141–9).
9 See MAA, CR 621, sentence Gerrit Geesinck (1800).
10 MA Amersfoort, CR 407/33 (1694).
11 See, for instance, Blok 1989, Schild 1980, Evans 1984, and especially E. Cohen 1989, 1990; cf. de Certeau 1979.
12 MA Amersfoort, CR 407/33 (1694).
13 See especially her sentence in DA at Hoorn, CR Enkhuizen 4924 (1688), which summarizes most of her previous convictions; cf. DA at Hoorn, CR Hoorn 4517 (1656). Trijn may have continued her career after 1688.
14 See MADe, CR 49 (20 July 1668). Among his colleagues were several 'famous thieves', including Stoffel van Reenen, who was hanged at Leiden just ten days before Jan's punishment at Delft.
15 See Egmond 1986 on the detention of several members of the Great Dutch Band at the Gevangenpoort in 1798–1800; cf. Calkoen 1906.
16 See ARA, CR Woerden 19, dossier Johan H. Himmelgarten.
17 Occasionally violence was used against the warders, as in the escape of Severain Louès from the prison at Breda. See SANB, RvB 1249, dossiers 511, 514, and van Haastert 1982.
18 Very little reliable information is available about Dutch crime rates, and comparisons between urban and rural crime rates are still lacking. The information provided by Faber 1983 and van de Pol 1987 on seventeenth- and eighteenth-century Amsterdam and by Beattie 1986 on London and the nearby countryside seems to indicate that urban crime rates were generally higher than rural ones.
19 ARA, CR Brielle 21.
20 MA Bergen op Zoom, CR 21.
21 See MA Vlaardingen, CR 11 (1798).
22 See, for example van den Eerenbeemt 1968, 1970, Hallema 1960, and the collection of documents in SANB, RvB Off. Fisc. 1297, 1301, 1304–5.
23 MA Amersfoort, CR 407/33 (1694).
24 For the London underworld see, among others, George 1985, Chesney

1972, Samuel 1981, McMullan 1982, and of course the famous Mayhew 1851–62; cf. Thompson & Yeo 1971.

25 With a small group of students at the University of Amsterdam I have tried to explore some of this evidence for the period 1680–1720 (mainly for Amsterdam and Haarlem). Papers by Luc de Ruijter on the urban geography of crime and by Harm Scholten on fences were of particular interest.

26 See MAR, CR 248 (1659–60).

27 See MAA, CR 581 (1654).

28 Both Isaac Lopes de Luna and Willem van Meckenum were arrested and sentenced to death by hanging at The Hague. De Luna was twenty-nine years old by then and had already been arrested five times in Amsterdam. This had resulted in only one previous conviction: to whipping, branding, and eight years' detention in the house of correction. Together with several other 'famous thieves' he soon broke out. De Luna, a Jew, was living with a Christian woman called Bregje Met Eeren (With honours) – a criminal offence at the time. Bregje was still married, moreover, and this added adultery to De Luna's already long list of criminal offences. See MATH, CR 106 (1690).

29 *Poffertjes* usually refers to a type of Dutch pastry (small pancakes), but at the time it was also a slang term for pocket pistols. On Genaer and his accomplices see the extensive documentation in ARA, HvH 5658, 5369/4; cf. HvH 5365/9.

30 MATH, CR 106 (1690).

31 The man was ordered by the local court to pay a substantial fine. See SANH, CR Winkel 5627 (1684); on folk-tales concerning the Achtkanten Boer see van der Kooi 1981–2.

32 See, ARA, HvH 5656 (1658), and ARA, CR Rijnland 8 (1663).

33 See DA at Oirschot, CR Oirschot 54 (1742).

34 The case of Cornelis Fredericksz Spalck, alias Freckled (Sprotten) Cees, shows some similarities. From childhood he had belonged to itinerant groups of chair-menders and tinkers. He served as a soldier in Dutch Flanders, deserted, worked as a sailor and joined a band of vagrant rural thieves in Holland. Cees finally wandered alone from one village to another in North Holland, begging and threatening people on the road. In 1696 he forced his way into a house brandishing a knife, shouted that he was a follower of the devil, and threatened to kill the woman who lived there as well as her visitors. He raped the woman twice before he could be arrested. See SANH, CR Schagen 5882 (1696).

35 See MA Axel 516 (1751).

36 See, for example, MAR, CR 255 (1746); DA at Purmerend, CR Beemster 4028 (1741, 1746); and MAL, CR 41 (1740).

37 For a group of boys and young men stealing from gardens and sheds and burgling houses in and near The Hague see MATH, CR 109 and dossiers (1773).

38 Some of the soldiers were later court-martialled and hanged. See SAZ, CR Vrije van Sluis 678 (1677).

39 See MA Alkmaar, CR 47 (1747).

Chapter 3 Post-war Bands: Holland and Zeeland, 1615–1720

1 The overall size of the Dutch army increased gradually in the course of the seventeenth century. In 1607, reaching its peak before the Twelve-years Truce of 1609, it formally numbered about 60,000 men. By 1672, when the armies were back to full strength, the official size amounted to 110, 000 men. See ten Raa & de Bas 1915 for the period 1609–25 and ten Raa & de Bas 1921 for the years 1648–72; cf. Zwitzer 1984 and Schulten & Schulten 1969. For the Spanish armies in the Netherlands see G. Parker 1972. See also Zwitzer 1991, which appeared after this manuscript was completed.
2 See MAR, CR 248 (1649).
3 See DA at Schoonhoven, CR Schoonhoven 2322 (1615), and SAZ, CR Zierikzee 3849 (1613).
4 See, for instance, the court records of the rural jurisdiction of the Egmonden near Alkmaar in North Holland, which present long lists of English-speaking vagrants and beggars. MA Alkmaar, CR De Egmonden 2054 (1620–1630s).
5 ARA, CR Rijnland 80 (1661).
6 See SANH, CR Amstelland (Nieuweramstel) 2347 (1655); MAR, CR 248, 140 (1656–7); ARA, CR Stein & Willens 17 (1657); ARA, CR Land of Strijen 1 (1657); MA Amersfoort, CR 407/27 (1657–9); SAU, HvU 99/8 (1657–61); MAL, CR 15 (1658); DA at Enkhuizen, CR Enkhuizen 4924 (1658); MA Gouda, CR 179 (1658–9); ARA, CR St Hubertsgerecht 3 (1659); MAA, CR 584–5, 312–13 (1659–61); ARA, CR Voorschoten 46 (1660); DA at Schoonhoven, CR Schoonhoven 2323, 2331 (1661); SANH, CR Blois 1293 (1661); and ARA, CR Rijnland 80 (1661, 1663).
7 MAA, CR 583 (May 1660).
8 See SAU, HvU CR 99/8 (1661).
9 DA at Schoonhoven, CR Schoonhoven 2323 (1661).
10 See SAU, HvU CR 99/8 (1661).
11 See MA Gouda, CR 179 (1658).
12 See ARA, CR Rijnland 80 (1661).
13 See MAA, CR 583 (1660).
14 See DA at Hoorn, CR Hoorn 4517 (1652).
15 I have not found his sentence among the rather fragmentary records of Gouda of this period.
16 See SANH, CR Blois 1293 (1661).
17 Other references to the use of a dead man's hand may be found in DA at Schoonhoven, CR Heeraartsberg 2 (1722), where a boy from the Odendaal Band describes how another band member used to carry a dead man's hand among his personal belongings, and in ARA, CR Woerden 5 (1724), where a woman living with a group of French vagrants states that 'entering the house, they put a dead man's hand, which Jacob the Leper used to carry, with a burning candle in it in front of the bed where people were lying asleep, expecting that they would not wake up'. Perhaps it is significant that such statements were apparently only made by women and children. Was this the kind of secret trade knowledge never spoken about by the

men in front of the authorities, or were women and children the only ones to believe in such customs?

18 MA Amersfoort, CR 407/27 (1659).
19 DA at Schoonhoven, CR Schoonhoven 2331 (1661).
20 See DA at Schoonhoven, CR Schoonhoven 2323, 2331 (1661).
21 DA at Schoonhoven, CR Schoonhoven 2331 (1661).
22 DA at Schoonhoven, CR Schoonhoven 2323 (1661).
23 For the Simons/Kaalkop group see SANH, CR Kennemerland 51 (1657); MAR, CR 248–9 (1662); MAL, CR 15 (1658–9); MAA, CR 581 (1651); DA at Hoorn, CR Hoorn 4517 (1658); and MADe, CR 49 (1659). For the Crabbe/Fransz group see MAA, CR 581–2 (1654–5, 1657) and MADe, CR 48 (1651). For the Maes/Jongejager group see MADe, CR 49 (1655–6).
24 Information about Stoffel's band may be found in MADe, CR 49, 58 (1665, 1668–9); MAL, CR 16 (1668); SAZ, CR Zierikzee 3850 (1668); MAR, CR 249 (1669); and SAU, HvU 99/9 (1669).
25 By 1669 Jacob was about twenty-five years old. In the past he had run away from an orphanage in Leiden. He had been convicted in Gorinchem and Beierland, and his final sentence contains a detailed list of about twenty-five recent thefts and burglaries. See MADe, CR 49 (1669).
26 See ibid.
27 See SANH, CR Kennemerland 51 (1657).
28 See SAU, HvU 99/9 (1669).
29 None of the three bands I have found for this period was of any real importance. The first one (1701–6) consisted of just four Brabanders and their wives or mistresses, who begged and committed petty thefts as well as a few burglaries in South Holland (see ARA, CR Rijnland 10, 1706). The second (1704–18) was a local band, made up of about fifteen inhabitants – friends, relatives, and neighbours at the fringe of local society – of Jaarsveld, near Utrecht.They mainly stole rye, cabbages, fish, straw, peas, cheese, and butter, partly for their own use, partly for resale (see SAU, CR Jaarsveld 854, 1718, and DA at Schoonhoven, CR Heeraartsberg 2, 1718). The third one (1706–7) consisted of six men (at least four of them deserted soldiers) and five women in their thirties; they toured South Holland, begged, extorted food and money, and broke into garden sheds, barns, and country houses (see MATH, CR 107, 1707, and MAL, CR 30, 1708).
30 Information about members of this band may be found in MATH, CR 107 (1715); MADe, CR 50 (1718); DA at Hoorn, CR Hoorn 4518 (1713); ARA, CR Rijnland 11 (1715); ARA, HvH 5659 (1717); SANH, CR Zijpe 6528 (1720); DA at Purmerend, CR Purmerend 3731 (1718); MAL, CR 34 (1718); and MA Alkmaar, CR 46 (1717).
31 Extensive sentences and interrogations of members of the Jaco Band may be found in: MAA, CR 608, 374 (1716–17); ARA, HvH 5659 (1718); SANH, CR Amstelland (Nieuweramstel) 2347 (1721); MAR, CR 253 (1716); MADe, CR 50 (1720). See also Mattheij 1986 and Buschman & Giele 1981a, 1981b.
32 Detailed information about all their activities may be found in MAA, CR 608, 374 (1716–17).

Chapter 4 'Foreign Soldiers': Military Bands in Brabant, 1690–1720

1 See SANB, CR Hoeven 33 (1741).
2 See MA Helmond, CR 176, 178/I (1747).
3 On the Brabant Zwartmakers see MAH, CR 39 and dossiers 164/11, 146/13, 131/24, 83/3 (1695–8, 1700); MAB, CR 112–13 (1694, 1697–8); DA at Heusden, CR Heusden 34 (1695); SANB, CR Land of Ravenstein 1 (1695); ARA, CR Rijnland 10, 61 (1697); SANB, CR Oosterhout 113 (1699); ARB, Drossaardschap van Brabant 61 (1696–8); MA Antwerp, Vierschaerboek 159 (1695–6); and SAG, HvG 4506, 1694/3 (1694). On the Gelderland branch see SAG, HvG 4506, 1693/2, 1694/2–3 (1693–5); MAA, CR 599, 341 (1695); SAU, HvG 99/9 (1694); MA Amersfoort, CR 407/33 (1694); MAH, CR 130/1 (1694).
4 Detailed descriptions of these and several more violent robberies may be found in the criminal records at 's Hertogenbosch – see MAH, CR 39 (1695). The most important expeditions generally figure in the sentences of more than one band member; versions told by different members and noted down by different courts can thus be compared.
5 MAH, CR 140/61 (1694).
6 MAH, CR 164/11 (1695).
7 MAH, CR 131/24 (1695).
8 See MAH, dossiers 164/11, 146/13, 131/24, 83/3 (1695–8, 1700).
9 MAH, CR 131/24 (1695).
10 SAG, HvG 1694/2 (dossier Willem Hermensz, 1694).
11 MAH, CR 131/24 (1695).
12 On Jantje van Emmenes see especially MAA, CR 599, 341 (1695). References to meetings at funeral meals are to be found in most of the records concerning the Gelderland branch mentioned in note 3. On meetings of vagrants, beggars, and thieves at rural wedding festivities in Flanders cf. Verhas 1991.
13 See ARB, Drossaardschap van Brabant 61.
14 See MAH, CR 39 (1696).
15 MAH, CR 39 (1695).
16 See MAB, CR 113 and dossiers 144/22–3 (1707), and MA Tilburg, CR 3 and unnumbered dossiers (1708, 1727).
17 MAB, CR 144/23 (1707).
18 According to a brief remark in some unpublished notes of the Breda historian van Haastert. Assistants at the Army Historical Section at The Hague have very kindly, but without success, tried to find any references to this company.
19 MA Tilburg, CR 3 and unnumbered dossier (1727).
20 See SANB, CR Putte 3, 5 (1713), and MAR, CR 145, 176 (1714).
21 See SANB, CR Putte 3 (1713).
22 SANB, CR Putte 5 (1713).
23 Ibid. SANB, CR Putte 5 (1713).
24 See MAR, CR 176 (1714).
25 Cf. on French nineteenth-century rural marginality Chauvaud 1990, and on English sixteenth- and seventeenth-century vagrancy Beier 1985.

26 The scarcity of such threats and, in general, of references by band members to bailiffs and public prosecutors is surprising. Whatever the reasons, it seems to point to a considerable distance between the judiciary and those on the wrong side of the law – and thus to a by no means self-evident lack of complicity between rural organized crime and the local bailiffs. Cf. van den Bergh 1857 on bailiffs and corruption.
27 MA Amersfoort, CR 407/33 (1694).
28 On the question of whether we should regard certain – if not all – robber bands, groups or burglars, thieves, and so on as social protest movements see Hobsbawm 1959, 1981, and the critical discussion of the latter in Blok 1972.
29 But cf. Blok 1976, 1991, on the eighteenth-century Bokkerijders bands in Limburg.

Chapter 5 Gypsy Bands, 1695–1730

1 DA at Hoorn, CR Sijbekarspel 5456 (1723).
2 This is hardly the place to go into the effects of exoticizing traditions or a biblical context on the representation of gypsies. Ingrid Janssens is at present preparing an MA thesis on the representation of gypsies in the Netherlandish art of the sixteenth to eighteenth centuries. I would like to thank her for showing me much of her information. See, for instance, illustrations in van Kappen 1965; cf. Dirks 1850, pp. 14–15. For France see de Vaux de Foletier 1961, esp. ch. 3, and 1966. French and German engravings seem to indicate that considerable changes occurred in gypsy dress between the mid fifteenth and late eighteenth centuries: wide cloaks and conspicuous hats remained a standard item, but among the men the wide shift-like garments of the sixteenth century had been replaced by trousers by the eighteenth century.
3 See MA Amersfoort, CR 407/32 (1692).
4 SAU, CR Oudewater OW24 (1734).
5 SANH, CR Weesp 2855 (1721).
6 See MA Haarlem, CR 55/8 (1740).
7 MAR, CR 145 (1714).
8 No such customs are mentioned in the principal studies about gypsy history in the Netherlands (Dirks 1850, van Kappen 1965, and L. Lucassen 1990). Mayall 1988 does not consider names. Okely, however, discusses a remarkably similar practice in her fascinating study of twentieth-century gypsies in England (1983): 'It is of primary importance that for the Gypsies or Travellers death is seen as a polluting event' (p. 217). 'The consequences of retaining a dead person's property were vividly described by a Gypsy' (p. 223). 'The name of the deceased must never be uttered ... Someone with the same name will generally be referred to by an alternative name, a derivation or a nickname' (p. 225). I would like to thank Mattijs van de Port for this reference.
9 See MA Haarlem, CR 55/8 (1740); cf. Okely 1983, pp. 174–5.
10 See, for instance, the sentences pronounced by the town court of Breda during 1721–3 (MA Breda, CR 114).
11 DA at Hoorn, CR Medemblik 5308 (1718).
12 SANH, CR De Nieuwburgen 6100 (1687); cf. cases at SANH, CR Diemen

2629 (1720); SANH, CR Amstelland (Nieuweramstel) 2347 (1720); DA at Hoorn, CR Sijbekarspel 5456 (1723); and SANB, CR Zegge 7 (1724).

13 MA Gorinchem, CR 37 (1754).

14 SAZ, CR Biervliet 1015a (1718).

15 See SANH, CR Assendelft 1971 (1723).

16 Cf. Okely 1975, an interesting essay on the role of twentieth-century gypsy women.

17 See DA at Purmerend, CR Purmerend 3723 (1725). For similar activities in seventeenth-century France see Asséo 1974. I would like to thank Arend Huussen for this reference.

18 See SANH, CR Zijpe 6524 (1687), and SANH, CR De Nieuwburgen 6100 (1687).

19 See MA Amersfoort, CR 407/32 (1692).

20 See ibid.

21 For the period 1650–98 Danker mentions eighteen ordinances against gypsies issued by the state of Braunschweig-Lüneburg, as well as eight issued by Württemberg (1988, p. 379). Dirks refers to the new Silesian rulings of 1683, 1685, 1688, and 1695, and to the Saxon ordinances of 1652, 1661, 1665, 1670, 1684, 1689, and 1697 (1850, pp. 32–8). The French authorities were almost equally active, proclaiming new measures in 1660, 1666, 1673, and 1682 (see Liégeois 1986, pp. 95–7, and Asséo 1974).

22 On Garneson and his involvement with the White Feather company see MAR, CR 145 (1714); cf. MA Amersfoort, CR 407/32 (1692).

23 MAR, CR 145 (1714).

24 Ibid.

25 See, for example, SANH, CR De Nieuwburgen 6101 (1712, 1716), and SANB, CR Oosterhout 113, 142/II (1716); cf. MAA, 610 (1724–6), and SANH, CR Assendelft 1971 (1723).

26 See ARA, CR Rijnland 11 (1720).

27 The bailiff as well as the defendants appealed. A move for a new trial was refused by the High Council (Hoge Raad) and the provincial estates of Holland. In the end the provincial Hof van Holland sentenced all four men to death. They were hanged at The Hague on Monday, 3 June 1720. See ARA, HvH 5659 (1720); cf. the sentence of Montagne Ysbrantsz published in van Kappen 1965, pp. 618–19.

28 See MAA, CR 609 (1722), and SANH, CR Weesp 2855 (1721).

29 Ibid.

30 Because of the wide and still partly obscure ramifications of the White Feather company, it is impossible to mention all relevant records here. For the older phases see the records concerning the Samel and Garneson groups mentioned in previous notes. The main records used for the period 1719–30 are, in Holland: ARA, HvH 5659, 5406/10 (1720, 1725); MAA, CR 609–10 (1722, 1724–6); MA Haarlem, CR 55/8 (1740); ARA, CR Zuid-Holland 114 (1723, 1727); SANH, Gooiland & Naarden 3042 (1718–20); SANH, CR De Nieuwburgen 6101 (1720–1); SANH, CR Amstelland (Nieuweramstel) 2347 (1721); SANH, CR Weesp 2855 (1721); ARA, CR Rijnland 11 (1720–1, 1725); ARA, CR Rijnsburg 48 (1724); ARA, CR Noordwijk 19 (1723); and MA Schiedam, CR 59 (1735); in Brabant: SANB, RvB 447/185–6; 447/188, 448 (1725–6); Off. Fisc. 519 (1725), 521 (1726), 523 (1726), 526 (1731); SANB, CR Zegge 7 (1724);

DA at Heusden, CR Heusden 34–5, 39 (1723–5); DA at Heusden, CR Woudrichem 15 (1725–6); SANB, CR Loon op Zand (or Venloon) 2 (1725–6); MAB, CR 114, 146/1–2, 146/7 (1722), 146/10–11, 146/14 (1725–6); in Zeeland: SAZ, CR Oostburg 1380 (1726). Publications about gypsy bands are scarce. Fragmentary information concerning the White Feather company may be found in Staats Evers 1865, 1869, and Dirks 1856. For some (insubstantial) information based on the records at Heusden see Kool-Blokland 1985, pp. 21–6. The principal publications are van Kappen 1965, pp. 460–506, and Hiemstra 1989. Neither uses more than a fraction of the above-mentioned records. Cf. for the southern Netherlands Deroisy 1964. Considering the huge amount of archival information, the period of at least fifteen to twenty years that should be taken into consideration, and the numerous courts – scattered all over Holland, Utrecht, Brabant, Gelderland, Overijssel, and Friesland (not to mention neighbouring foreign territories) – involved in the prosecution of these bands, it is not surprising that a full-scale study of the gypsy companies has not yet been undertaken. Research focusing on these companies and covering the whole of the Netherlands might uncover particularly interesting information about patterns of mobility, connections (both between contemporaneous companies and between successive groups), gypsy culture, and contacts between gypsies and non-gypsies.

31 The encampment at the Zandschel is mentioned in many of the above-named records. See also van Kappen 1965, pp. 460–506, and Hiemstra 1989. Even at present – in spite of drainage and reallotment – the distinction between the sandy soils and the clay areas is still clearly visible. The old provincial boundary between Brabant and Holland can likewise still be traced. (The modern one lies considerably further to the north.) A wall plaque of a gypsy (or, to be more precise, an oriental-looking person) can be seen above the front door of an old farmhouse close to the spot where the gypsy encampment must have been.

32 See MAA, CR 610 (1726).

33 Extensive information about this robbery may be found in the records at Breda, Amsterdam, and Rijnland mentioned in note 30. See also van Kappen 1965, pp. 460–506, whose report about the robbery is mainly based on the statements of gypsies detained by the court of Friesland.

34 ARA, CR Rijnland 11 (1725).

35 A distinction should be made not only between death penalties and lighter forms of punishment but between the different forms of death penalty as well. During the 1720s the courts frequently imposed aggravated death penalties on gypsies involved in robberies. Johannes Montagne Ysbrantsz, for instance, was broken on the wheel – in itself the most severe form of death penalty. Ordinarily, judges set limits to the convict's suffering by allowing a first stroke on the breast, which would kill instantly. In this case the court explicitly stated that the breaking of the limbs should proceed 'van onderop', starting with the legs, while the stroke on the breast came last; afterwards his head was cut off and exposed on a pike.

Chapter 6 Jewish Networks, 1690–1800

1 For all information on Moses see SANH, CR Weesperkarspel 2858 (1734–5), and MA Vlaardingen, CR10 (1736).

2 Diederiks 1987 reaches the same conclusion, and demonstrates convincingly that Jansen's contrary opinion (1986) is based on a misinterpretation of current criminal procedure. See also Huussen 1979. In Germany the legal situation was similar, but prosecution policies differed. There, large numbers of Jews were regularly arrested, but a high percentage were subsequently released because of lack of evidence. See Glanz 1968, pp. 28–30, and cf. Rohrbacher 1984.

3 See MATH, CR 108, 89 (1739, 1741); ARA, HvH 5461/4 (1750); and MAR, CR 255 (1742, 1751). Similar networks operated during 1764–70 and in the 1780s.

4 MATH, CR 106 (1695).

5 On this band see SANB, CR Grave 4 (1730).

6 For extensive information see SANH, CR Amstelland (Nieuweramstel) 2343 (1765); MAA, CR 615, 616 (1765, 1733); and SANH, CR Gooiland & Naarden 3046 (1763).

7 See ibid. and DA at Hoorn, CR Hem & Venhuizen 4817 (1743). There may also have been links with a group of Jewish robbers operating out of Amsterdam in the early 1750s who were involved in the murder and robbery of a clergyman at Groningen. See SANH, CR Weesperkarspel 2956 (1760).

8 The Estates General's official policy was directed at counteracting Roman Catholic influence in the still largely Roman Catholic southern parts of the Dutch Republic, where, contrary to formal regulations, Roman Catholics continued to act as bailiffs and judges. Perhaps that is why southern courts imposed extremely harsh punishments (involving burning or scorching) on both Jewish and non-Jewish church robbers during the first half of the eighteenth century. See also Blok 1989. I have not found any similar punishments in the predominantly Protestant north.

9 See SANB, RvB 448 (10.665–10.674) and 447/325–6, and MAH, CR 44A (1794).

10 Ferrand 1989 also points to the prominence of marginal or excluded groups among the perpetrators of church robberies in eighteenth-century southern France. On social protest, the role of skinners, and the church robberies committed by the Bokkerijders bands in Limburg see Blok 1989, pp. 42–6, and 1991.

11 See Reijnders 1969, pp. 18–33, Bloom 1937, Brugmans & Frank 1940, Huussen 1989, esp. pp. 114–20, Diederiks 1987, and Schama 1987, pp. 587–95; cf. Löwenstein 1985 and Gijswijt-Hofstra 1989. On Jews and their involvement in crime see also Egmond 1990.

12 I have found no cases of Jewish women having affairs with or marrying Christian men. The theme of sexual relations between Christians and Jews deserves further study. It may throw light on the self-images of both groups as well as on notions of purity and gender roles and relations. See brief discussions in Huussen 1989, pp. 115–16, and Roodenburg 1990, pp. 81–4; cf. Schama 1987, pp. 591–92.

13 See MAR, CR 255 (1751–3).
14 For all information on this family see DA at Hoorn, CR Hem & Venhuizen 4817 (1743).
15 But cf. Hulst 1989, p. 168, who refers to witness accounts by rural inhabitants of the eastern provinces which mention conspicuous dark garments, black curls, and earrings.
16 ARA, HvH 5496/3 (1769).
17 See MAH, CR 44 (1785), and SAU, CR Loosdrecht 1198 (1786, 1794, 1800).
18 For all details on Joseph see MA Dordrecht, CR 186 (1801).
19 The prosecutor had demanded whipping, branding, and twenty years' detention. See ibid.
20 Jewish fences deserve a separate study, if only because of their crucial role as middlemen between Jews and Christians. Cf. Endelman 1979, pp. 206–7.
21 ARA, CR Vianen 75 (1712).
22 See MAR, CR 253 (1712).
23 On the restrictive measures see, for example, Beem 1981, Zwarts 1940, Mansfeld 1961, and Reijnders 1969, esp. pp. 42–59.
24 As Wischnitzer notes, 'these Jews represented a constant danger of felony and even criminality and were a permanent source of embarrassment to the well-settled communities' (1965, p. 26). See especially Glanz 1937 and 1968. Cf. Endelman 1979, pp. 176–9, Shulvass 1971, pp. 67–111, and Danker 1988, pp. 352–3. For the Netherlands see Mansfeld 1961, p. 188.
25 See Bloom 1937, Israel 1985, pp. 106–9, 154–6, van Dillen 1940, and Diederiks 1984.
26 On increasing poverty and deplorable housing conditions in the late eighteenth century see Boekman 1930; cf. Bloom 1937, pp. 217ff, and Diederiks 1984.
27 See ARA, HvH 5496/3 (1769). In the rather smaller Jewish networks of the late seventeenth and early eighteenth centuries German and east-European Jews also formed the majority. The same was true of the Great Dutch Band of the 1790s (see Chapter 7 below and Egmond 1986, pp. 52–6).
28 The prominence of recent immigrants among those sentenced should not be taken as evidence that immigrants were arrested more readily; immigrants were just as numerous among those who were mentioned by detainees but were not arrested or sentenced.
29 On patterns of migration and the numbers of Jewish immigrants in the Netherlands see Shulvass 1971, esp. p. 73, Israel 1985, pp. 104–5, 145–55, and Bloom 1937, pp. 24–9, 31–2. Both Boekman (1929, p. 104) and van Dillen (1940, p. 595) report that about 19,000 of the 24,000 Ashkenazim living in Amsterdam in 1805 were poor. Cf. Diederiks 1984.
30 See Shulvass 1971, p. 73, and Bloom 1937, pp. 24–9, 31–2. Bloom presents the following figures for Ashkenazim living in Amsterdam: 1674: 5,000; 1720: 9,000; 1748: 10,000; 1780: 19,000; 1795: 21,000; 1805: 24,000. The numbers should be seen in the context of a more or less stable total population of about 200,000.
31 On Amsterdam see Diederiks 1984, p. 117, who refers to: 332 marriages for the period 1700–10; 382 for 1711–20; 989 for 1721–30; 1,067 for 1731–40; the figures continue to rise, reaching 1,577 for 1791–1800. For Leiden see Zwarts 1940, pp. 441–3.
32 For the geographical origins of Jewish immigrants who were not involved

in crime see Shulvass 1971, Israel 1985, pp. 104–5, 145–55, Sluijs 1940, esp. pp. 340—4, and Beem 1969, pp. 92ff.

33 See DA at Hoorn, CR Hoorn 4519 (1730).

34 For all information see SANH, CR Weesperkarspel 2956 (1760).

35 Ibid.

36 This seems to apply to Jewish bands active in Germany as well. See Glanz 1968; cf. Danker 1988, pp. 297–301.

37 On occupational activities see Bloom 1937, van Dillen 1940, Endelman 1979, Katz 1973, and Reijnders 1969.

38 In these respects too Jewish bands operating in the Dutch Republic closely resemble Jewish *Gauner* in Germany. Cf. Glanz's fascinating chapter on gender relations, kinship ties, and the role of women (1968, pp. 183–97).

39 See MAH, CR 44 (1783). Obviously these examples concern 'exceptional' women who did accompany their husbands and kinsmen, otherwise I would never have heard about them.

40 See Moses's lengthy interrogations and sentence in MA Alkmaar, CR 48BII (1786). For each decade the list of his accomplices and companions takes up at least half a page.

Chapter 7 Mixing Minorities, 1720–1800

1 Archival documentation concerning the Rabonus Band is abundant: ARA, VROA Collection van Maanen 1900–15 (list of accomplices named by three men sentenced at Alkmaar in 1768); ARA, CR Schieland 83 (sentences), 35 (interrogations), and 12–13 (correspondence) (1765); DA at Heusden, CR Woudrichem 3 (1767); SANB, RvB Off. Fisc. 547 (1763); MA Alkmaar, CR 48, 48BII, 48BIII (1767–8); MAR, CR 256 (sentences), 160, 161 (interrogations) (1765); MAR, CR Slot van Capelle aan de IJssel 3045 (1765); MADe CR 51 (1765); MA Dordrecht, CR 168 (1768); and SAG, Landdrostambt Zutphen 6 (including a sentence by the Hof van Gelre) (1762). For some related smaller groups see DA at Heusden, CR Woudrichem 2, 16 (1754); SANH, CR Gooiland & Naarden 3046 (1762); and in particular the records concerning the group of Hazemondse Kaat & Dirk de Kletsoog in ARA, HvH 5665 and 5482/4 (1764–5); and MA Gorinchem, CR 38 (1763).

2 The Rotterdam sentences of Arorus Florusse, Christina van den Bergh, and Anne Mie Bilouw (MAR, Cr 256) mention several criminal sentences pronounced against band members in the northern provinces during the 1750s.

3 See ARA, CR Schieland 35 (1765).

4 See MAR, CR 161 (1765).

5 See MAR, CR 257, sentence Arorus Florusse (1765).

6 See SAG, Landdrostambt Zutphen 6, sentence Joseph Bilouw (1762).

7 Descriptions may be found in ARA, CR Schieland 83, 35, sentence and examinations Rabonus (1765), and MAR, CR 256, sentence Elisabeth Josephs (1765).

8 See DA at Heusden, CR Woudrichem 3, sentence Henke (1767).

9 See DA at Heusden, CR Woudrichem 3, sentences Henke, Marie Elisabeth, Marie Josephs, and Dirck or Tobias (1767).

10 DA at Heusden, CR Woudrichem 3, sentence Marie Elisabeth (1767); cf.

MA Alkmaar, CR 48BII, sentences Alemondus Sjouwele, Cornelis Labans, and Nathan Moses (1768). This same part of North Holland had been the site of gypsy encampments at the beginning of the century, just like the moorlands near Rotterdam, the environs of Woudrichem, and a region called the Vlasmeer (which I have not been able to locate).

11 DA at Heusden, CR Woudrichem 3, sentence Henke (1767). Information about these ritual occasions is extremely scarce: Johanna Florusse mentions another one 'last summer near Veenhuizen in North Holland in the woods' (MAR, CR 161, 1765).

12 For a copy of the report see ARA, CR Schieland 35 (1765).

13 DA at Heusden, CR Woudrichem 3, sentences Henke and her family (1767).

14 See the interrogations of Rabonus and his relatives in ARA, CR Schieland 35 (1765).

15 SAG, Landdrostambt Zutphen 6 (1762).

16 See MAR, CR 161 (1765).

17 Ibid.

18 ARA, CR Schieland 35 (1765).

19 MAR 161 (1765).

20 ARA, CR Schieland 35 (1765).

21 MAR, CR 161 (1765). The Dutch *speellieden* includes not only itinerant musicians but all entertainers performing at fairs and so on, as well as those pedlars who sell and sing songs.

22 ARA, VROA Collection van Maanen 1900–15, and see also a copy in MA Alkmaar, CR 48.

23 See MAR, CR 161 (1765).

24 ARA, CR Schieland 35 (1765).

25 Ibid.

26 Ibid.

27 Ibid.

28 See the interrogations of the young boy in ARA, CR Schieland 35 (1765), who said that the captain and his two lieutenants carried special instruments for breaking through walls and were the first ones to enter a house during a burglary. Cf. the statement by Johanna Florusse (MAR, CR 161, 1765) declaring that Frederik Jansse had been leader of the band since his release from the house of correction at Rotterdam about one year before. Previously a certain Hermanus had acted as captain for five to six years. The captain received a large part of the stolen goods: half according to some.

29 Fat Piet's daughter Lena was married to Michiel Arendse, the son of Jan Rijnhoud, whose family belonged to Rabonus's band.

30 On Fisone, her companions in 1740, and her previous associates see MA Haarlem, CR 55/8 (sentences), 28 (correspondence), 52/1 (minutes), 26.26 (resolutions) (1740). For earlier sentences and references see ARA, CR Schieland 82 (1738), and SAU, CR Oudewater OW134 (1734). References to Knolletje's activities may be found in several documents concerning the Band of the White Feather.

31 For all quotations see MA Haarlem, CR 55/8 (1740).

32 See MA Alkmaar, CR 48, 48BII, 48BIII (1768).

33 On Moses's role as a guardian see ibid.

34 See MA Alkmaar, CR 48 (1768).

35 The only case I have found concerns a 45-year-old man who called himself master Isaac Jansz, Christian and surgeon, and his 40-year-old wife, who were found begging and camping with a group of about fifteen gypsies in North Holland during the 1680s. They continued to travel together: by the late 1690s Isaac, his wife, and various other members of their group had been convicted at least four times. The whole band was involved in numerous petty thefts and a small number of burglaries. Both Isaac and his wife were eventually hanged at Delft. See DA Waterland, CR Beemster 4027 (1688), and MADe, CR 50 (1698).

36 The term is untranslatable. I am using it here because it combines the notion of class (*schicht*, meaning 'layer', 'stratum') with that of illegality (*Gauner*, meaning 'thieves', 'vagrants').

37 Records concerning the Freduwa group may be found in MA Haarlem, CR 55/11–12 (sentences), 58/1–2 (interrogations), 29/8 and 25/12 (minutes and correspondence) 1787, 1797; MAR, CR 257–8 (1779, 1783, 1784, 1786); and MA Dordrecht, CR 175 (1776).

38 MA Haarlem, CR 55/11 (1787).

39 Records concerning the Calotte Band are to be found in MAH, CR 43 (sentences), and 91/1, 137/11, 126/6, 112/4 (dossiers) 1765–6); ARA, VROA Collection van Maanen 1900–15 (list of band members, which can also be found in SANB, RvB Off. Fisc. 547); and ARA, HvH 5495. For further information about particular robberies and band members see MA Tilburg, CR 4 (sentences) and 1765/2 (dossiers) (1765); SANB, CR Beek & Donk 39 (1765); MAB, CR 116 (1765); MA Roosendaal, CR 82 (1766); and SANB, CR Grave 5, 21 (1766–7).

40 See the lists mentioned in the previous note.

41 On de Bast and Rijckaart see MAA, CR 615 (1765); on the Feijtsburger Band in general see MAA, CR 615, 616 (1765, 1773); SANH, CR Amstelland (Nieuweramstel) 2343 (1765); and SANH, CR Gooiland & Naarden 3046 (1763).

42 The band had previously been active in Groningen. On the Gossels Band, see MAA, CR 616, 438 (1773–4), and ARA, CR Wassenaar & Zuidwijk 53 (1766). Cf. the pamphlet in which an inhabitant of Amsterdam describes how several band members were arrested: *Brief van een Amsterdammer* 1773. I am grateful to Marten Buschman for the reference.

43 On culture and identity of poor east-European Jews in the Netherlands in the seventeenth and eighteenth centuries see Kaplan 1989a, 1989b, and Egmond in press.

44 For this quotation and all other information about Wijl see SANH, CR Amstelland (Nieuweramstel) 2343 (1765).

45 MA Alkmaar, CR 48BII (1768). Chance played some part in these contacts, but of course they were not completely fortuitous. Mozes Wijl would not even have known about the Calotte group if there had been no Christian–Jewish cooperation in his own Feijtsburger Band as well as in the Calotte network. Nor would Nathan Moses and Heijntje van Gog have concluded a deal if they had not recognized and apparently trusted each other as colleagues in crime. A shared language helped, of course, and might in itself indicate a measure of unity in the world of thieves, but it would hardly have been reason enough to trust a complete stranger with the sale of valuable booty.

46 For all information concerning the Great Dutch Band see Egmond 1986 and the records mentioned there; for the Jacob family see especially Becker 1972.
47 See ARA, CR Den Briel 3 (1780), and MAR, CR 257 (1780).
48 See MAH, CR 44, 133/1 (1783–5), and SANB, RvB Off. Fisc. 568 (1783).

Chapter 8 The Brabant Connection, 1730–1810

1 See, for instance, the patterns of labour migration during the late eighteenth century as mapped and analysed in J. Lucassen 1984.
2 Many other local bands can be found in Brabant, but not in Holland. Around 1787, for instance, the Dintelse Band operated in the area of the small river Dintel in western Brabant; it consisted largely of rural labourers, who stole cattle and quantities of wheat and oats from their former employers and other farmers. They regularly transported the stolen goods by barge and much of it was sold. This group was active during years of both political unrest and high grain prices. See MAB, CR 117, 149/10 (1788).
3 On the Coppens family and the Zundert Band see GAB, CR 114, 52, 145/9–12 (1714); cf. SANB, CR Rucphen 12 (1728).
4 See DA at Heusden, CR Heusden 35, 39; MAH, CR 40, 41, and dossiers K 68/5, 128/16, 106/8 and old no. 183; MA Eindhoven, CR Woensel unnumbered (list *c.* 1731); SANB, CR Waalwijk 23, 77 (1727); MA Tilburg, CR 3 and unnumbered dossier (1729); ARA, CR Zuid-Holland 112 (1727); and SANB, CR Lith 11 (1725).
5 Accounts of this case of arson and of the drawing of cards may be found in most of the records mentioned in note 4.
6 MAH, CR 42, sentence Caspar Frits (1736).
7 For their final sentences see MAH, CR 42 (1736), and SANB, CR Loon op Zand 2 (1736). For further information about this group see MAB, CR 115 and dossiers 146/26, 146/28, 146/30–1 (1730–1); SANB, CR Deurne 32 (1736); MA Roosendaal, CR 81 (1737); SANB, CR Standdaarbuiten 7 and dossiers 9–10 and 16 (1731); MA Eindhoven, CR Woensel dossiers in box 1725–47 (1739); DA at Zevenbergen, CR Wouw 98 and dossiers 257, 260 (1731).
8 See SANB, CR Waalwijk 23 (1727, 1736); ARA, HvH 5665 and 5482/4 (1765); cf. MA Gorinchem, CR 38 (1763).
9 See MAH, CR 43 (1765), and SANB, CR Asten 20 (1735).
10 Both had previously belonged to the bands of Black Cas and Engele Jantje. See MAH, CR 42 (1741).
11 See SANB, CR Oud- & Nieuw-Gastel 17 (1758). Anthonie was hanged at Brussels.
12 See ARA, VROA Collection van Maanen 1900–15 (1783); ARA, CR Leerdam 191 (1783); and MA Gorinchem, CR 39 (1782).
13 Nicknames current in rural vagrant groups in Brabant can hardly be distinguished from nicknames commonly used among the non-vagrant part of the rural population. Very little has been published about the sociolinguistic aspects of naming in the Netherlands. On nicknames in Belgian Brabant see van Langendonck 1978; cf. Crott 1989.
14 See SANB, CR Rucphen 12 (1729).

15 Members of the Jaspers family may be found in the criminal records of Oudenbosch, Zegge, Roosendaal, Hoeven, Breda, Oud- & Nieuw-Gastel, and Rucphen itself.
16 See SANB, CR Zegge 7 (1756); SANB, CR Rucphen 12 (1759); and MAB, CR 116 (1763).
17 See MA Roosendaal, CR 83, 126–7, (1773–4, 1777) and SANB, CR Oudenbosch 47 (1778).
18 See SANB, CR Zegge 7 (1756).
19 For extensive information about the Catoen Band see MAB, CR 117 and 149/34–6 (1793–4); the printed version of the Breda sentences in ARA, HvH 5599; SANB, CR Oud- & Nieuw-Gastel 17 (1796); MA Roosendaal, CR 84 (1794); SANB, CR Oudenbosch 47 (1789, 1792); SANB, CR Rucphen 13–14 (1787–94); SANB, CR Hoeven 33 (1789–90); SAZ, CR Vrije van Sluis 593 (1792); and DA at Zevenbergen, CR Wouw 100, 292, 289 (1797). See also the printed *Sententien* 1802; cf. Sinninghe 1939, van Oosten 1928, Rijk 1972, and Lepoeter 1980.
20 See the records mentioned in the previous note, in particular SANB, CR Oud- & Nieuw-Gastel 17, sentence Piet Catoen (October 1796).
21 See the records mentioned in note 19. For the band's activities in Zeeland see Egmond 1986, pp. 52–6 and appendices. See also SAZ, Archieven Gewestelijke Besturen 298, 318 (1802).
22 The quotation is from a list of personal descriptions based on information provided by Little Thorn-bush to the court of Leerdam. See ARA, VROA Collection van Maanen 1900–15 (1783).
23 See ARA, CR Leerdam 191 (1783); MA Gorinchem, CR 39 (1782); and SANB, RvB Off. Fisc. 568 (letter referring to a court case against Christ the Skinner at Druten, 1783).
24 See SANB, RvB 448, nos 10665–74 (1794), and dossiers 447/325, 447/329.
25 Seven men were sentenced by the Raad van Brabant (four were hanged); investigations into Kappel's ventures precluded his further involvement in the band's activities.
26 See SANB, RvB 448, no. 10668 (1794).
27 See ibid.
28 On the strategic position of innkeepers see Blok 1991.
29 Geerts's nickname is nearly untranslatable. *Lui* means lazy; *Maan* is an abbreviation of Hermanus (another name used by Geerts); it also means moon. For this band see ARA, VROA Collection van Maanen 1900–15 (list 1792–3); SANB, CR Beek & Donk 40 (1798); and some personal descriptions in SAZ, CR Vrije van Sluis 593 (1792).
30 On the Blok Band see ARA, CR Zuid-Holland 125–6, 129 (1797–9).
31 For this band see ARA, VROA Collection van Maanen 1900–15 (1802); SANB, RvB 1249 dossiers 474, 502 (1799, 1802); SANB, RvB Off. Fisc. 1296 (printed sentences by the Hof van Gelre, 1803); MAH, CR 3361a (1805); SANB, RvB 1251 (1803); cf. SANB, CR Drunen 2 (1787), and van Kervel 1908.
32 See SANB, RvB Off. Fisc. 1296 (printed sentences by the Hof van Gelre, 1803).
33 The phenomenon of the Walloon immigrants and their involvement in several bands of the period 1780–1805 deserves further study. For some other Walloon bands see MA Eindhoven, CR Waalre 19 (1778–9); SANB,

CR Oudenbosch 47 (1786); MAB, CR 117, 149/12–13 (1778–9); SANB, RvB 447/450, 447/475, 1249/482 (1799–1800); and especially MA Roosendaal, CR 83–4, 86, and dossiers 126 (1787–8, 1800). See also Goyarts 1992, which appeared too late to be used here.

34 See the printed sentences in note 31.

35 Extensive information concerning the Zwartjesgoed may be found in ARA, VROA Collection van Maanen 1900–15 (list of members, 1805); ARA, CR Woerden 10, 19 (1805); MATH; CR 113 (1806–7); SAU; CR Oudewater OW25, OW28, OW43–4 (1805–6); MAR, CR 218 and interrogations 182–5 (1805–6); ARA, CR Rijnland 17, 39 (1804–6); SANH, CR Gooiland & Naarden 3052, 3063 (1806); and SANH, CR Schagen 5884 (1805–6). For earlier sentences of peripheral band members see, for example, MA Dordrecht, CR 176 (1778). Several authors (but no modern historians) have discussed aspects of the Zwartjesgoed Band: Christemeijer 1828, Moorman 1956, Sinninghe 1956, and Wiersma 1969, 1970.

36 ARA, CR Woerden 19 (15 May 1805).

37 MAR, CR 183, seventh interrogation Mie Albert.

38 References to *rommisceers* may be found both in the correspondence quoted in the text and in many interrogations.

39 See especially the list in ARA, VROA Collection van Maanen 1900–15.

40 See the records mentioned in note 35.

41 Sentences pronounced by bailiff Blok's court of Rijnland: ARA, CR Rijnland 17.

42 See MAR, CR 263, 182–5.

43 ARA, CR Woerden, 10, 19.

44 See, for instance, the correspondence between bailiffs Meuleman (at Woerden) and Montijn (at Oudewater) in ARA, CR Woerden 19, dossier J. H. Himmelgarten (1805).

45 In 1813, of course, the Netherlands regained their independence. This is not the place to go into developments in the nineteenth and twentieth centuries. For general surveys of Dutch legal and administrative history see de Monté ver Loren & Spruit 1972, Fockema Andraea 1972, and Gerbenzon & Algra 1987. On extradition and inter-jurisdictional contacts within the Dutch Republic see van Weel 1989 and Zwaardemaker 1939. Cf. the perceptive discussion of the organizational differences and inequalities between the modern (nineteenth- and twentieth-century) Dutch judiciary and police, and criminal organizations in Fijnaut 1989.

46 Little is known as yet about organized crime in the Dutch countryside during the nineteenth century, but evidence provided by van Ruller 1987 suggests that very few people were sentenced to death on account of major robberies – not because the courts imposed lighter penalities but, in all likelihood, because few bands commited such crimes.

Chapter 9 Contrasting Designs

1 This phase of relative quiet seems to have occurred in every type of property crime. Faber describes the pattern for Amsterdam, where the number of prosecutions remained low for an even longer period (1740 to about 1780). Since the same phenomenon is evident in almost every (urban and rural) jurisdiction in Holland, Zeeland, and Brabant (at least in the field of

organized property crime), an explanation in terms of changing prosecution patterns can only account for part of it. The spectacular fall of prosecutions during the 1740s and 1750s may after all have been caused simply by a decline of criminal activities. See Faber 1983, esp. pp. 69, 299. Prosecution in eighteenth-century England followed different, war-related patterns. See Beattie 1986, pp. 199–223.

2 See especially Boomgaard 1992 concerning Amsterdam. Cf. Jansma 1987 and Abelmann 1976–8.

3 For sensitive descriptions of the life of the poor in France during this period see Hufton 1974 and the work of Richard Cobb.

4 Cf. Richard Cobb's superb reconstruction of the journey of three men after committing a double murder in 1809, 'L'Affaire Perken' (Cobb 1975c, pp. 49–76).

5 See Hobsbawm 1981, Weisser 1979, and McIntosh 1975. Cf. Küther 1976, 1984 (on Bavaria, Hessen, Spessart, Odenwald, Hunsrück), Danker 1988 (more about Germany), Blok 1991 (Maastricht area), MacFarlane 1981 (Westmorland), and Beier 1985 (England).

6 Evidence concerning the economic, social, and cultural unity of this coastal region (and thus indicating major differences between the urbanized coastal zone and its continental hinterland) strengthens this hypothesis. It points to common migration patterns (from inland zones to the whole North Sea coast from Bruges to Bremen), strong economic ties (shipping, harbours, trade) and frequent communication between coastal towns, a common language and architecture, quite apart from the early urbanization and commercialization of agriculture in the coastal zone, a weak feudal tradition, and so on. Direct evidence can, of course, only be provided by systematic research comparing rural organized crime in, for instance, the coastal regions of northern Germany and central Germany, or south-east England and the northern counties, or the urbanized western part of the southern Netherlands and the inland provinces.

7 MA Alkmaar, CR 48BIII (1768); SANH, CR Amstelland (Nieuweramstel) 2347 (1721); and MA Breda, CR 113 (1707).

8 ARA, CR Woerden 10, 1805–6.

9 SANH, CR Abbekerk 5427 (1765).

10 ARA, CR Schieland 35 (1765).

11 For the first quotation see ARA, CR Strijen 1 (1661); for the second, which concerns the Band of Hees, see SANH, CR Kennemerland 51 (1658). See also the interesting chapter 'Un groupe réprouvé: délits imputés' in Asséo 1974, pp. 41–53.

12 MAR, CR 256 (1765).

13 See Vandenbroeck 1987, whose term *negatieve zelfdefiniëring* (negative self-definition) I have borrowed here. This is one of the important themes in the growing literature on symbolic inversion and the representation of 'others'. See, for instance, Burke 1978, 1987, Davies 1975, Le Roy Ladurie 1979, Babcock 1978, Pleij 1985, 1988, and Mason 1990. For a discussion of *asymmetrische Gegenbegriffe* in a very different context see Koselleck 1979.

14 MA Gorinchem, CR 37 (1754).

15 Cf. A. Cohen 1985 on community and boundaries. See E. Cohen 1989, 1990, Blok 1989, and de Certeau 1979 on symbolic aspects of public executions. See also Moore 1987 on stigmatization and persecution.

16 See especially Ginzburg's brilliant reading and use of court records in several essays in Ginzburg 1990b, and also Ginzburg 1980, 1983.

Appendix The Organization of Dutch Criminal Justice

1 Only very few institutions were entitled to infringe on the territorial autonomy of these first-instance courts. Certain categories of people were subject to special courts: officers and soldiers were generally court-martialled; professors and students of Leiden University could only be prosecuted by a university court; and people belonging to the staff of the Court of Holland were dealt with by the Court itself. A few administrative institutions had special judicial prerogatives: some of the polder and dyke boards – *hoogheemraadschappen* – for instance, might prosecute in criminal cases concerning drainage, dykes, and some. The Court of Holland, moreover, shared first-instance competence with the local courts regarding all vagrant people and all crimes threatening public safety. See Huussen 1976 and Egmond 1987a.

2 See, for instance, ARA, CR Beierland 8 (1720), and SAZ, CR Zierikzee 3850 (1723).

Archival Sources

The archival sources consist of the criminal sentences and other criminal records of the courts listed below. With the exception of the provincial courts, all the names mentioned here refer to local courts of first instance with full competence in criminal matters: the so-called high jurisdictions. They range from big towns (Amsterdam, Rotterdam) and large rural areas (South Holland, Schieland) to only one village or even a polder without inhabitants. The years refer to the extant series of criminal sentences, all of which have been gone through systematically; additional criminal records have been used for the more important bands. Archival records outside these provinces have been used incidentally and are referred to only in the notes.

The Province of South Holland[1]

Algemeen Rijksarchief at The Hague

Hof van Holland	1600–1800
Abbenbroek	minor frags
Achttienhoven	see under Nieuwkoop & Noorden
Albrandswaard & de Kijvelanden	minor frags
Alkemade	1761–1809
Ameide & Tienhoven[2]	1714–59
Asperen	1672–87; 1692–1732; 1741–81; 1792–1803
Beierland (Nieuw)	1716–1805 (fragm.)
De Beierlanden	1673–7; 1682–1811
Benthuizen	1680–1806
Bleiswijk	minor frags
Blois	1649–1752; 1761–1806 (fragm. before 1700)
Blokland (Laag)	1650–1771 (fragm.)
Boskoop	1795–1811

Brielle	1614–34; 1671–1810
Delfland	1776–1811
Esselijkerwoude & Jacobswoude	1667–71; 1695–1721
Geervliet	1732–94
Giessen-Nieuwkerk & Oudekerk	1665–1781
Godschalksoord	nothing left
Goedereede	1689–1811
Goudriaan	1650–1808
's Gravenzande & Zandambacht	1638–98 and 1750–3 (for both); 1760–1810 ('s Gravenzande); 1786–1803 (Zandambacht)
Grijsoord	1727–1810
Haastrecht	1659–1799
Hazerswoude	1699–1796
Hekendorp & IJsselveer	1762–1808
Heukelum	1706–1803 (fragm.)
Hofwegen	minor frags
Hondertland & de Oranjepolder	minor frags
Hoogeveen	nothing; area mainly covered by water
Hoogmade	1739–1807
Katwijken & 't Zand	1655–62; 1706–95
Klinkerland	minor frags
Koudekerk	1738–1810
Langerak	1669–80; 1689–1705; 1723–8; 1785
Leerdam	1779–1810
De Lier	1655–1756 (very fragm. after 1729); see also under Wateringen
Liesveld	1656–1737
Middelharnis	1694–1811
Monster etc.	1645–1809
Naaldwijk	1652; 1688–1716; 1742–54; 1764–9; 1778–1809
Naters & Pancras Gors	minor frags
Nieuweveen	nothing left
Nieuwkoop, Noorden & Achttienhoven	1660–1712; 1721–42; 1763–1811
Nieuwpoort	1618–1725 (fragm.); 1783–90
Noordeloos & Overslingeland	minor frags
Noordwijk-Binnen, Noordwijk aan Zee, Langeveld & Offem	1654–1738
Noordwijkerhout, Voorhout Hillegom & Lisse	1747–76; 1800–10
Oegstgeest	1645–1810
Papendrecht & Matena	1795–1810
Putten, Land of	1740–99
Rhoon & Pendrecht	1669–76; 1699–1720; 1749–1802
Rijnland	1653–1811

Rijnsburg	1703–1801
St Hubertsgerecht	1650–1799; 1801
Schieland	1678–90; 1708–1810
Slingeland	nothing left
Spijk	nothing left
Stein & Willens	1647–62; 1684–1810 (fragm. after 1738)
Strijen, Land of	1633–1787; 1795–1802
Tempel	nothing left
Valkenburg	1739–1811
Veur	minor frags
Vianen	1634–1754; 1765–1810
Vliet	nothing left
Voorne, Land of	1724–1810
Voorschoten	1646–90; 1701–44; 1795–1810
Voshol	1654–1810
Warmond	1663–1800
Wassenaar & Zuidwijk	1652–1811 (bad quality before 1700)
Wateringen etc.	1730–92
Wijngaarden & Ruybroek	1701–89 (fragm.)
Woerden	1652–65; 1695–1811
Zuid-Holland	1723–1811

MA at Delft

Abtsrecht	nothing left apparently
Delft	1619–1811

MA at Dordrecht

Dordrecht	1706–49 (fragm.); 1749–1805

MA at Gouda

Bloemendaal	nothing left apparently
Broek, Tuil & 't Weegje	nothing left apparently
Gouda	1663–1810

MA at Gorinchem

Gorinchem, Hardinxveld & Land of Arkel	1654–8; 1700–1809

MA at The Hague

The Hague & Haagambacht	1670–1811

DA Krimpenerwaard at Schoonhoven

Gouderak	1646–1810 (fragm.)
Heeraartsberg, Bergambacht & Klein Ammers	1654–1774; 1783–1808
Lekkerkerk & Zuidbroek	1686–1803 (fragm.)
Schoonhoven	1612–1806 (fragm. 1703–30)

MA at Leiden

Leiden	1647–1811

MA at Rotterdam

Rotterdam	1644–1811
Slot van Capelle aan de IJssel	1689–1808 (fragm.)

MA at Schiedam

Schiedam	1647–67; 1672; 1683–97 (fragm.); 1697–1811

MA at Vlaardingen

Vlaardingen	1595–1611; 1641–1811

The Province of North Holland

Algemeen Rijksarchief at The Hague

Hof van Holland	1600–1800

SA North Holland at Haarlem

Abbekerk	1671–1810
Amstelland (Nieuweramstel)	1650–1737; 1765–79; 1794–1811
Amstelland (Ouderamstel)	1690–1700; 1730–61; 1700–1811
Assendelft	1673–1738; 1769–1808
Barsingerhorn	1730–1802
Beverwijk	1724–34; 1752–1810
Bijlmermeer	1650–85; 1712–52; 1778–1807

Blois	1660–87; 1722–78; 1797–1802
Brederode	1743–53; 1798–1811 (fragm.)
Diemen	1685–1808 (fragm. 1740–60)
Gooiland & the town of Naarden	1682–1811
Haringkarspel	1657–94
Heerhugowaard	1789–94 (fragm.)
Den Helder & Huisduinen	1733–1802; 1802–10
Hoog-Bijlmer	1699–1804 (fragm. 1739–71)
Kallandsoog	1689–1811
Kennemerland	1657–99; 1795–1811
Muiden & Muiderban	1662–1795
Niedorp	1687–1758; 1774; 1806–10
De Nieuwburgen	1647–1700; 1709–41; 1761–72; 1773–88; 1789–1810
Oud-Karspel	1653–80; 1722–45; 1758–90; 1803–4 (fragm. after 1760)
Petten	1668–1702; 1713; 1717–18; 1729–34; 1800–10
Schagen	1684–1766; 1774–1809
Veenhuizen	1741–7; 1778; 1803–4
Waterland	1676–1811 (fragm. 1745–95)
Weesp	1668–98; 1711–1810
Weesperkarspel & Hoog-Bijlmer	1737–60; 1760–97 (fragm.); 1794–1811
Wieringen	1701–20; 1742–1807
Wieringerwaard	1688–1749; 1756–7; 1777–99
Winkel	1676–1734; 1752; 1770–87; 1791; 1796–1808; additional frags 1718–69
Zijpe & Hazepolder	1641–1723; 1733; 1775–9; 1805–10

MA at Alkmaar

Alkmaar	1665–1768; 1776–1810
Bakkum	1672–1749 (fragm.)
Bergen	1644–98; 1711; 1739–1810
De Egmonden	1619–34; 1676–1706; 1716–19; 1728–36; 1780; additional frags 1795–1810
Warmenhuizen etc.	1729–1809 (fragm. after 1770)
Wimmenum	1655–78; 1699–1700; 1709; 1730–5; 1749–50

MA at Amsterdam

Amsterdam	1651–1811

MA at Haarlem

Haarlem	1673–1811

DA Waterland at Purmerend

Beemster	1683–1811
Edam	1710–1810
Monnikendam	1669–1729; 1734–40; 1745; 1750–2; 1763–9; 1771–9; 1782–3; 1787–1810
Oosthuizen, Hobreede & Etershem	1711–1810 (fragm.)
Purmerend	1648–1770; 1787–1810
Purmerland & Ilpendam	1686–1726; 1751; 1764–9; 1781–8; 1796–1808
Wormer (Enge)	1707–1810 (fragm.)
Wormer (Wijde)	1653–63; 1685–6; 1704; 1726–8; 1738; 1774–6; 1800–03

DA Westfriese Gemeenten at Hoorn

Enkhuizen	1654–96; 1701–1810
Grootebroek	1661–1811
Hem & Venhuizen	1691–1811
Hensbroek	1781–1805
Hoogwoud & Aartswoud	1664–1742; 1762; 1778; 1792–4; 1804–10
Hoorn	1643–1811
Medemblik	1659–1710; 1717–1811
Obdam	1753–1800 (fragm.)
Opmeer	1748–66 (fragm.)
Schellinkhout	1650–68; 1679–1811 (fragm.)
Sijbekarspel	1688–1743; 1771–83
Spanbroek	1692–1785; 1800–01; 1808–10
Westwoud	1704–55; 1763–4; 1786; 1791–1811
Wijdenes & Oosterleek	1658–1804

The Province of Utrecht[3]

SA Utrecht at Utrecht

IJsselstein (town & Land of)	1654–1811
Jaarsveld	1715–28; 1739–1806
Kabauw	nothing left
Lange Linschoten &	1704–42; 1795–1808 (fragm.)

Snelrewaard	
Loenen Kroonenburgs	1756–72
Loosdrecht, Mijnden & Tekkoop	1679–96; 1707–1801; 1807–10
Oudewater	1679–1811
Waveren, Botshol & Ruige Wilnis	1727–1808
Zevender	nothing left
Zuid-Polsbroek	1652–1807 (fragm.)

North Brabant

SA North Brabant at 's Hertogenbosch

Raad van Brabant (and its successors)	1650–1810
Asten	1713; 1718–1802
Beek & Donk	1716–1808
Berlicum & Middelrode	1677–1761; 1775–1801
Borgvliet	1759; 1790–3 (fragm.)
Boxmeer, barony of[4]	nothing
Boxtel	1673–81; 1689–1805 (fragm. before 1720)
Budel	1723–66
Deurne & Liessel	1660–91 (fragm.); 1711–1801
Dinteloord & Princeland	1658–70; 1679–1803
Dinther	1673–93; 1740–1802 (fragm.)
Drunen	1690–1755; 1767–96; 1802
Empel	1729–80 (fragm.)
Fijnaart	1685–1803
Geertruidenberg	1628–1711 (but hardly any criminal cases)
Geffen	1704; 1718–82 (fragm.)
Gemert[5]	1669–1811 (fragm.)
Grave & the Land of Cuijk	1679–1803
Halsteren	1699–1810
Heeswijk	1763–1801 (fragm.)
Heÿningen	see under Fijnaart
Hilvarenbeek	minor frags
Hinkelenoord	nothing
Hoeven	1675–1803
Hoge & Lage Zwaluwe	1690–1811
Hoogerheide	minor frags
Huijbergen	1725–73 (fragm.)
Kessel	1725–57; 1779–85; 1793
Klundert (or Niervaart)	1696–1810
Liempde	1699–1779
Lieshout	1763–1810
Lith	1717–91; 1798–1805
Loon op Zand (or Venloon)	1680–90; 1724–1802

Maarheeze & Soerendonk	1678–1715 (fragm. before 1700); 1724–1802
Megen	1680–1802 (minor frags)
Mierlo	1749–1800
Moergestel	1702–26; 1732–1800 (fragm.)
Oud- & Nieuw-Gastel	1733–96
Nuland	1694–1757 (fragm.); 1785–99 (fragm.)
Oosterhout	1666–1803
Oploo	nothing
Ossendrecht	1731–1802
Oudenbosch	1674–1806
Oyen	1712–71 (fragm.)
Putte	1713–90
Ravenstein, land of[6]	1694–1741; 1750–61; 1770–91; 1800–11
Rucphen	1715–46; 1759–1803
St Anthonis[8]	nothing
St Michielsgestel	1690–1794
Sambeek[7]	nothing
Standdaarbuiten	1715–1803
Steenbergen	1679–1716; 1720–1803
Vlierden	minor frags
Vlijmen	1661–2; 1675–7; 1690–1707; 1713–21
Vorenseinde	minor frags
Waalwijk	1664–1715; 1727–48; 1765–1807 (all fragm.)
Wernhout	1667; 1694; 1801–2
Willemstad	1715–1811
Woensdrecht	1714; 1780–94
Zegge	1700–1802 (fragm.)
Zevenbergen	1687–1810
Zuidgeest	1722–55 (fragm.)

MA at Bergen op Zoom

Auvergne & Glymes polders	nothing
Beijmoer polders	nothing
Bergen op Zoom	1642–1738; 1749–1802
Noordgeest	nothing

MA at Breda

Breda (town & barony)	1626–1811

MA at Helmond

Helmond	1709–1801 (fragm.)
Stiphout	1705–47; 1753–1801 (fragm.)

MA at 's Hertogenbosch

Bokhoven	1687–1770; 1797–1806 (fragm.)
Engelen	minor frags
's Hertogenbosch (town & the larger part of the surrounding Meijerij)	1676–1811

DA Land van Heusden & Altena at Heusden

Eethen & Meeuwen	1715–91
Gansoijen	minor frags
Hagoort	nothing
Heusden (town & Land of)	1670–1810
Oudheusden	1685–1802
Woudrichem & the Land of Altena	1729–1808

DA Nassau-Brabant at Zevenbergen

Moerstraten	minor frags
Wouw	1616–60 (fragm.); 1675–1803

DA Oirschot at Oirschot

Oirschot	1685–1742; 1742–1802 (minor frags)

DA Oosterhout at Oosterhout

's Gravenmoer[10]	1753–1802

MA at Roosendaal

Roosendaal & Nispen	1675–1810

DA Southeast Brabant at Eindhoven

Aalst	1683–97; 1713–18; 1806
Eckart	nothing
Eindhoven	1742–95; 1790–6; 1802–7
Geldrop	1714–49; 1754–91 (fragm.)
Gestel, Stratum & Strijp	1625–1801 (fragm.)
Heeze & Leende	1659–1790

Waalre & Valkenswaard	1705–1800
Woensel	1674–1747

MA at Tilburg

Tilburg & Goirle	1764–1803

MA at Vlijmen

Nieuwkuijk	1644–1809
Onsenoort	1659–1721; 1749–51; 1784–1809 (fragm. after 1749)

MA at Waalwijk

Baardwijk	1663–92; 1715–18; 1735–6; 1766–1810

ARA at The Hague

Nassause Domeinraad	1707–76

The Province of Zeeland

Algemeen Rijksarchief at The Hague

Hof van Holland (and Zeeland)	1600–1800
Departementaal Gerechtshof Zeeland	1803–7
Raad van Vlaanderen[11]	1676–86; 1713–94

SA Zeeland at Middelburg

(Jurisdictions on the islands of Zeeland)

Arnemuiden	1644–8; 1683–1811 (seventeenth century fragm.)
Bommenede	1722–1800
Borssele	1618–60; 1764–1807
Brouwershaven	1661–1783
Bruinisse	1661–1799
Domburg	1708–13; 1762–3; 1784; 1802
Dreischor	1672–1705
Duijveland	nothing

Kortgene	1764–87; 1801–11
Middelburg & Zeeland Bewester Schelde[12]	no series left; scattered information for 1625–1733; 1783
Oosterland	1671–1807
Reimerswaal	nothing after 1630
Sir Jansland	1698–1810
Vlissingen[13]	1712–45
Westkapelle	1695–1809
Zierikzee & Zeeland Beooster Schelde	1612–1810

(Jurisdictions in Dutch Flanders)

Aardenburg	1662–1794
Biervliet	1708–80 (fragm. after 1740)
Breskens & Breskenszand	1703–37; 1757; 1777–91 (fragm.)
Filippine	1664–1704; 1754–68 (fragm.)
Hulsterambacht	1659–1700 (fragm.); 1700–91
Nieuwvliet	1642–1738; 1750–94
Oostburg	1713–26; 1741–59; 1768–90
Polder of Namen[14]	nothing
Sas van Gent	1660–1794 (fragm. after 1716)
St Anna ter Muiden	1702–95 (fragm.)
St Janssteen	1686–1706; 1711–18; 1720–89
Sluis	1694–1755
Terneuzen	minor frags
Vrije van Sluis	1609–1795
Westdorpe	1776–90 (fragm.)

MA at Axel

Axel & Axelambacht	1657–1795

MA at Goes

Goes	1635–1811

MA at Hulst

Hulst	1666–1793

MA at Tholen

St Maartensdijk	1621–1703; 1712–27; 1734–1809
Scherpenisse	1683–1710; 1770s (fragm.)
Tholen	1741–58; 1774–1800; 1804–11
Vosmeer (Oud & Nieuw)	1683–5; 1695–8; 1725–40; 1758–93
Vrijberge	1733–7; 1752–1807 (minor frags)

MA at Veere

Veere	1663–1808

Notes

1 This is the modern Dutch province of Zuid-Holland, not to be confused with the former high jurisdiction Zuid-Holland.
2 There were regular conflicts about competence with the neighbouring town of Vianen, which may have taken over criminal justice in this area during certain periods.
3 The following jurisdictions belonged to Holland during the seventeenth and eighteenth centuries but are now part of the province of Utrecht.
4 The barony of Boxmeer and the area of Gemert did not belong to the Dutch Republic but formed part of German territory. Their differently organized criminal records often mention only procedural matters and not offences.
5 See note 4.
6 The Land of Ravenstein did not form part of the Dutch Republic.
7 Sambeek, like St Anthonis, formed part of the barony of Boxmeer.
8 See note 7.
9 Bokhoven did not form part of the Dutch Republic but belonged to Liège.
10 From the early eighteenth century until 1735 criminal justice at 's Gravenmoer was usurped by the bailiwick of South Holland, which already controlled most of the adjacent territory.
11 The Raad van Vlaanderen is of only marginal importance to this study; its archives contain hardly any criminal cases.
12 Middelburg had high jurisdiction over both the town itself and large parts of several islands; nearly all its court records were burnt during World War II. An eighteenth-century index summarizes some of the criminal sentences.
13 Most of the criminal records of Vlissingen were burnt during the years 1808–9; some eighteenth-century copies are all that remain.
14 By the eighteenth century this polder had disappeared under the waters of the Westerschelde.

Works Cited

Abelmann, L. J. 1976–8: Vagebonden van de zelfkant. *Historisch Jaarboek voor Zuid- en Noord-Beveland*, 2: 57–61, 3: 22–3; 4: 15–21.

Agulhon, Maurice (ed.) 1990: *Les Marginaux et les autres*. Mentalités: histoire des cultures et des sociétés, no. 4. Paris.

Asséo, Henriette 1974: Le Traitement administratif des bohémiens. In Robert Mandrou (ed.), *Problèmes socio-culturels en France au XVIIe siècle*, Paris, 9–87.

Babcock, Barbara (ed.) 1978: *The Reversible World: symbolic inversion in art and society*. Ithaca/London.

Beattie, J. M. 1974: The pattern of crime in England, 1660–1800. *Past and Present*, 62: 47–95.

——1986: *Crime and the Courts in England, 1660–1800*. Oxford.

Becker, B. 1972: *Aktenmässige Geschichte der Räuberbanden an den beyden Ufern des Rheins*. 2 vols: Reprint. Leipzig. 1st edn Cologne 1804.

Beem, Hartog 1969: Joodse namen en namen van Joden. *Studia Rosenthaliana*, 3: 82–94.

——1981: Historical aspects of the small Jewish communities in the Netherlands. *Studia Rosenthaliana*, 15: 101–5.

Beier, A. L. 1985: *Masterless Men: The vagrancy problem in England, 1560–1640*. London.

Berents, D. A. 1976: *Misdaad in de Middeleeuwen: een onderzoek naar de criminaliteit in het laat-Middeleeuwse Utrecht*. Utrecht.

——1985: *Het werk van de vos: samenleving en criminaliteit in de late Middeleeuwen*. Zutphen.

Bergh, L. Ph. C. van den 1857: De baljuwen. *Het Nederlandsche Rijks-archief*, 235–303.

Blok, Anton 1972: The peasant and the brigand: social banditry reconsidered. *Comparative Studies in Society and History*, 14: 494–503.

——1975: *Wittgenstein en Elias: een methodische richtlijn voor de antropologie*. Amsterdam.

——1976: The Bokkerijders bands 1726–1776: preliminary notes on brigandage in the southern Netherlands: In *Papers on European and Mediterranean Studies*, vol. 7, Amsterdam.

——1988: *The Mafia of a Sicilian Village, 1860–1960: a study of violent peasant entrepreneurs*. Reprint. Prospect Heights, Ill. 1st edn 1974.

——1989: The symbolic vocabulary of public executions. In Jane F. Collier & June Starr (eds), *History and Power in the Study of Law: new directions in legal anthropology*, Ithaca, 31–55.

——1991: *De Bokkerijders: roversbenden en geheime genootschappen in de Landen van Overmaas (1730–1774)*. Amsterdam.

Bloom, H. I. 1937: *The Economic Activities of the Jews of Amsterdam in the 17th and 18th Centuries*. Williamsport, Pa.

Boekman, E. 1929: Demografische en sociale verhoudingen bij de Joden te Amsterdam omstreeks 1800. *De Vrijdagavond*, 3, 10 and 17 May, 72–4, 89–91, 103–6.

——1930: De bevolking van Amsterdam in 1795. *Tijdschrift voor Geschiedenis*, 45: 278–92.

Boomgaard, J. E. A. 1992: *Misdaad en straf in Amsterdam: een onderzoek naar de strafrechtspleging van de Amsterdamse schepenbank 1490–1552*. Zwolle/Amsterdam.

Brewer, John, & John Styles (eds) 1980: *An Ungovernable People: the English and their law in the seventeenth and eighteenth centuries*. London.

Brief van een Amsterdammer 1773: *Brief van een Amsterdammer, aan zyn vriend te Utrecht: Behelzende eenige byzonderheeden, over het gevange-nemen der bewuste negen roovers, op sondag s'morgens, den 22 deezer by't ontsluyten van de boom aan de oude stadsherberg te Amsterdam* (pamphlet), (University Library Amsterdam Pfl. Q.n.27.)

Brugmans, H., & A. Frank (eds) 1940: *Geschiedenis der Joden in Nederland*. Vol. 1. Amsterdam.

Buijnsters, P. J. 1980: *Levens van beruchte personen: over de criminele biografie in Nederland*. Utrecht.

Burke, Peter 1978: *Popular Culture in Early Modern Europe*. New York.

——1987: *The Historical Anthropology of Early Modern Italy*. Cambridge.

Buschman, M., & J. Giele 1981a: De ongeloofwaardige lotgevallen van Sjako en zijn bende. *De Tand des Tijds*, 30/31: 5–7.

——1981b: Sjako, voor de duvel nog niet bang. *Vrij Nederland*, 10 October.

Calkoen, G. C. 1906: *De Gevangenpoort of Voorpoort van den Hove*. The Hague.

Certeau, Michel de 1979: Des outils pour écrire le corps: inscriptions de la loi sur le corps. *Traverses*, 14/15: 3–14.

Chartier, Roger 1974: Les élites et les gueux: quelques représentations (XVIe-XVIIe siècles). *Revue d'histoire moderne et contemporaine*, 21: 367–88.

——1979: La 'Monarchie d'Argot' entre le mythe et l'histoire. In *Les Marginaux et les exclus dans l'histoire*. Cahiers Jussieu, no. 5, Paris, 275–311.

Chauvaud, Frédéric 1990: Les Îlots de la marginalité rurale au XIXe siècle. In Maurice Agulhon (ed.); *Les Marginaux et les autres*, Paris, 119–34.

Chesney, Kellow 1972: *The Victorian Underworld*. Reprint. Harmondsworth. 1st edn 1970.

Christemeijer, J. B. 1828: *Nieuwe Tafereelen uit de geschiedenis der lijfstraffelijke regtspleging*. Amsterdam.

Cobb, Richard 1970: *The Police and the People: French popular protest 1789–1820*. Oxford.

——1972a: La Bande d'Orgères. In R. Cobb, *Reactions to the French Revolution*, London, 181–215.

——1972b: La Vie en marge: Living on the fringe of the French Revolution. In R. Cobb, *Reactions to the French Revolution*, London, 128–79.

——1975a: La Route du nord: the Bande à Salembier. In R. Cobb, *Paris and Its Provinces 1792–1802*, London, 194–210.

——1975b: La Route du nord: the Bande Juive. In R. Cobb, *Paris and Its Provinces 1792–1802*, London, 141–93.

——1975c: *A Sense of Place*. London.

——1978: *Death in Paris, 1795–1801*. Oxford.

Cohen, Anthony P. 1985: *The Symbolic Construction of Community*. Chichester/London.

Cohen, Esther 1989: Symbols of culpability and the universal language of justice: the ritual of public executions in late medieval Europe. *History of European Ideas*, 11: 407–16.

——1990: 'To die a criminal for the public good': the execution ritual in late medieval Paris. In Bernard S. Bachrach & David Nicholas (eds), *Law, Custom, and the Social Fabric in Medieval Europe: essays in honor of Bryce Lyon*, Kalamazoo, Mich., 285–304.

Crott, J. 1989: Bokkerijders en hun bijnamen: *Veldeke*, 2: 54–60.

Danker, Uwe 1988: *Räuberbanden im Alten Reich um 1700: ein Beitrag zur Geschichte von Herrschaft und Kriminalität in der frühen Neuzeit*. 2 vols. Frankfurt am Main.

Davis, Natalie Zemon 1975: *Society and Culture in Early Modern France*. Stanford, Calif.

——1983: *The Return of Martin Guerre*. Cambridge, Mass.

——1988: *Fiction in the Archives: pardon tales and their tellers in sixteenth-century France*. Cambridge.

Deroisy, Armand 1964: La dispersion d'une bande d'Egyptiens en Brabant au début du XVIIIe siècle. *Études tsiganes*, 10: 17–25.

Deursen, A. Th. van 1977: *Het kopergeld van de Gouden Eeuw*. Vol 3. Assen.

Diederiks, Herman 1984: Structures ethniques et espace social: Amsterdam à la fin du XVIIIe siècle. In Maurice Garden & Yves Lequin (eds), *Habiter la ville, XVe–XXe siècles*, Lyons, 107–26.

——1987: Strafrecht en stigmatisering: de Joden in de achttiende-eeuwse Republiek. In H. Diederiks & C. Quispel (eds), *Onderscheid en Minderheid: sociaal-historische opstellen over discriminatie en vooroordeel*, Hilversum, 77–98.

Dijkhuis, H. Tj. 1937–9: De Jordaan: de ontwikkeling van een volkswijk in een grote stad. *Economisch-historisch Jaarboek*, 21: 1–91.

Dillen, J. G. van 1940: De economische positie en betekenis der Joden in de Republiek en in de Nederlandsche koloniale wereld. In H. Brugmans & A. Frank (eds), *Geschiedenis der Joden in Nederland*, vol. 1, Amsterdam, 561–616.

Dirks, J. 1850: *Geschiedkundige onderzoekingen aangaande het verblijf der Heidens of Egyptiërs in de Noordelijke Nederlanden*. Utrecht.

——1856: Nieuwe bouwstoffen voor de geschiedenis van het verblijf der Heidens of Egyptiërs in Nederland. *Bijdragen voor Vaderlandse Geschiedenis en Oudheidkunde* 1st series, 10: 271–84.

Eerenbeemt, H. F. J. M. van den 1968: *In het spanningsveld der armoede: agressief pauperisme en reactie in Staats Brabant*. Tilburg.

——1970: *Van mensenjacht en overheidsmacht: criminogene groepsvorming en afweer in de Meijerij van 's-Hertogenbosch, 1795–1810*. Tilburg.

Egmond, Florike 1986: *Banditisme in de Franse Tijd: profiel van de Grote Nederlandse Bende, 1790–1799*. Amsterdam.

——1987a: De hoge jurisdicties van het 18e-eeuwse Holland: een aanzet tot de bepaling van hun aantal, ligging en begrenzingen. *Holland, regionaal-historisch tijdschrift*, 19: 129–61.

——1987b: The noble and the ignoble bandit: changing literary representations of west-European robbers. *Ethnologia Europaea*, 17: 139–56.

——1989a: Fragmentatie, rechtsverscheidenheid en rechtsongelijkheid in de Noordelijke Nederlanden tijdens de 17e en 18e eeuw. In Sjoerd Faber (ed.), *Nieuw licht op oude justitie: misdaad en straf ten tijde van de Republiek*, Muiderberg, 9–22.

——1989b: Georganiseerde misdaad en de overheid in het verleden: Nederland tijdens de 17e en 18e eeuw. In C. J. Fijnaut (ed.), *Georganiseerde misdaad en strafrechtelijk politiebeleid: rechtshistorische, politieke, journalistieke en rechtsvergelijkende beschouwingen*, Lochem, 11–22.

——1990: Crime in context: Jewish involvement in organized crime in the Dutch Republic. *Jewish History*, 4: 75–100.

——In press. Contours of identity: poor Ashkenazim in the Dutch Republic. In *Dutch Jewish History Proceedings of the 6th International Symposium on the History of the Jews in the Netherlands, Jerusalem, 1991*.

Einstadter, Werner J. 1969: The social organization of armed robbery. *Social Problems*, 17: 64–83.

Endelman, Todd M. 1979: *The Jews of Georgian England, 1714–1830: tradition and change in a liberal society*. Philadelphia.

Evans, Richard 1984: Öffentlichkeit und Autorität: zur Geschichte der Hinrichtungen in Deutschland vom Allgemeinen Landrecht bis zum Dritten Reich. In Heinz Reif (ed.), *Räuber, Volk und Obrigkeit: Studien zur Geschichte der Kriminalität in Deutschland seit dem 18. Jahrhundert*, Frankfurt am Main, 185–258.

Faber, Sjoerd 1983: *Strafrechtspleging en criminaliteit te Amsterdam, 1680–1811: de nieuwe menslievendheid*. Arnhem.

Faller, Lincoln B. 1987: *Turned to Account: the forms and functions of criminal biography in late seventeenth- and early eighteenth-century England*. Cambridge.

Farge, Arlette 1979: *Vivre dans la rue à Paris au XVIIIe siècle*.

——1993: *Fragile Lives: violence, power and solidarity in eighteenth-century Paris*. Trans. C. Shelton. Cambridge, French edn. 1986.

Feit en fictie 1985: *Feit en fictie in misdaadliteratuur (ca. 1650-ca. 1850)*. Amsterdam.

Ferrand, Renaud 1989: Le Vol dans les églises en Lyonnais et en Beaujolais (1679–1789): le sacrilège des exclus. *Bulletin du Centre d'Histoire économique et sociale de la région Lyonnaise*, 2: 43–76.

Fijnaut, Cyrille 1985: Georganiseerde misdaad: een onderzoeksgerichte terreinverkenning. *Justitiële Verkenningen*, 9: 5–42.

Fijnaut, Cyrille (ed.) 1989: *Georganiseerde misdaad en strafrechtelijk politiebeleid: rechtshistorische, politieke, journalistieke en rechtsvergelijkende beschouwingen*. Lochem.

Fockema Andraea, S. J. 1972: *De Nederlandse staat onder de Republiek*. 4th edn. Amsterdam; 1st edn 1904.

Gatrell, V. A. C. 1980: The decline of theft and violence in Victorian and Edwardian England. In V. A. C. Gatrell, Bruce Lenman & Geoffrey Parker (eds), *Crime and the Law: the social history of crime in western Europe since 1500*, London, 238–337.

Gatrell, V. A. C., Bruce Lenman & Geoffrey Parker (eds), 1980: *Crime and the Law: the social history of crime in western Europe since 1500*. London.

George, M. Dorothy 1985: *London Life in the Eighteenth Century*. 2nd edn. Harmondsworth 1st edn. 1925.

Gerbenzon, P., & N. E. Algra, 1987: *Voortgangh des rechtes: de ontwikkeling van het Nederlandse recht tegen de achtergrond van de Westeuropese cultuur*. 6th end. Alphen aan den Rijn. 1st edn 1969.

Gijswijt-Hofstra, Marijke (ed.) 1989: *Een schijn van verdraagzaamheid: afwijking en tolerantie in Nederland van de zestiende eeuw tot heden*. Hilversum.

Ginzburg, Carlo 1980: *The Cheese and the Worms: the cosmos of a sixteenth-century miller*. London.

——1983: *The Night Battles: witchcraft and agrarian cults in the sixteenth and seventeenth centuries*. London.

——1990a: *Ecstasies: deciphering the witches' sabbath*. London.

——1990b: *Myths, Emblems, Clues*. London.

Glanz, Rudolf 1937: Die unterste Schicht von deutschen Judentum im 18. Jahrhundert. *Yivo-Bleter*, 11: 356–86.

——1968: *Geschichte des niederen Jüdischen Volkes in Deutschland: ein Studie über historisches Gaunertum, Bettelwesen und Vagantentum*. New York.

Gorp, H. van 1978: *Inleiding tot de picareske verhaalkunst of de wederwaardigheden van een anti-genre*. Groningen.

Goyarts, C. B. 1992: Een Luikse bende actief in Staats-Brabant. *Jaarboek de Ghulden Roos*, 52: 18–61.

Groot Placaet-boeck 1705: *Groot Placaet-boeck, vervattende de placaten, ordonnantien ende edicten van de Staten Generael der Vereenighde Nederlanden ende van de . . . Staten van Hollandt en West-Vrieslandt; mitsgaders van de . . . Staten van Zeelandt . . . tot den jaare 1794 in geslooten in het licht gegeeven door Cornelis Cau, Simon van Leeuwen e.a.* Vol 4. The Hague.

Haastert, J. van 1982: Beschouwingen bij de criminele vonnissen van Bredase rechtbanken in de periode 1796–1811. *Jaarboek van de Geschied- en Oudheidkundige Kring van Stad en Land van Breda 'De Oranjeboom'*, 35: 62–119.

Hallema, A. 1960: De Politie te Breda en in de Baronie gedurende de 17e eeuw. *Jaarboek van de Geschied- en Oudheidkundige Kring van Stad en Land van Breda 'De Oranjeboom*, 13: 180–219.

Ham, W. van, & J. Vriens 1980: *Historische Kaart van Noord-Brabant 1795: de gebieden van de schepenbanken binnen de huidige provincie Noord-Brabant omstreeks 1795*. 's-Hertogenbosch.

Hay, Douglas 1982: War, dearth and theft in the eighteenth century: the record of the English courts. *Past and Present*, 95: 117–60.

Hay, Douglas, Peter Linebaugh, John G. Rule, E. P. Thompson & Cal Winslow 1988: *Albion's Fatal Tree: crime and society in eighteenth-century England*. Reprint. Harmondsworth, 1st edn 1975.

Hiemstra, Minke E. 1989: Bendeleven en -structuur in de heerlijkheid Venloon: de bende van 'De Veeren', 1717–27. *Bijdragen tot de Geschiedenis*, 72: 59–80.

Hobsbawm, E. J. 1959: *Primitive Rebels: studies in archaic forms of social movement in the 19th and 20th centuries*. Manchester.

——1981: *Bandits*. Rev. edn. New York. 1st edn London 1969.

Hufton, Olwen 1974: *The Poor of Eighteenth-century France, 1750–1789*. Oxford.

Hulst, Frank 1989: Een brutale overval te Een in 1744. *Ons Waardeel*, 5: 165–72.

Huussen, A. H., Jr 1976: De rechtspraak in strafzaken voor het Hof van Holland in het eerste kwart van de achttiende eeuw. *Holland, regionaal-historisch tijdschrift*, 8: 116–39.

——1978: Jurisprudentie en bureaucratie: het Hof van Friesland en zijn criminele rechtspraak in de achttiende eeuw. *Bijdragen en Mededelingen betreffende de Geschiedenis der Nederlanden*, 93: 241–98.

——1979: De emancipatie van de Joden in Nederland: een discussiebijdrage naar aanleiding van twee recente studies. *Bijdragen en Mededelingen betreffende de Geschiedenis der Nederlanden*, 94: 75–83.

——1989: De Joden in Nederland en het probleem van de tolerantie. In Marijke Gijswijt-Hofstra (ed.), *Een schijn van verdraagzaamheid: afwijking en tolerantie in Nederland van de zestiende eeuw tot heden*, Hilversum, 107–29.

Israel, Jonathan I. 1985: *European Jewry in the Age of Mercantilism, 1550–1750*. Oxford.

Jansen, J. C. G. M. 1986: Strafrechtspraak en joden in Limburg in de 18e en vroege 19e eeuw. *Studies over de sociaal-economische geschiedenis van Limburg*, 31: 78–101.

Jansma, L. G. 1987: Misdaad in de 16e eeuw in de Nederlanden: de Batenburgse benden na 1540. *Doopsgezinde Bijdragen*, n.s., 12/13: 40–55.

Kaplan, Yosef 1989a: Amsterdam and Ashkenazic migration in the seventeenth century. *Studia Rosenthaliana*, 23: 7–21.

——1989b: The Portuguese community in 17th-century Amsterdam and the Ashkenazi world. In *Dutch Jewish History*, vol. 2, Assen, 23–45.

Kappen, O. van 1965: *Geschiedenis der Zigeuners in Nederland: de ontwikkeling van de rechtspositie der Heidens of Egyptenaren in de Noordelijke Nederlanden (1420-ca. 1750)*. Assen.

Katz, Jacob 1973: *Out of the Ghetto: the social background of Jewish emancipation, 1770–1870*. Cambridge, Mass.

Kervel, L. A. A. van 1908: Struikrovers en chauffeurs een eeuw geleden: de bende van Joseph Anzee in Gelderland. *Tijdspiegel*, 2nd section, 171–9.

Kooi, Jurjen van der 1981–2: Schinderhannes en de Achtkante Boer 1 and 2. *Driemaandelijkse Bladen voor Taal en Volksleven in het Oosten van Nederland*, 33: 81–95, 34: 43–58.

Kool-Blokland, J. L. 1985: *De elite van Heusden 1700–1750, een prosopografische studie*. Tilburg.

Koselleck, Reinhart 1979: Zur historisch-politischen Semantik asymmetrischer Gegenbegriffe. In Reinhart Koselleck, *Vergangene Zukunft: zur Semantik geschichtlicher Zeiten*, Frankfurt am Main, 211–59.

Küther, Carsten 1976: *Räuber und Gauner in Deutschland: das organisierte Bandenwesen im 18. und 19. Jahrhundert*. Göttingen.

——1983: *Menschen auf der Strasse: vagierende Unterschichten in Bayern, Franken und Schwaben in der zweiten hälfte des 18. Jahrhunderts*. Göttingen.

——1984: Räuber, Volk und Obrigkeit: zur Wirkungsweise und Funktion staatlicher Strafverfolgung im 18. Jahrhundert. In Heinz Reif (ed.), *Räuber, Volk und Obrigkeit: Studien zur Geschichte der Kriminalität in Deutschland seit dem 18. Jahrhundert*, Frankfurt am Main, 17–42.

Langbein, John H. 1977: *Torture and the Law of Proof: Europe and England in the ancien régime*. Chicago.

Langendonck, W. van 1978: De persoonsnaamgeving in een Zuidbrabants dialect. *Naamkunde*, 10: 92–144, 234–67.

Lepoeter, G. J. 1980: De Zeeuwse episode uit het leven van Jan Catoen. *Varia Zelandiae*, 16: 32–43.

Le Roy Ladurie, Emmanuel 1979: *Le Carnaval de Romans: de la Chandeleur au Mercredi des Cendres, 1579–1580*. Paris.

Liégeois, Jean-Pierre 1986: *Gypsies: an illustrated history*. Trans. Tony Berrett. London, French edn 1983.

Löwenstein, Steven M. 1985: Suggestions for study of the Mediene based on German, French and English models. *Studia Rosenthaliana*, 19: 342–54.

Lucassen, Jan 1984: *Naar de kusten van de Noordzee: trekarbeid in Europees perspektief, 1600–1900*. Gouda.

Lucassen, Leo 1990: *'En men noemde hen zigeuners': de geschiedenis van Kaldarasch, Ursari, Lowara en Sinti in Nederland: 1750–1944*. Amsterdam.

Lüsebrink, H. J. 1983: *Kriminalität und Literatur in Frankreich des 18. Jahrhunderts: literarische Formen, soziale Funktionen und Wissenskonstituenten von Kriminalitätsdarstellungen im Zeitalter der Aufklärung*. Munich/Vienna.

MacFarlane, Alan 1981: *The Justice and the Mare's Ale: law and disorder in seventeenth-century England*. Oxford.

McIntosh, Mary 1971: Changes in the organisation of thieving. In S. Cohen (ed.), *Images of Deviance*, Harmondsworth, 98–133.

——1975: *The Organisation of Crime*. London.

McMullan, John 1982: Criminal organization in sixteenth and seventeenth century London. *Social Problems*, 29: 311–23.

Mansfeld, R. G. 1961: Een Joodse roversbende in Gelderland en Overijssel in de eerste helft van de 18e eeuw. *Bijdragen en Mededelingen Gelre*, 60: 185–208.

Mason, Peter 1990: *Deconstructing America: representations of the other*. London/New York.

Mattheij, T. M. M. 1986: *Uitvoerig verhaal van alle schelmstukken, gepleegd door Jacob Frederik Muller, alias Jaco*. Muiderberg.

Mayall, David 1988: *Gypsy-travellers in Nineteenth-century Society*. Cambridge.

Mayhew, Henry 1851–62: *London Labour and the London Poor*. Vols 1–3 (1851–2) and vol. 4 (with J. Binny, B. Hemyng & A. Halliday, 1862). London.

Meer, Th. van der 1984: *De wesentlijke sonde van sodomie en andere vuyligheeden: sodomietenvervolgingen in Amsterdam 1730–1811*. Amsterdam.

Monté ver Loren, J. Ph. de, & J. E. Spruit, 1972: *Hoofdlijnen uit de ontwikkeling der rechterlijke organisatie in de Noordelijke Nederlanden tot de Bataafse Omwenteling*. 5th edn. Deventer.

Moore, R. I. 1987: *The Formation of a Persecuting Society*. Oxford.

Moormann, J. G. M. 1955: Jan H. Himmelgarten en het Zwartjesgoed: geschiedenis van een moordenaarsbende. *Neerlands Volksleven*, 6: 13–26.

Muchembled, Robert 1989: *La Violence au village (XVe–XVIIIe siècle)*. Brepols, Belgium.

Muir, Edward, & Guido Ruggiero (eds) 1991: *Microhistory and the Lost Peoples of Europe*. Baltimore/London.

Müller-Fraureuth, C. 1894: *Die Ritter- und Räuberromane*. Halle, Repr. Hildesheim 1965.

Okely, Judith 1975: Gypsy women: models in conflict. In Shirley Ardener (ed.), *Perceiving Women*, London, 55–86.

——1983: *The Traveller-gypsies*. Cambridge.

Oosten, G. D. van 1928: De bende of 't rot van Jan Catoen. *Sinte Geertruydtsbronne*, 5: 16–20, 74–9.

Parker, Alexander A. 1967: *The Picaresque Novel in Spain and Europe, 1599–1753*. Edinburgh.

Parker, Geoffrey 1972: *The Army of Flanders and the Spanish Road, 1567–1659: the logistics of Spanish victory and defeat in the Low Countries' wars*. Cambridge.

Pleij, Herman 1985: *Het gilde van de blauwe schuit: literatuur, volksfeest en burgermoraal in de late middeleeuwen*. 3rd ed. Amsterdam. 1st edn 1979.

——1988: *De sneeuwpoppen van 1511: literatuur en stadscultuur te Brussel tussen middeleeuwen en moderne tijd*. Amsterdam.

Pol, Lotte van de 1987: Vrouwencriminaliteit in Amsterdam in de tweede helft van de 17e eeuw. *Tijdschrift voor Criminologie*, 29: 148–55.

Raa, F. J. G. Ten, & F. de Bas (eds) 1915: *Het Staatsche Leger 1568–1795*. Vol. 3. Breda/The Hague.

——1921: *Het Staatsche Leger 1568–1795*. Vol. 5. Breda/The Hague.

Reijnders, C. 1969: *Van 'Joodsche Natien' tot Joodse Nederlanders: een onderzoek naar getto- en assimilatieverschijnselen tussen 1600 en 1942*. Amsterdam.

Rijk, P. 1972: Voetenbranders en rovers op Zuid-Beveland. *Varia Zelandiae*, 8: 2–3.

Rijpperda Wierdsma, J. V. 1937: *Politie en justitie: een studie over den Hollandschen staatsbouw tijdens de Republiek*. Zwolle.

Rohrbacher, Stefan 1984: Räuberbanden, Gaunertum und Bettelwesen. In *Köln und das rheinische Judentum: Festschrift Germania Judaica 1959–84*, Cologne, 117–24.

Roodenburg, Herman 1990: *Onder censuur: de kerkelijke tucht in de gereformeerde gemeente van Amsterdam, 1578–1700*. Hilversum.

Rousseau, G. S. 1987: The pursuit of homosexuality in the eighteenth century. In R. Maccubbin (ed.) , *'Tis Nature's Fault*, Cambridge, 132–68.

Ruller, Sibo van 1987: *Genade voor recht: gratieverlening aan ter dood veroordeelden in Nederland, 1806–1870*. Amsterdam.

Samuel, Raphael 1981: *East End Underworld: chapters in the life of Arthur Harding*. London.

Schama, Simon 1987: *The Embarrassment of Riches: an interpretation of Dutch culture in the golden age*. New York.

Schild, Wolfgang 1980: *Alte Gerichtsbarkeit: vom Gottesurteil bis zum Beginn der modernen Rechtsprechung*. Munich.

Schöffer, I., H. van der Wee & J. A. Bornewasser 1985: *De Lage Landen van 1500 tot 1800*. Amsterdam.

Schreurs, A. F. A. 1947: *Het kerkdorp St Willibrord (het Heike): een sociaalgeografische en criminologische studie*. Utrecht.

Schulten, C. M., & J. W. M. Schulten 1969: *Het leger in de zeventiende eeuw*. Bussum.

Sententien 1802: *Sententien van president en rechteren der stad Middelburg . . . tegen Francis Mertens, Jan Catoen en Modestus van de Perre . . . 20 September 1802*. Middelburg, (Provincial Library of Zeeland at Middelburg, no. 438 B 112.)

Shulvass, Moses A. 1971: *From East to West: the westward migration of Jews from Eastern Europe during the seventeenth and eighteenth centuries*. Detroit.

Sinninghe, J. 1939: Het bewogen leven van Jan Catoen, gauwdief en roover: *Sinte Geertruydtsbronne*, 16: 107–22.

——1956: Het Zwartjesgoed. *Neerlands Volksleven*, 6: 98–9.

Slootmans, C. J. F. 1956: Uit Rucphen's verleden voor 1800. *Jaarboek van de Geschied- en Oudheidkundige Kring van Stad en Land van Breda 'De Oranjeboom'*, 9: 158–89.

Sluijs, J. M. 1940: Hoogduits-Joods Amsterdam, van 1675 tot 1795. In H. Brugmans & A. Frank (eds), *Geschiedenis der Joden in Nederland*, vol. 1, Amsterdam, 306–81.

Spierenburg, Pieter 1984: *The Spectacle of Suffering: executions and the evolution of repression: from a preindustrial metropolis to the European experience*. Cambridge.

Staats Evers, J. W. 1865: *Bijdragen tot de geschiedenis der regtspleging in Gelderland, bijzonder te Arnhem*. Arnhem.

——1869: Belangrijkste vonnissen uit de criminele sententieboeken van het Geldersche Hof (1571–1752). *Nieuwe Bijdragen voor Regtsgeleerdheid en Wetgeving*, 19: 190–211.

Stone, Lawrence 1983: Interpersonal violence in English society 1300–1980. *Past and Present*, 101: 22–33.

Thompson, E. P., & Eileen Yeo (eds) 1971: *The Unknown Mayhew: selections from the 'Morning Chronicle' 1849–50*. Harmondsworth.

Vandenbroeck, Paul 1987: *Beeld van de andere, vertoog over het zelf: over wilden en narren, boeren en bedelaars*. Antwerp.

Vaux de Foletier, François de 1961: *Les Tsiganes dans l'ancienne France*. Paris.

——1966: Iconographie des 'Egyptiens', precisions sur le costume ancien des tsiganes. *Gazette des Beaux-arts*, 68: 165–72.

Verhas, Christel 1991: Mentaliteitsverandering tegenover de misdaad in de kasselrij Oudburg, doorheen de moderne tijd. MA thesis, University of Ghent.

Vrugt, M. van de 1978: *De Criminele Ordonnantien van 1570: enkele beschouwingen over de eerste strafrechtcodificatie in de Nederlanden*. Zutphen.

Weel, Toon van 1989: De interjurisdictionele betrekkingen in criminele zaken van het Amsterdamse gerecht (1700–1811). In Sjoerd Faber (ed.), *Nieuw licht op oude justitie: misdaad en straf ten tijde van de Republiek*, Muiderberg, 23–48.

Weisser, Michael 1979: *Crime and Punishment in Early Modern Europe*. Hassocks, West Sussex.

Wiersma, D. 1969: *Moord en sensatie in de negentiende eeuw*. Leiden.

——1970: Nadere gegevens over het Zwartjesgoed. *Tijdschrift voor Strafrecht*, 79: 205–12.

Wischnitzer, Mark 1965: *A History of Jewish Crafts and Guilds*. New York.

Wittgenstein, L. 1958: *Philosophical Investigations*. 2nd edn. Oxford. 1st edn 1953.

Zwaardemaker, A. F. 1939: De interjurisdictioneele verhoudingen in het strafrecht van de Republiek der Vereenigde Nederlanden. *Tijdschrift voor Strafrecht*, 49: 221–67.

Zwarts, J. 1940: De Joodse gemeenten buiten Amsterdam. In H. Brugmans & A. Frank (eds), *Geschiedenis der Joden in Nederland*, vol. 1, Amsterdam, 382–453.

Zwitzer, H. L. 1984: The Dutch army during the ancien regime. *Revue internationale d'histoire militaire*, 58: 15–36.

——1991: *'De militie van den staat': het leger van de Republiek der Verenigde Nederlanden*. Amsterdam.

Index